REVOLUTION AND EVOLUTION IN THE TWENTIETH CENTURY

To Larry

With great resp
and app
Continue mo   onward
Towards our best humanity.

Vincent
12/21/77

REVOLUTION AND EVOLUTION IN THE TWENTIETH CENTURY

JAMES AND GRACE LEE BOGGS

MONTHLY REVIEW PRESS
NEW YORK AND LONDON

Library of Congress Cataloging in Publication Data
Boggs, James.
    Revolution and evolution in the twentieth century.   1. Revolution—
History.   2. Negroes—Politics and suffrage.   3. United States—Civili-
zation—1945.   I. Boggs, Grace Lee, joint author.   II. Title.
D445.B63   301.6′333   73-90076
ISBN 0-85345-322-5

First Modern Reader Paperback 1975
Third Printing

Monthly Review Press
62 West 14th Street, New York, N.Y. 10011
21 Theobalds Road, London WCIX 8SL

Manufactured in the United States of America

CONTENTS

PREFACE

We have written this book for those Americans of our time who have become aware of the need for profound and drastic change in this country, who want to do something to improve human life and are ready to dedicate their lives to this goal, but who are unable to see a path, a direction for their dedication; who are convinced that they must do something of a sustained character to change this country if they are to realize their own human identity and if this country is ever to get back on the human road, but who are not sure whether what they are now doing is helpful or futile, relevant or irrelevant.

During the more than thirty years of our participation in the labor, radical, and black movements in this country, we have made countless speeches and written countless documents, pamphlets, leaflets, and articles. We have also written two books on the contradictions in U.S. society and the state of the movements which have emerged to resolve these contradictions.

In *The American Revolution* (New York: Monthly Review Press, 1963), we focussed on the tremendous technological development which has taken place in this country, the economy of abundance and the Welfare State which it has made possible, and the transformations which these have brought about in the work force and in the relations between the races and classes in this country. Most radicals have never reflected upon this unique development. Instead of using the dialectical method which was Marx's landmark contribution to revolutionary thought, they have been chiefly concerned with proving the correctness of what Marx wrote about capital and labor in the middle of the nineteenth century at the beginning of the Industrial Revolution. The aim of *The American Revolution* was to create a consciousness of historical development in the U.S. movement and thus finish up with those so-called Marxists who will never be able to do the creative thinking necessary to lead a revolution in the United States, because for them Marx has written the last word on revolution and the world might as well have been standing still for the last one hundred years.

Racism and the Class Struggle (New York: Monthly Review Press, 1970), contained a selection of our many articles and speeches from the 1960s. Our main purpose in these articles and speeches was to make clear the specific role which exploitation of the black underclass has played in the rapid development of American capitalism and hence the strategic political role which blacks can now play in revolutionizing this country as a whole.

The central theme in these publications has been the fundamental and dangerous contradiction in our society between economic overdevelopment and political, or human, underdevelopment. This political underdevelopment pervades our society. Every American, black or white, rich or poor or middle class, suffers from it because over the years everyone has gone his/her merry and not so merry way, pursuing individual life, liberty and happiness, and evading political responsibility in the delusion that economic development will resolve all human questions.

Now the chickens have come home to roost.

When *The American Revolution* was published in 1963, the idea of a American Revolution in our generation was so remote that most people assumed it was a book about the revolution of 1776. Now, on the eve of the two hundredth anniversary of the Declaration of Independence, this country has undergone nearly twenty years of sustained rebellion, the longest such period in our history.

In this period of social upheaval, most Americans have done what others have done in other countries in similar times. First, they have tried many different ways to resolve their problems and their conflicts. Then, having been frustrated in these efforts, most people have gone back to being apathetic, while a few continue to search for a new way. These few must now move on to a higher level, a higher plateau, in order to get a perspective on where they have been and where they still have to go.

We hope these people will find in this book food for much thought, and from that thought, the energies for the protracted struggle necessary to create a new nation out of these United States, a nation which all Americans, regardless of race, sex, or national origin, will be proud to call their own.

The ideas in the following pages are the product of collective struggles and collective discussion continuing over many years. They are ours only in the sense that we take responsibility for them.

—James Boggs
—Grace Lee Boggs

Detroit, Michigan
July 4, 1973

REVOLUTION AND EVOLUTION IN THE TWENTIETH CENTURY

1
REVOLUTION AND EVOLUTION

There is a dangerous and terrifying gap between the emotions with which most people respond to the critical state of affairs in this country and their understanding of how our struggles relate to the continuing struggle of humankind down through history.

All too often people believe that once an issue has been identified, the next step is action and the more militant the action the better. In their haste to find a quick and simple solution, militant activists usually disregard the evolution of man/womankind. All they can see is man/woman as he/she is now. They fail to recognize that what we are today is the result of a long and continuing process of evolution, and that this process of evolution is still going on and will go on as long as there are men and women on this planet. All too often, militants fail to understand the links between the struggles that we are carrying on today in this country and the struggles that other men and women have carried on in the past and are still carrying on in other parts of the world. They do not stop to reflect on how man/womankind's revolutions have been an essential part of their evolution, and their evolution an essential part of their revolutions.

Man/woman did not suddenly appear on this earth planet a few years ago nor did man/woman begin with Adam and Eve as the Bible tells us. Long before there were any gods, there were the men and women whose imaginations invented and created the gods. Nature and the universe existed before human beings, but the world in which we live has been created by the ideas, the work and the deeds of human beings. Therefore it can be changed by the ideas, the work and the deeds of human beings.

Humanity has been in the process of developing for the last twenty million years, ever since some creatures, looking more like apes than people, began using sticks and stones as tools. *Homo sapiens,* or the beings who have left behind evidences of their ability to reflect, did not come into being until approximately fifty thousand years ago. Thinking about themselves, reflecting upon their past, their present and their future, is the unique ability which separates human beings from all other living creatures. It is the ability which enables them to learn from the past and project into the future. Animals only react and spend their entire existence living by their instincts. Man/womankind, on the other hand, has been continuously evolving through the thoughts and actions of living men and women.

In every period, when most men and women were still doing what they had been doing all along and when this was creating more problems than it was solving, a few, a very few, individuals began to reflect, i.e., to have second thoughts. They began to examine what man/woman was doing and to wonder how we might behave differently in order to create a better life for humankind. In this process of creative thinking, or of thinking differently from the norm or average, a few individuals have always pioneered for the great majority.

Humanity as a developing species has undergone and surmounted many crises in the past. We are in a critical period today, and if we are going to get to the root of our crisis, some individuals will have to do some serious and creative thinking. Some individuals, some people, have to take the responsibility.

Once the new ideas have been developed, some individuals, some people will have to put them into practice and from their practice, enrich or correct the new ideas. Putting ideas into practice is always necessary; it is always a concrete and difficult problem. But for man/woman to behave in a new and different way, the thoughts, the new ideas, have to come first—whether it is a new way of making things or a new way of people living together.

This concept of the relation between revolutionary ideas and revolutionary practice is very different from that which is held by most militants in the United States, and especially young militants. In their impatience they see the relation between theory and practice as an antagonistic one. What they call "practice" is activism: "Enough of this talk, let's do something even if it's wrong." They have no concept of the flow from revolutionary theory to revolutionary practice and then back again to enriched theory through the evaluation of systematic practice.

New ideas come out of reflection upon past experiences. They do not come from out of the sky. Nor do they come from just reacting to what someone or the system does to you. The process of reflection is as important as the experiences themselves because in the reflection lies the possibility of something new and original.

As human beings concerned with revolutionary social change, we must have a philosophy of revolution. That is to say, we must have some very fundamental ideas about what a revolution means to the continuing advance of humanity.

To get ourselves into the proper setting for thinking about what a revolution is, we have to begin with some fundamental questions. Once you begin to think, that is, once you pause in your many activities, which to one degree or another have been only reactions, and start to use your mind, then it is crucial which questions you ask.

What is a revolution? How do you project the notion of revolution? Today, as we look or listen to the mass media, we are being given its concept of revolution. Its concept is inevitably ours as well until we have examined and repudiated it.

There is an urgent necessity today to combat the widespread tendency, propagated by the mass media, to think of revolution in terms of a single tactical event or episode, as a D-Day confrontation or shoot-out between the violence of the state and the violence of the oppressed. The idea which most of us have of revolution, encouraged by the FBI as well, is that of barricades, a Wild West shoot-out, an assault upon a police headquarters or even hijacking an airplane or robbing a bank. Most people, including most militants, think of a revolution in terms of "Instant Revolution" rather than in terms of a protracted struggle. Revolution to them is one confrontation after another. They have not stopped to wonder about the advance in human evolution which is the only justification for a revolution and which can only be achieved when the great masses of the people at the bottom of a society make a tremendous leap forward in their own humanity.

To understand what a revolution *is*, we must be very clear about what a revolution *is not*. The first step in defining anything is differentiation. A revolution is not the same as a rebellion or an insurrection or a revolt or a coup d'état.

A *rebellion* is an attack upon existing authority by members of an oppressed group with no intention on the part of the rebels to take state power. It is usually spontaneous.

An *insurrection* is a concentrated attack upon existing authority by members of an oppressed group, usually with the intention of taking power, if only temporarily, during the course of revolutionary struggles or at the culmination of a process of revolutionary struggle.

A *revolt* is an organized attempt to seize power, usually by a section of the armed forces, without prior organization of the masses in struggle and without any clear set of social objectives.

A *coup d'état* is the successful overthrow of existing authority in one audacious stroke, usually by a section of the armed forces. Another name for a coup d'état is a putsch.

All these are single events, limited in time as well as in target and objective. Each has distinct characteristics although the line between them is not always rigid, and a particular event may take on the characteristics of more than one of these categories. The first two, rebellion and insurrection, may take place in the course of revolutionary struggle, but they do not constitute revolution.

Rebellion is a stage in the development of revolution, but it is not revolution. It is an important stage because it represents the "standing up," the assertion of their humanity on the part of the oppressed. Rebellions inform both the oppressed and everybody else that a situation has become intolerable. They establish a form of communication among the oppressed themselves and at the same time open the eyes and ears of people who have been blind and deaf to the fate of their fellow citizens. Rebellions break the threads that have been holding the system together and throw into question the legitimacy and the supposed permanence of existing institutions. They shake up old values so that relations between individuals and between groups within the society are unlikely ever to be the same again. The inertia of the society has been interrupted.

Only by understanding what a rebellion accomplishes can we see its limitations. A rebellion disrupts the society, but it does not provide what is necessary to establish a new social order. In a rebellion the oppressed are reacting to what has been done to them. Therefore rebellions are issue-oriented. They tend to be negative, to denounce and expose the enemy without providing a positive vision of a new future. They also tend to be limited to a particular locality, or to a particular group—workers, blacks, women, chicanos. For all these reasons the time span of a rebellion tends to be limited—usually to a few days or a few weeks.

When those in rebellion talk about power, they are employing the rhetoric of revolution without the substance. In fact, they are simply protesting their condition. They see themselves and call on others to see them as victims and the other side as villains. They do not yet see themselves as responsible for reorganizing the society, which is what revolutionary social forces must do in a revolutionary period. Hence a rebellion begins with the feeling by the oppressed that "*we* can change the way things are," but it usually ends up by saying "*they* ought to do this and *they* ought to do that." So that while a rebellion generally begins with the rebels believing in their right to determine their own destiny, it usually ends up with the rebels feeling that their destiny is, in fact, determined by others.

It is very hard for those who have been oppressed to get beyond the stage of asking others to do things *for* them. It is particularly difficult in the United States. The Welfare State and the abundance created by exploitation of other countries and by advanced technology have made possible a vast apparatus of social workers and welfare workers whose economic well-being depends on expanding the agencies for helping the oppressed. This country has also had the wealth to create a vast network of programs by which the oppressed are pacified and the most militant leaders are rewarded with high-paying jobs in community projects.

It is hard to go beyond rebellion to revolution in this country because of the widespread belief that revolutions can be made as simply and instantly as one makes coffee. Therefore the tendency is to engage in acts of adventurism or confrontation which the rebels believe will bring down the system quickly. It is always much easier for the oppressed to undertake an adventuristic act on impulse than to undertake a protracted revolutionary struggle. A protracted revolutionary struggle requires that the oppressed masses acquire what they never start out with—confidence in their ability to win a revolution. Without that confidence, the tendency of many militants is toward martyrdom, in the hope that their death may at least become an inspiration to others.

In a period of sustained rebellion such as the present, the oppressed begin to feel the need for some philosophy, some general body of ideas to bind them together and enable them to make an appeal to others. Since it is not easy to create a philosophy of revolution, their first efforts in this direction are usually very idealistic, romantic or escapist.

In the United States today most militants refer constantly to "the struggle," implying that they are engaged in a revolutionary struggle whose importance is so obvious that only a reactionary would raise questions. Most of them think of revolution as a "Day of Reckoning," when those who have been exploited or oppressed (the "good guys") wipe out those who have exploited them (the idle rich, the capitalists, the "bad guys") in a sudden angry upheaval. By some miracle, these angry masses are assumed to have been imbued with all the moral and political virtues and qualities necessary to create a new society. This metaphysical concept of revolution as miracle is closely linked with the tendency to think of revolution as a spontaneous, unpredictable act of god or of other forces outside human control—something like a forest fire or earthquake.

This scenario has not only been encouraged by the mass media but by romantic historians who spend their lives in studies of what has already happened rather than in the creative and arduous activity of making or leading a revolution. Few of them have even stopped to reflect on the fact that revolutionary thinking is itself only two hundred years old. Oppression and rebellion against oppression have been an integral part of human history. But only in the last two hundred years have people believed that the oppressed could not only rise against their oppressors but go on to create a new, more advanced society.

Revolutionary thinking begins with a series of illuminations. It is not just plodding along according to a list of axioms. Nor is it leaping from peak to peak. Revolutionary thinking has as its purpose to discover where man/woman should be tomorrow so that we can struggle systematically and programmatically to arouse the great masses of the people to want to go there.

A revolution is not just for the purpose of correcting past injustices. A revolution involves a projection of man/woman into the future. It begins with projecting the notion of a more human human being, i.e., a human being who is more advanced in the specific qualities which only human beings have—creativity, consciousness and self-consciousness, a sense of political and social responsibility.

A revolutionary period is one in which the only exit is a revolution. Revolution is a specific way in which the evolution of man/woman is advanced. The only justification for a revolution is that it advances the evolution of man/woman. A revolution is a phase in the long evolutionary process of man/woman. It initiates a new plateau, a new threshold on which human beings can continue to develop, but it is still situated on the continuous line between past and future. It is the result both of long preparation and a profoundly new, a profoundly original beginning. Without a long period for maturing, no profound change can take place. But every profound change is at the same time a sharp break with the past.

Man/woman is obviously at a threshold, a border, a frontier. How should people live today? What changes are necessary in our values, in our morality? Today we know that moral progress is not an automatic byproduct of technological development, that in fact economic overdevelopment exists dangerously side by side with political and moral underdevelopment. How can we achieve the political and moral development required to cope with the present stage of technological development? Not by more development of economic forces or of technology. Not simply by making what already exists more available to more people on a more equitable basis. Not by depending upon spontaneous rebellion of the oppressed.

A conscious struggle, that is, a struggle governed by conscious values, conscious goals, conscious programs and conscious persons, is required. Yet for so long have Marxists and most radical social scientists relegated morality and consciousness to the "superstructure" that most radicals are hesitant even to talk about the values that are the product of tens of thousands of years of the cultural development of humankind.

The contradictions are within man/woman, internal as well as external. Because man/woman has crossed the threshold of reflection, and because each man and woman is a conscious individual, there are thousands of choices which each must make, including how and where and when he/she would like to live with his/her fellow men and women, and how he/she will think about him/herself, about society and about humankind.

These choices can only be posed by those who have developed the capacity to think historically, in terms of the development of men and women over tens of thousands of years.

Who are the antagonists in the present struggle? In the United States today there is far more antagonism on questions of social relations than on questions of economic relations. The conflict is not just between rich and poor, not just between one generation and another, but between different concepts of what a human being is and how a human being should live. We must know what is the principal contradiction before we can decide who is on the right side and who is on the wrong side.

Man/womankind today needs to redefine what are appropriate social relations. This can't be done by a plebiscite, by counting noses, or by any other kind of numbers game. It must be done by particular kinds of people projecting another way to live and testing it against certain classes, certain races, certain groups, certain people.

Clearly we are at a threshold of a new relation between necessity and choice. But what does any American today know about necessity or the concept of necessity? Necessity and choice used to be clearly separate. Today the borders between the two are no longer clear. One cannot be defined without the other. Once you accept the idea that people are no longer dominated by necessity in the way that they used to be, then you must see that our freedom to choose carries with it new responsibilities.

At this point we have to ask ourselves: can a worker or a black person be exonerated from responsibility because of class or race or because he/she has been and is oppressed? Are the ideas, the contributions of upper-class persons to be rejected out of hand because of their class origins? Or are ideas, actions, to be judged on their merits, in relation to how they contribute to the advancement of humanity?

How should people spend their lives? Is it sufficient to say that capitalism is responsible for the present state of affairs and that we are all its victims? Or is it necessary to develop new conceptions of appropriate social and human relations and then the concrete programs of struggle necessary to realize these conceptions?

What is the relation between wants and thoughts? Between wants and needs? Between masses and revolutionists? Masses have wants which are not necessarily related to human needs. Revolutionists must have thoughts about human needs. They cannot just rely on the spontaneous outburst of the masses over their wants. A revolutionist must absorb and internalize the lives, the passions, and the aspirations of great revolutionary leaders and not just those of the masses. It is true that revolutionary leadership can only come from persons in close contact with masses in movement and with a profound conviction of the impossibility of profound change in society without the accelerated struggle of the masses. But leaders cannot get their thoughts only from the movement of the masses.

A revolution begins with those who are revolutionary exploring and enriching their notion of a "new man/woman" and projecting the notion of this "new man/woman" into which each of us can transform ourselves.

The first transformation begins with those who recognize and are ready to assume the responsibility for reflecting on our experiences and the experiences of other revolutionary men and women. Thus the first transformation can begin with our own re-thinking. That is why we believe it is so crucial that before we undertake to project the perspectives for an American revolution, we review what previous revolutions of our epoch have meant in the evolution of man/womankind. As we study these revolutions, the first thing we shall learn is that all the great revolutionists have projected a concept of revolution to the masses. They did not just depend on the masses or the movement of their day for their idea of what should be done. They evaluated the state of the world and their own society. They internalized the most advanced ideas about human development which had been arrived at on a world scale. They projected a vision of what a revolution would mean in their own country. They analyzed the different social forces within their country carefully to ascertain which forces could be mobilized to realize this vision. They carried on ideological struggle against those who were not ready to give leadership to the masses or who were trying to lead them in the wrong direction. Only then did they try to lead their own masses and every other possible sector of the society in struggle.

We review these revolutions not as scholars but as revolutionists, for the help that they can give us in clarifying the perspectives for a revolution in the United States. We are very much aware that our problems are very different from those of people in Russia, China, Vietnam, and Guinea-Bissau. But by reviewing these revolutions we can view the revolutions that have taken place in different parts of the world in our epoch as a historical whole, a continuous process of human liberation which advances one step at a time and whose forms move from country to country, from people to people. We can gain some insight into how far world humanity has already advanced towards the conscious creation by men and women of a new expanded human identity. We can draw some universal lessons from particular revolutions which will contribute to the next advancement. And we can begin to appreciate the protracted commitment, the refusal to be confined by dogma, the creative boldness, the readiness to practice new ideas as well as to compel others to choose between opposing roads, the tireless struggle against the new contradictions and obstacles which never cease to appear—all of which are the awesome responsibility of revolutionary leadership.

As we struggle in the second part of this book to understand our choices in the United States, we must not allow our thoughts to be paralyzed by fear of repression and fascism. One must always think realistically about the dangers, but in thinking about the counter-revolution a revolutionist must be convinced that it is a "paper tiger."

Revolution and counter-revolution both involve social upheaval, but they are not equal opposites. The revolution creates the future; the counter-revolution seeks to maintain the present or restore the past. The counter-revolution is invariably anti-historical. It narrows and limits human beings, whereas a revolution expands and enriches human identity.

An American revolution will enable the American people to renew and enlarge their sense of their own humanity. It will give them a new sense of time, of duration, of development, and of progress. It will instill in them a new love both for themselves and for men and women everywhere as they begin to see themselves as an integral part of the history of all man/womankind. An American revolution will give Americans real and continuing opportunities to make responsible choices—opportunities which at the present time they do not even know they lack.

2
REVISITING THE RUSSIAN REVOLUTION

A successful revolution exerts a powerful influence on revolutionary-minded people all over the world. It not only lifts their hopes. It also shapes their concepts of how social change is brought about. Consciously or unconsciously, would-be revolutionaries begin to adopt the successful revolution as a model or blueprint for their own. The dynamics of the successful revolution tend to take on the force of inexorable law, making it difficult for the revolutionary to remember that every revolution is unique—the product of the creative energies of specific leaders, specific organizations and specific masses in a specific country under very specific conditions, all of which have been developed over a number of years, at a particular time and in a particular historical period, and which, therefore, cannot possibly be repeated at another time in another place.

Moreover, in the excitement and jubilation which every progressive person naturally feels at the sight of formerly downtrodden and submissive masses rising up to take control of their own destiny, it is easy to overlook the setbacks and retreats, the protracted struggles by which this great historical leap was arrived at, as well as the difficult problems and decisions that the new revolutionary government must now make. The tendency is to borrow intact the most spectacular strategy and tactics, the most striking statements of the successful revolutionary leaders or organizations, and turn them into rituals or catchwords.

All this which we have witnessed in this period in relation to the Chinese, the Algerian, the Korean, the Vietnamese, and the Cuban revolutions took place for practically a whole generation of radicals all over the world after the October Revolution in Russia, the first, *and actually the only*, socialist workers revolution in history. Revolutionists everywhere began looking forward to their own October—predicting, in reality hoping for, a similar conjuncture of circumstances: military defeat and chaos on the battlefront coupled with economic and political chaos on the home front, exposing the bankruptcy of the existing regime, provoking mass rebellion, and thereby creating the objective conditions for a disciplined Communist Party to lead the workers to power.

Today we should know better. First of all, we have witnessed the success of and know a great deal about other revolutions—the Chinese, the Cuban, the Vietnamese—all of which have been quite different from the Russian Revolution, despite the deceptively similar formulations. We know a lot more about what led up to the Russian Revolution and about what has transpired since. And most important, we are now faced with real rebellions and real social crises in this country, which, as the world's technologically most advanced and militarily most powerful nation, with the highest standard of material living that the world has ever known, bears no resemblance to pre-revolutionary Russia.

That does not mean that we have nothing to learn from the Russian Revolution. On the contrary. The Russian Revolution is an essential link in the continuing struggle of humanity to create the new social relations and political forms by which men and women can achieve greater control over their own lives and a higher level of social responsibility for each other. And anyone who refuses, for whatever reason, to take seriously both the achievements of the Russian Revolution, *and therefore the problems it has bequeathed to future generations of revolutionists*, cannot be taken seriously as a revolutionary leader.

The Russian Revolution announced to the world that the capitalist system, far from being permanent, would probably end up as the shortest-lived economic and social system in history. It thus gave hope and inspiration to those who have been victimized by capitalism and imperialism as well as to those who had been its beneficiaries but were repelled by its single-minded pursuit of material values at the expense of human values. But it also challenged those who called themselves socialists to stop relying on the inevitability of capitalist collapse and to start assuming the awesome responsibilities of revolutionary leadership. Revolutionary leadership, it made clear, involves far more than sympathy for the oppressed or hatred for the oppressor. No occupation is more demanding of continuing, creative, and disciplined thinking and action. Revolutionary leadership is not for the fainthearted, the flamboyant, or the fly-by-night, the easily flattered, the easily satisfied, or the easily intimidated, the seekers after excitement or popularity or martyrdom. More valuable than those who would die for the revolution are those who would give the rest of their lives to it.

As practically everyone, friend or foe, agrees, the Russian Revolution was successful because it was led by Lenin at the head of a vanguard party which not only had dedicated itself for nearly twenty years to the continuing escalation of the revolutionary struggles of the masses, but which was ready to assume the responsibility for taking power when the old power structure collapsed. This kind of party, consisting of a continuing revolutionary leadership growing in numbers, experience, and organization, made its first historical appearance at the beginning of this century in Russia. Fortunately, the almost complete documentation of its creation and development is available for everybody to study in the voluminous writings of its founder, Lenin, who was untiring in explaining the necessity for a vanguard party, how it should be organized, what it should and what it should not do in the many differing circumstances with which the Russian movement was involved over a period of many years. Therewith he has illuminated certain key concepts of revolutionary politics: e.g., the concepts of *revolutionary social forces,* of *tendencies,* the limitations of *spontaneous rebellion,* the difference between *propaganda* and *agitation,* the purpose of a revolutionary *convention* or congress.

Lenin was born in 1870 in Simbirsk, a small town on the Volga River about five hundred miles east of Moscow. His father, who died when Lenin was sixteen, was a schoolteacher who had risen from the ranks to become an official responsible for organizing elementary schools in the province. His mother, an educated woman, knew several languages which she taught her six children.

The class of educated Russians from which Lenin came supplied most of the revolutionaries in Russia at that time. Teachers, lawyers, doctors and engineers, they were very conscious of the political and economic backwardness of Russia as compared with the rest of Europe. They found it intolerable to have no voice in the Russian government, which was run according to the whims of the Tsar and his family. In Russia there were no institutions of the kind which are generally called bourgeois-democratic—no elected Congress; no freedom of speech, of the press, or of assembly—and anyone who spoke out about political matters risked arrest and exile. Thus, more than half of Lenin's thirty-odd years of political life was spent in exile, in prison, or in hiding. On a number of occasions he voluntarily left Russia to work abroad because it was easier to print his paper in Switzerland or Sweden and smuggle it back across a number of borders than to risk arrest and the confiscation of his printing presses inside Russia. Only during those brief periods when the workers, through their Soviets, exercised de facto power and guaranteed freedom of the press and assembly to revolutionaries was Lenin able to move about freely and address meetings.

Russia was extremely backward economically. The great majority of the population lived in ignorance, poverty, and squalor on the vast countryside. Not until 1861 had the Russian peasants been emancipated from serfdom. After their emancipation, tens of thousands of the poorest peasants migrated to the cities where they worked in factories for fifteen or sixteen hours a day under the most inhuman conditions.

Faced with these obvious social evils, many Russian intellectuals became convinced that the society in which they lived had to be changed; that the change had to bring an improvement in the material conditions of life of the masses of people and give them greater control over their lives; that this change could only be brought about by a forceful displacement of those in economic and political power; and that a socialist society based on collective ownership must be created to break the power of the large property holders over the propertyless.

In the pursuit of these convictions the intellectuals of late nineteenth-century Russia had already developed a tradition of social and political consciousness and of selfless dedication to revolutionary causes. In this sense, the Russia of Lenin's youth was already much further advanced than the United States today where the movement is only just beginning to recognize the opportunists and careerists, and has not even begun to develop the programs to weed out these freedom hustlers and consolidate those who are ready for the long haul.

Lenin came out of this tradition. What distinguished him from his predecessors and his contemporaries was his aggressiveness in grappling with and doing ideological battle around certain key questions at critical periods in the development of the revolutionary struggle. These questions were not invented by Lenin. They were posed by the actual situation in Russia. Lenin's contribution was his insistence that those in the movement take clear positions on these questions. In this way he made clear that there actually are different *tendencies* inside any movement. Different people not unnaturally have different evaluations and perspectives, and you only run around in circles if you try to build a continuing political organization and develop a political program with people with different political perspectives. Having made the differences clear, Lenin separated himself politically from those whose evaluations and perspectives differed from his and proceeded to build an organization and develop a program with those who shared his evaluations and perspectives.

For us the important thing is not so much what Lenin's position was at any particular time or even if it was correct, but that he was ready to pose the alternative positions sharply, make clear where he stood, and then organize and mobilize people to act on the basis of the choice he had clearly made. By the way in which Lenin took political positions and organized around them, his whole political life is a demonstration of how the questions which the revolutionist poses and the answers which he/she chooses become a means to shape social reality. Thus the next series of questions and answers are themselves the product of the way in which the questions of the preceding stage have been resolved. That is why revolutionary politics is not just a way of contemplating reality but changes reality. The revolutionists who build an organization take responsibility for projecting their answers to the masses. This interaction produces new questions which require new answers and so on. When you become convinced that society must make a sharp break with past values and practices, you become *revolutionary*. But you do not become a *revolutionist* until you have organized with others in an organization which takes responsibility for this continuing process of answers and questions.

The first question around which Lenin had to do ideological battle was the question of which section or sections of Russian society had the greatest potential for revolutionary struggle. When Lenin was a young man, it seemed obvious that the Russian peasants were the most revolutionary social force. First of all, they were the over-whelming majority of the population. Secondly, they had a tradition of great militancy. Between 1826 and 1861, for example, there had been 1186 peasant uprisings. In fact, Tsar Alexander II had decreed the emancipation of the peasants from serfdom in 1861 because he felt it was better to liberate the peasants from above than to wait until they took their freedom from below. Moreover, the Russian peasants had a kind of self-governing organization in the *commune*, a traditional institution through which each Russian village council regulated the sale and inheritance of land, supervised the collection of taxes, and in theory acted as an equalizing institution for the villagers. In this situation it was reasonable to believe that if you just got rid of the landlords, and particularly of the Tsar who was the biggest landlord of all, you could at one and the same time liberate the peasants from their oppressors and liberate their communal organization as the foundation of a new socialist society.

This was the position adopted by the group known as the Friends of the People (*Narodniks*). The Narodniks dressed like peasants and went into the villages trying to rouse the peasants to struggle. When the Russian peasants failed to respond, the Narodniks turned their efforts to getting rid of the Tsar, hoping thereby to trigger peasant uprisings. In 1881 they had succeeded in blowing up Tsar Alexander II with a bomb, and in 1887, Lenin's twenty-one-year-old brother Alexander had been hanged for participating in a plot that almost succeeded in blowing up Alexander III.

In opposition to this group of intellectuals was another much smaller group which was organized around the ideas of Karl Marx. This group insisted that capitalist development in Russia was inevitable and that it had already begun, both in the country, where rich peasants were buying up the land of poor peasants and actually controlling the communes, and in the cities, where foreign capital, state capital, and private capital were being invested in huge factories. They thought that this capitalistic economic activity would develop the country industrially, while creating a working class which would be forced to struggle against both the capitalists and the autocracy. This working class, they thought, would be a better foundation for socialism than the peasants because of the unity, the organization, the discipline, and the training in industrial processes which it would receive in capitalist production. These intellectuals, led by George Plekhanov, attacked the Narodniks both for their romanticism and for their terrorist methods.

The youthful Lenin aligned himself with the Marxists even though it meant a political repudiation of his recently martyred brother. Sentenced to exile in 1887–1888 because of his participation in some student demonstrations, Lenin began to read Marx and Engels. In their writings he found a philosophy of human development which enabled him to combine the struggle against Tsarist oppression with the struggle for a more advanced society, and to relate the struggles of the Russian masses to those of oppressed people everywhere. Armed with these prerequisites for sustained revolutionary struggle, Lenin was able to break once and for all with the unhistorical and idealistic thinking of the Narodniks.

Upon his return to law school in 1888, Lenin organized a small Marxist group, in which his remaining brother and two of his sisters participated. After graduating from law school in 1893, he went to St. Petersburg, where he joined a group of Plekhanov's followers, the Emancipation of Labor.

Having joined the Marxists, Lenin's ideological struggles were just beginning. *In any movement which is actually moving, every unity is the starting point for further differentiation.* The new differentiation developed between those who were only interested in theoretical discussions in small study groups with other intellectuals or politically advanced workers and those ready to carry out propaganda and agitation among the Russian workers who were just beginning to display the militancy in struggle which the Marxists had predicted.

Out of those who were ready to go to propagandize and agitate the workers, Lenin formed a new group, the Social-Democratic League of Struggle of the Working Class.

In 1895, again in prison, Lenin began to draft a program for a Social-Democratic Labor Party. Written in invisible ink, it was smuggled out of the prison. His article "The Tasks of Social Democracy" written shortly thereafter, reveals how Lenin was beginning to move *from theory to practice:*

> At the present time the most urgent question is the question of the practical activities of Social-Democrats . . . Now the main and fundamental features of the theoretical views of the Social-Democrats are sufficiently clear. This, however, cannot be said in regard to the practical side of Social-Democracy, its political program, its methods of activity, its tactics. . . .
>
> The socialist work of *Russian Social-Democrats* consists of propagating the doctrines of scientific socialism, of spreading among the workers a proper understanding of the present social and economic system, its foundations and its development, an understanding of the various classes in Russian society, of the mutual relations between these classes, the struggle between them, of the role of the working class in this struggle, the attitude of this class towards the declining and developing classes, towards the past and the future of capitalism, of the historical task of the International Social-Democracy and of the Russian working class.
>
> Inseparably connected with propaganda is *agitation* among the workers. . . . Agitating among the workers means that the Social-Democrats take part in all the spontaneous manifestations of the struggle of the working class, in all the conflicts between the workers and the capitalists over the working day, wages, conditions of labor etc. . . .
>
> To organize study circles for workers, to establish proper and secret connections between those and the central group of Social-Democracy, to publish and distribute literature for workers, to organize correspondence from all centres of the labor movement, to publish agitational leaflets and manifestos and to distribute them, and to train a corps of experienced agitators—such, in the main—are the manifestations of the *socialist activity of Russian Social-Democracy.*

Thus Lenin clarified for the revolutionary organizer the forms of socialist activity and the difference between propaganda and agitation. The difference is valid to this day. The *content* of the propaganda and agitation which he outlines, however, was for the Russian Social-Democracy of 1897, nearly a century ago.

Once he had engaged in practical activity among workers, Lenin began to recognize the danger in just reacting to issues with good ideas. Without an organization which has developed the perspective and programs to direct the consciousness and the activities of the masses towards some goal, the best ideas and the best slogans can only get lost in the shuffle. Worse still, without an organization to follow through on agitation and propaganda, the aroused masses become confused and therefore open to all kinds of demagogic leadership.

Lenin began drafting a program for a Russian vanguard party in 1895, and his ideas were widely circulated among Russian radicals. But it was not until 1903 that he was ready to call a congress to unite the various Marxist groupings into a united party. The delay was deliberate. A gathering calling itself the Congress of the Russian Social-Democratic Workers Party (which has become known as the First Congress) had been held in 1898, but it had not resulted in the adoption of a program or of party rules or in the election of a centralized leadership. Lenin was not in any hurry to bring Russian radicals together just so that they could talk about how bad the Tsar was or how beautiful the workers were.

By the late 1890s and early 1900s Marxism had become the fashion in Russia. The Russian workers had become militant, spontaneously striking for economic demands and even raising political demands against the autocracy. Intellectuals wrote articles about the workers, and militants formed local committees to organize workers.

Before it made any sense to unite into a party, Lenin said, it was necessary to draw some hard and firm lines between the different tendencies in the movement, so that those who came together to form the party would be those who had chosen the revolutionary line.

The tendency which Lenin considered the most dangerous obstacle to the creation of a revolutionary vanguard party and which he therefore attacked with the greatest vigor in his famous pamphlet "What is to be done?" was that of the Economists. This was the name given to those radicals who encouraged and made a great fuss over the militancy of the workers and their spontaneous outbursts and strikes over their immediate grievances. It is important to understand the Economists because an analogous tendency emerges in any period of revolutionary ferment. A period of revolutionary ferment is characterized by innumerable spontaneous rebellions and explosions by oppressed masses who find their conditions intolerable. As the rebellions spread, the most natural tendency on the part of a great many intellectuals or leadership types is to rush to become the spokesman of the masses, articulating their grievances and stirring them to more militant protests without raising their political consciousness of how far they will have to go in order to solve their problems. Such people, Lenin said, profess to lead the masses but actually they lag way behind them. They have not accepted the responsibility of revolutionary leadership, which is not just to sympathize with the masses over their wrongs or encourage them in their militancy. That is what the liberal does. Revolutionary leadership, as distinct from liberal leadership, has the duty to help the masses understand what their political goals must be if they are going to achieve any fundamental solution to their problems. In refusing to do this, Lenin said, the Economists were guilty not only of neglect, but of forcing the masses to follow the bourgeois liberals for lack of any alternative. On the other hand, those who recognized that the spontaneous rebellion of the workers was just the beginning and who also recognized that the bourgeois liberals were incapable of revolutionary leadership had the duty to form a revolutionary party which would lead the workers in revolutionary struggle against the autocracy.

In "What is to be done?" Lenin also outlined plans for a newspaper which would both attack the Economists and put forward the ideas of a revolutionary party. Such a newspaper would be the mechanism for sifting out those who were ready to form a revolutionary party as demonstrated in their willingness to undertake the risks of distributing the newspaper in the police state that was Tsarist Russia. Lenin's newspaper *Iskra* (the Spark) served not only to propagandize and agitate the workers; it tested the courage and commitment of comrades. Distributing a revolutionary paper in Tsarist Russia was an objective test comparable to armed struggle.

The Congress organized by Lenin to begin the party, called the Second Congress, was held in 1903, meeting first in Brussels and then, when the Belgian police interfered, in London. Those who attended were those who accepted the purpose of the Congress, namely, "to create a real party on the basis of principles and organizations which had been advanced and elaborated by *Iskra*."

Only forty-three delegates, representing twenty-six organizations, attended.

The Congress adopted the party program following extensive debate around the inclusion of three points upon which Lenin insisted: 1. that the goal of the revolution was the dictatorship of the proletariat; 2. that peasant demands be included in the program even though the party based itself essentially on the working class; 3. that the right of nationalities to self-determination be supported.

These three questions—the goal of the revolution, how to gain the support of the majority of the population, and the rights of minorities—are bound to arise in the course of the adoption of any revolutionary program, and differences over them should be anticipated by any revolutionary leadership. But it would obviously be ridiculous to expect that debate in the United States would be around the same goals or in relation to the same majorities and minorities as in the Russia of 1903.

The debate around the program was relatively harmonious compared to that which followed around the question of party rules and regulations. The agenda was now moving into the sphere of concrete implementation, where underlying political differences can usually be brought to a head and decided in a political fashion.

Lenin proposed three conditions for party membership: 1. acceptance of the party program; 2. financial support of the party; and 3. membership in a party organization. Martov, who had been a close associate and friend of Lenin's since 1895, made a substitute motion, accepting the first two requirements but rejecting the third. In these opposing motions is contained the fundamental difference between those who are only ready for a loose organization and those who are ready for a tightly disciplined one. This is not just a question of temperament. In political practice a loose organization means that those who are sympathetic to the revolution but unwilling or unable to accept the discipline and carry out the tasks of the party nevertheless have the right to influence and make party decisions. Those in favor of loose organization are usually intellectuals or careerists who want to be part of the leadership of the struggle while continuing to pursue their individual careers. This attitude to organization is usually characterized as petty-bourgeois. Conscious of the popularity of Marxism at the time, Lenin recognized that a loose organization would mean the inclusion of all kinds of floaters and rhetorical revolutionaries in party decision-making. The conflict between Lenin and Martov has gone down in history as that between the Bolsheviks and the Mensheviks. Bolsheviks is the Russian word for majority and Mensheviks the Russian word for minority, but the difference is by no means exclusively Russian. It is bound to recur in the organization of any revolutionary party, and, as with Lenin and Martov, usually requires a painful choice between personal friendship and political principle.

Later the polarization between the Mensheviks and the Bolsheviks, which had erupted first over an organizational question, developed into a conflict over the perspectives for socialism. More and more Martov and his intellectual friends began to see socialism as a natural consequence of the development of productive forces and therefore dependent upon objective forces outside human control. Meanwhile, Lenin became more determined to build human forces who would be able to take advantage of objective opportunities.

Three years later, in 1905, the first Russian Revolution erupted with the spontaneous outburst of the workers. Like all great spontaneous outbursts, it served to sharpen as well as to clarify the fundamental differences between tendencies inside the Russian movement.

The revolution broke out because of events in which the Bolsheviks had played little or no role. Since 1904 Russia had been fighting—and losing—a war with Japan for control of Manchuria. Hundreds of thousands of Russian peasants, the bulk of the Russian army, were being slaughtered or taken prisoner at the front. The obvious incompetence of the Tsarist government and of the Tsarist army encouraged the workers to begin militant actions to improve their conditions. Against this background, Father Gapon, a priest who wanted to improve the image of the church among the workers, led a march on Sunday, January 9, of hundreds of thousands of workers to the Tsar's palace to petition for relief. Their demands were elementary: they asked for an eight-hour day, for an increase in wages of one ruble a day, and for better working conditions. The march was not very different from the many marches on Washington which we have witnessed in this country since 1963. But the Tsar's troops fired on the marchers, killing nearly a thousand and wounding twice that many.

Immediately mass political protest strikes broke out all over Russia. These were followed by revolts in the armed forces, including the refusal of soldiers to fire on striking workers, and a mutiny on the battleship *Potemkin*. In the countryside the peasants rose, burning down the homes of landlords and demanding or often confiscating land for themselves.

Trying to pacify the mounting revolutionary ferment, the Tsar issued a promise in August that he would grant a Constitution and a Duma, an elected representative body. But the Duma promised was so obviously inadequate—it was to be chosen only on a limited franchise and to be only advisory—that nobody paid much attention to it.

As the unrest spread, the Tsar hastened to sign a peace treaty with Japan in September, which made it possible for him to bring the troops home for action on the domestic front. Ending the war appeased the peasants, but it did not satisfy the workers. At the beginning of October the St. Petersburg workers organized a Soviet, or council, and soon other cities followed suit. Originally the Soviets were conceived chiefly as coordinating strike committees, but they soon began to exercise a form of de facto power; for example, assuring the right of publication and assembly to radicals, and enforcing the eight-hour day.

The organization of the Soviets forced the Tsar to think in terms of more serious concessions, and a few days later he issued another manifesto, in which he promised freedom of speech and assembly, the right to form unions, amnesty for political prisoners, lower taxes for the peasants, and a broadening both of the voting base and the powers of the Duma.

Not until November did Lenin return from exile in London. Meanwhile he had been hailing the new stage of the revolution and calling upon the Bolsheviks to escalate the demands and organization of the workers. The workers were now carrying out the mass political strikes against the autocracy which the Bolsheviks had been urging all along. The soldiers' refusal to fire on striking workers and the *Potemkin* mutiny, he said, were the first steps in the formation of a revolutionary army that would be necessary to take power. Lenin hailed the Soviets as the embryonic elements for a new revolutionary self-government of the people, if an alliance could be made with the peasantry.

In line with Lenin's interpretation, the Moscow Soviets, under the leadership of the Bolsheviks, attempted an armed uprising in December 1905. The uprising was crushed, and by the middle of 1906, despite sporadic armed struggles, the first Russian Revolution had been defeated.

Following the defeat, a bitter political struggle developed between the Bolsheviks and the Mensheviks. The Mensheviks charged the Bolsheviks with trying to rush the workers into revolutionary leadership and armed struggle and with trying to skip the stage of the bourgeois revolution which could only be led by the bourgeoisie. The Bolsheviks defended the Moscow uprising and attacked the Mensheviks for seeking every possible excuse to avoid or postpone armed struggle by the workers, for encouraging the workers to have democratic illusions about what they could expect from the Russian bourgeoisie, and for interpreting Marxism to mean a fatalistic reliance upon the peaceful development of the contradictions of capitalism to create socialism. Despite the Moscow defeat, the Bolsheviks insisted, the attempted uprising had taught the Russian workers very important lessons about the lengths to which they would have to go to smash the Tsarist autocracy.

It is possible to say, and many Monday morning quarterbacks have said, that the Bolshevik evaluation of the situation in December 1905 was a mistaken one; that they had not appreciated the extent to which the Tsar had managed to isolate the revolutionary forces by the concessions of the October Manifesto. That kind of discussion is a pretty futile one, made to order for armchair generals who spend so much time replaying yesterday's battles that they have no time to plan tomorrow's.

For us the most important point to be made about the first Russian Revolution is that it was a dress rehearsal for the 1917 Revolution. What happened in 1917 could not have happened without the lessons which the workers, the party, and especially Lenin drew from the experiences of 1905.

A revolutionary movement, a revolutionary organization, a revolutionary leadership cannot develop unless people are ready to *learn* from experience and *teach* from experience. That may sound very obvious and elementary, but it stands repetition and emphasis in this country where an unbelievable reluctance exists on the part of those with experience to teach and those just coming into the movement to learn. This phenomenon has deep roots in the anti-intellectualism, the individualism, the youth-cultism of the country, all of which have led people in the movement to reject one of the chief advantages which human beings have over animals—the capacity to reflect on the past. This does not mean, of course, that the young must accept uncritically the information and judgments of their elders. But every great leap forward is always both a continuation and a critique of or struggle against the past.

The second Russian Revolution began twelve years later. In February 1917, military disaster for the Tsarist armies, joined with the Allies in World War I, and the ensuing economic chaos, again precipitated a spontaneous eruption of the workers and the organization of Soviets. This was followed in October by the insurrection through which the Bolshevik Party took power. Essentially what took place in 1917 was a repetition on a larger scale of what had happened in 1905, except that this time the Soviets were organized not only by workers, but by soldiers and peasants; *and,* instead of trying to carry out an armed uprising through street battles and barricades as in 1905, the Bolsheviks seized power practically in the dead of night, by occupying the chief centers of government, communications, and transport.

It is not necessary here to go into detail about the 1917 revolution since the objective conditions in the Russia of 1917 are very unlikely to occur in the United States. Much more important for our purposes is what we can learn from the Russian Revolution about the responsibilities of power.

In June 1917, during a meeting of the All-Russian Congress of Soviets, the Menshevik Tsereteli, trying to defend the Provisional Government in which he held a Cabinet post and fully aware that this government was powerless to check the spreading chaos, challenged his critics to put up or shut up. "At the present moment," he said, "there is no political party which would say, 'Give the power into our hands; go away, we will take your place.' There is no such party in Russia." From the audience a voice rang out. "There is." It was Lenin, ready to assume the responsibilities of power at the head of the Bolshevik Party.

In every revolutionary situation there is a critical point when those who have been agitating the masses against the power structure must face this question. In this country those who talk about revolution have not even reached the point of wondering how they would govern if they had the power.

The responsibilities of the new Soviet government were gigantic. The war with Germany had to be brought to a close without delay for two reasons: first, the Bolsheviks had won the support of the masses in practically a bloodless insurrection on a promise of peace; and, second, the German army seemed likely to wipe out the disintegrating Russian army. The army, the economy, the political apparatus had all collapsed. If the productive and distributive machinery were not gotten into order at once, millions would die from cold and hunger. Sabotage by the bourgeoisie, banditry under the flag of anarchism, rioting by drunken mobs—all had to be dealt with quickly and firmly.

As a first step towards solving these problems, the new government expropriated the holdings of private capitalists; nationalized large enterprises, such as banks; turned the land of the large landlords over to the peasants; decreed equality for women and the right of self-determination for all the minorities.

A few days after the seizure of power, Lenin drafted his appeal: "To the population: Comrade Workers! Remember that you yourselves now administer the state. Nobody will help you if you yourselves do not unite and take all the affairs of the state into your own hands. Your Soviets are henceforth the organs of state power, organs with full powers, organs of decision."

The unhesitating way in which the new government took measures against those who had so cruelly oppressed the workers and peasants, and its direct appeal to the population to take the affairs of state into their own hands, created that sense of exhilaration, social confidence, and mass initiative in the armed workers, soldiers, and peasants which impressed all foreign observers. As contrasted with what the counter-revolution would have done, practically no force was expended in the creation of a sense of social order.

But very real problems remained. If the new regime was even going to survive and have an opportunity to create a new society, the first prerequisite was the end of the war with Germany. In theory, the German workers and soldiers should feel more solidarity with the new Russian regime than with the Junker government. The Bolsheviks had always believed that the success of a Russian revolution was dependent upon the success of a revolution in Germany. Germany

being economically more advanced than Russia, the German workers, according to Marxist theory, were better prepared for socialism.

Fervent appeals were made to the German soldiers in the name of
solidarity with the new workers' society. Mass strikes by German
workers in January 1918 encouraged the hope of an immediate
German revolution. But the strikes did not lead to revolution, and
the German army continued to advance. Finally, in March 1918, the
Bolsheviks had no alternative but to sign the Treaty of Brest-Litovsk
with Germany on terms that involved the loss of 40 percent of the
industry and industrial population of the former Russian Empire, 70
percent of the iron and steel production, and 90 percent of the sugar.

A bitter debate in the Bolshevik Party preceded the acceptance of
these harsh terms. In the course of the debate the German army
continued to advance and the terms became progressively harsher.
The debate brought to the surface a fundamental dilemma facing any
revolutionary movement which regards itself as part of the world
revolution. How much can a revolution in one country base its
strategy on the support of the revolution in other countries? Does the
defense of the socialist state ever take precedence over the needs of
the revolutionary movement in another country? Following the
Russian Revolution, an entire generation of communists was to
debate and split over this question, which was most dramatically
brought to the attention of the world when Stalin signed the pact
with Hitler in 1940 in order to gain time to prepare the Russian army
for the inevitable German attack. These are hard questions but a
revolution is full of hard questions.

The war over, the Bolshevik government was freed to tackle the
pressing problems of economic reconstruction. A week later the
All-Russian Congress of Soviets issued an appeal to the toiling
masses:

> The Congress most insistently draws the attention of all workers,
> soldiers and peasants, of all the toilers and the oppressed masses to the
> main, current and indispensable task of the present moment: the raising
> of the activity and self-discipline of the workers, the creation every-
> where and in all directions of strong solid organizations covering as far
> as possible all production and all distribution of goods, a relentless
> struggle with the chaos, disorganization and disintegration which are
> historically inevitable as the consequence of a devastating war but are
> at the same time the primary obstacle to the final victory of socialism
> and the reinforcement of the foundations of socialist society.

The urgency of the appeal brought to light the difficulties inherent in governing the Russia of 1917 on the basis of theoretical conceptions developed by Marx more than half a century before. Marx's original contribution to socialist theory had been his concept of the working class as a socialized, organized, united, and disciplined force growing up within capitalist production. Marx did not only describe and sympathize with the misery of the workers. He saw in them a positive basis for constructing a new socialist society, because of their organization and discipline which was prevented from expressing itself by the capitalist integument of private property. Theoretically, once this integument was destroyed by the revolutionary expropriation of private property, the socialist energies of the workers would be released to establish a rational system of production. Toward the end of his life, Marx began to recognize that "planning" would be necessary but he said that "society" would do it.

Along the same lines, Lenin, writing *State and Revolution* on the eve of the seizure of power, had envisaged a kind of "direct democracy," providing that great vision of the new society without which it is difficult, if not impossible, for a revolutionary leadership to assume the awesome responsibility of power. "Under socialism," he wrote, "much of 'primitive' democracy will inevitably revive, since for the first time in the history of civilized societies the mass of the population will be raised to independent participation not only in voting and elections, but in day-to-day administration. Under socialism all will administer in turn and will quickly become accustomed to nobody administering."

And again: "According to Marx, what the proletariat needs is only a state in process of dying away, i.e., so constituted that it will at once begin to die away and cannot help dying away. . . . The proletarian state will begin to die away immediately after its victory, since in a society without class contradictions, the state is unnecessary and impossible."

Now the bourgeoisie had been expropriated and the Tsarist state destroyed. But who was going to organize and plan production? In life the expropriation of private property had resulted in something far different from the organization and administration from below which Marx and Lenin had both envisaged. The Bolsheviks had not been surprised by the individualism of the peasants; the social weaknesses of the peasant had been diagnosed and anticipated since the early days of the disputes with the Narodniks. But they *were* surprised at the extent to which the workers and the factory committees acted as if the individual plants belonged to them, at their tendency to take independent piecemeal action without regard for the needs of the economy, and at their extremely low level of political and social consciousness and responsibility.

Typically, Lenin viewed the problem first of all as a historical challenge:

> We have knowledge of socialism, but as for knowledge of organization on a scale of millions, knowledge of the organization and distribution of commodities—that we have not. . . . This the old Bolshevik leaders did not teach us. . . . Nothing has been written about this yet in Bolshevik textbooks, and there is nothing in Menshevik textbooks either. . . .
>
> All that we knew, all that had been precisely indicated to us by the best experts, the most powerful brains, of capitalist society who had foreseen its development was that a transformation must, by historical necessity, take place along the certain broad line, that private ownership of the means of production, had been condemned by history, that it would break, that the exploiters would inevitably be expropriated. This was established with scientific exactitude. We knew it when we raised in our hands the banner of socialism, when we declared ourselves socialists, when we founded socialist parties, and when we seized power in order to embark on socialist reorganization. But the forms of the transformation and the rapidity of the development of the concrete reorganization we could not know. Only collective experience, only the experience of millions, can give decisive indications in this respect.

Lenin is saying plainly that Marx's theories, developed in response to questions raised by the French Revolution, were no longer adequate to the new historical problems that had now been posed by a twentieth-century revolution in a capitalist country and that socialists would have to create new theories based upon the new questions raised by the experiences of revolutionary Russia. Life had caught up with and made a critique of theory.

Having acknowledged the historical and theoretical problem, Lenin saw no concrete alternative to setting up the machinery for centralized planning and controls with all the dangers of a bureaucratic apparatus this entailed and which were soon to become a monstrous fact.

He was to spend the few remaining years of his life warning against this bureaucratic machine and trying to mobilize the masses of the people in positive struggles to undermine it. The chief problem that he faced was the mobilization of the masses themselves for creative organizational work. Over and over again he stated this, constantly seeking to create new forms by which the masses could exercise independent initiative and social responsibility from below: competition, Workers' and Peasants' Inspection, mass accounting and control, volunteer work, independent trade unions. Against the bitter opposition of his more doctrinaire colleagues who held on tenaciously to the abstract advantages of collective property, he even encouraged free enterprise among the peasants through the New Economic Policy. He called on the nationalities to organize, hoping that their awareness of historical and cultural identity would give them the impetus to structure themselves politically.

Lenin's last articles and speeches are full of demands upon the masses to organize themselves from below and thereby struggle against bureaucracy. In language anticipating the cultural revolution in China, he said, "After the problem of the greatest political revolution in the world had been solved, other problems confronted us, cultural problems. . . . The time when it was necessary politically to depict great tasks has gone; the time has come when these tasks must be carried out in practice. Now we are confronted with cultural tasks, the task of assimilating this political experience, which must, and can be put into practice. . . . We must try to make the ability to read and write serve the purpose of raising the level of culture, try to make the peasant learn to read and write for the purpose of improving his farm and his state.

"I hope very much that we shall expel a hundred thousand to two hundred thousand Communists who have attached themselves to the party and who are not only unable to fight against red tape and bribery but even hinder the fight." Note that he made these demands on the masses themselves, instead of mobilizing the masses to make demands on others.

Lenin died in early 1924. What happened after his death is now history. In the ensuing struggle for power, the two ablest and strongest men in the Central Committee were pitted against one another. Stalin, whom Lenin had described in his posthumously published testament as "too rude and inconsiderate of comrades," won out against Trotsky, whom Lenin described in the same document as "the most able man in the present Central Committee —but distinguished also by his too far-reaching self-confidence and a disposition to be too much attracted by the purely administrative side of affairs." Stalin went on to build Russia into what it is today—one of the world's most economically developed and militarily powerful countries, second only to the United States and under the direction of an equally powerful bureaucratic machine.

If Lenin had lived, would he have been able to bring about the cultural revolution which he was obviously trying to mobilize in the last years of his life? If Trotsky had won out in the struggle with Stalin, would he have been able to prevent the bureaucratic degeneration of the first workers' state? Those who occupy themselves with such questions and speculations are living in the past, the fantasy land of "what might have been." Much more important to us should be the fundamental questions which the Russian Revolution has bequeathed to future generations of revolutionists, questions with which Lenin was grappling in the last years of his life.

1. Following the great historical experience of the Russian Revolution, can revolutionists continue to base their activities chiefly on Marx's analysis of the socialist revolution as a revolution in property relations which will release the socialized labor of the working class?

2. Would workers in industrially more advanced countries prove themselves as much in need of a cultural transformation to develop political and social consciousness and responsibility as the backward Russian workers were?

3. What transformations in people, i.e., what kind of cultural revolution, does an oppressed social grouping or potentially revolutionary social force have to undergo to become an effective force in building a new society? What is the most effective way to mobilize a potentially revolutionary social force to make such a transformation in itself? Can the masses be mobilized to transform themselves in the course of the struggle for power so that they will be more capable of preventing the rise of bureaucracy after the revolution?

These are the questions Lenin was asking himself in the last few years of his life with the same seriousness as in his early years he had been trying to decide whether the workers or the peasants were the most revolutionary social force. The contradiction to which he returned time and again in his last articles and speeches was the one between the bold theoretical constructions of the Bolsheviks and their timidity in making the most minor practical changes. "The more abrupt the revolution," he realized, "the longer this contradiction would last." In other words, the less protracted the struggle prior to taking power, the more protracted would be the cultural remolding required thereafter. He urged his comrades to "admit that there has been a radical modification in our whole outlook on socialism . . . formerly we placed, and had to place, the main emphasis on the political struggle, the revolution, on winning political power, etc. Now the emphasis is changing and shifting to peaceful, organizational, 'cultural' work. I should say that emphasis is shifting to educational work, were it not for international relations. If we leave that aside, however, and confine ourselves to internal economic relations, the emphasis in our work is certainly shifting to education."

From our vantage point, it would not be too difficult to infer from this statement that had the new workers' state not been under such pressure from international capitalism, Lenin might have been ready in 1923 for a cultural revolution as drastic as that launched by Mao Tse-tung in 1966.

In his last years Lenin also repeatedly criticized his comrades and the whole International for the European chauvinism implicit in their assumption that the next wave of revolution would come from the Western capitalist countries. It is "the hundreds of millions of the people of Asia which is destined to follow us on the stage of history in the near future," he warned, as he attacked those "European philistines" who "never dream that revolutions might be made otherwise" or that the "subsequent revolutions in Oriental countries, which possess much vaster populations and a much vaster diversity of social conditions, will undoubtedly display even greater distinctions than the Russian Revolution."

Meanwhile, socialists from all over the world flocked to Moscow seeking support, encouragement, advice, spiritual refueling, and all the other blessings which a revolutionary government in power is able to provide. At congress after congress of the Third International, they sang, with the same fervor and the same optimism as we used to sing "We Shall Overcome" in the early 1960s, the battle song of the world working class: "Tis the final conflict/let each stand in his place/the International Party shall lead the human race."

At the Fourth Congress—the last he attended—Lenin criticized the previous year's resolution on organization as being too exclusively Russian and concluded with these somber words:

> I think that the most important thing for us, Russian and foreign comrades alike, is that after five years of the Russian Revolution, we must study. Only now have we secured the possibility to study. I am convinced that we must say in this matter not only to our foreign comrades that the most important task in the period now beginning is to study. We are learning again in a general sense. We must learn in a special sense in order really to achieve organization, structure, method and content of revolutionary work. If this is done, then I am convinced that the prospects of world revolution will be not only good but excellent.

While some members of the Central Committee were giving advice to delegates from other countries who hoped to imitate the Russian success, and others were giving fiery speeches which ended in "long live the Russian Revolution; long live the world revolution" in a half-dozen languages, Lenin was quietly trying to get people to understand that the Russian Revolution was far from the last word, that they must not try to copy what the Russians had done, but rather to study their own experiences and learn from their own problems. "If this is done," he said as he picked up his books and tried to slip to his seat in order to forestall applause, "then I am convinced that the prospects of world revolution will be not only good but excellent."

Today we would only make one change in Lenin's next-to-last public speech. Instead of saying "If this is done," we would say, "if *we* do it." The responsibility begins with those who call themselves revolutionists.

3
THE CHINESE REVOLUTION: PUTTING POLITICS IN COMMAND

The Russian Revolution was the first socialist revolution in history. It is not surprising therefore that it fell short of the great expectations which it had aroused in revolutionary and progressive-minded people all over the world. Unexpectedly isolated by the failure of revolutions in the advanced countries of Western Europe, anticipating attack from a Germany which was being encouraged by other Western powers to build itself into an anti-Bolshevik bridgehead, the new workers' state became preoccupied with defending itself as the only socialist country in the world. Rushing pell-mell into industrialization, it ended up by creating a society as hierarchical, bureaucratic and materialistic as any in the capitalist world.

Many, especially in the West, who had invested their hopes in the Russian Revolution, felt betrayed by these developments. Others refused to see what was taking place before their very eyes. Both reactions testify to how difficult it is to understand that there is no "final struggle," and that the shortest distance between two historical points is not a straight line.

Meanwhile, the idea that the capitalist system is not eternal and that it can be overthrown by the working masses under the leadership of a vanguard party had been loosed upon the world. In China it was seized upon and put into massive practice by a people who, since the middle of the nineteenth century, had been searching for a political philosophy which would be forward-looking rather than backward-looking, i.e., which would enable them to make scientific and economic progress without the exploitation and dehumanization of capitalism.

Today, after more than five decades of incredible struggles, during which they have made maximum use both of their own past and of what has transpired in Russia and the West, the Chinese have created a society in socialist struggle which bears no resemblance to the Soviet Union. In so doing, they have opened up to the world a new vision of revolution as the continuing struggle to create a new more advanced humanity.

The modern crises of Chinese society date back to China's defeat by Britain in the Opium Wars of 1841–1842. This defeat began the disintegration of Chinese society on two levels, ideological and economic. It discredited the ideas of Confucius and of the intellectual bureaucracy on which successive Chinese dynasties and the society as a whole had depended for stability for nearly two thousand years. The result was ideological chaos. It also opened up China to the invasion of Western manufactured goods and Western capital and destroyed the traditional economic and social structure of the country. *At the bottom,* artisans and working people were displaced, including not only the millions of men and women who made the cotton to clothe the Chinese masses, but also such marginal types as pirates and smugglers whose interstitial occupations were now squeezed out by the omnipresent foreign navies and tax collectors. *At the top,* landlords became capitalists, which meant that they not only had to squeeze more money out of the peasants for the purposes of investment, but that they left the villages where they had traditionally exercised authority and began to live in the cities as absentee landlords. *In the middle,* the merchants, traditionally next to the bottom in the social hierarchy, began to rise to the top as their ties with the landlords and Western capital became cemented by "Green Power."

The net result of this introduction of capitalist dynamics into feudal China was pauperization and disintegration on a scale and at a rate hitherto unknown by the Chinese. As the class most materially affected, the Chinese peasants were the first to react to the Western challenge. Their response was rebellion, the traditional reaction of peasants to increasing misery. First, there was the Taiping Rebellion, a rebellion chiefly of Southern peasants who between 1850 and 1864 brought nearly half of China under their control. The Taiping leader, Hung Hsiu-ch'üan, represented himself as the younger brother of Jesus Christ and the second son of God, and developed a remarkably advanced program of what has been called "fantasy socialism." In the same period, between 1852 and 1868, the Northern peasants were led by a dissident Buddhist group in what has been called the Nien Rebellion. Both these rebellions developed within a religious framework, reflecting the way that peasants usually seek metaphysical or supernatural sanction for their struggles.

The Boxer Rebellion of 1900–1901 was the first clearly nationalistic rebellion. Foreign powers had become increasingly aggressive following the exposure of China's weakness by its defeat in the Sino-Japanese War of 1894–1895 and were establishing their spheres of influence all over the country. At the same time, a reform movement had begun to mushroom among Chinese intellectuals who sought the modernization of China. Helpless to check foreign aggression, threatened by the intellectual reform movement, and anxious to divert growing mass discontent, the Manchu Empress Dowager encouraged the growing street force in and around the cities to turn their wrath against the foreigners. Thus encouraged, a wave of anti-foreign violence exploded under the leadership of various secret societies and gangs. This in turn was crushed by a coalition of foreign troops who looted and killed Chinese civilians with the vengefulness which the United States has since made familiar to the world in Vietnam.

In order to defeat the Taiping and Nien Rebellions, the Manchu Dynasty had encouraged the formation by the landlords of regional armies. The new military leaders of these armies, after crushing the peasant rebels, proceeded to establish their own ties with Western capitalism. At the same time they continued to build up their own private armies from the increasing number of unemployed or underemployed youth who thereby gained official sanction for their banditry and pillage of the peasants. In this way the defeated rebellions actually contributed to the further disintegration of the society, since in order to crush them the central government had brought into existence a new social grouping combining the roles of warlord, landlord, and merchant. This new social grouping was powerful enough to create a continuing reign of terror among the peasants, and to weaken the authority of the central government. But it was powerless to resist the increasing foreign incursions on Chinese territorial, economic, and political integrity.

In 1911 Dr. Sun Yat-sen, hoping to establish a Western-style democracy, came back from exile to take over the central government after local revolts in various provinces and cities had led to the establishment of independent local governments. But Dr. Sun was taking over only a powerless apparatus—the authority of the central government had already been destroyed. It was therefore only a matter of time before Dr. Sun, the liberal democrat, was forced to retire by Yuan Shih-kai, one of the warlords. Under Yuan the country continued to disintegrate as the various provinces, under untrammeled warlord governments, were consolidated into spheres of influence by the various imperialist powers.

On May 4, 1919, giant student demonstrations against Western and Japanese imperialism heralded the beginning of the attempt by Chinese intellectuals to reclaim their historic role as the nation's political leaders. In the wake of these demonstrations a number of Chinese intellectuals, including the youthful Mao, then only in his twenties, began to look toward Marxist-Leninism for a revolutionary theory which would enable them to cope with the two critical and increasingly desperate problems of China: its growing helplessness in the face of foreign powers, and, consequently, the deepening impoverishment of the Chinese masses. These intellectuals were attracted towards Marxist-Leninism not only because of the success of the Russian Revolution but also because over a period of seventy-five years every other method which the Chinese had tried in an effort to cope with these two problems had only resulted in their worsening.

Peasant rebellion under religious leadership, nationalist rebellion under secret society leadership, democratic revolution under Western-style patriotic leadership—all had been tried, each in turn had failed. It is impossible to overemphasize the importance of this historical experience of failure. What it meant was that each of these methods, these alternatives, these choices, had not only been eliminated as solutions but that the actual historical recourse to all of them had already contributed substantially to the weakening and destruction of the central government and the authority of the ruling class. The entire society was thus plunged into the chaos which follows widespread and continuing rebellion—vice, crime, armed bandits of both the official and unofficial variety, extortion, rape, kidnapping—in high places and low, in the city streets as well as the rural hinterland. All the old values had been destroyed and no new ones had been created to take their place. No wonder that the Chinese intellectuals, aroused to social responsibility by the May 4 demonstrations, were ready for a comprehensive philosophy which would enable them to transform rebellion into revolution.

During the next decade they would find that their efforts to make a Chinese revolution simply by importing Marxist-Leninism from Russia would prove equally disastrous. But meanwhile Marxist-Leninism provided them with what they urgently needed: a dialectical concept of historical movement towards a modern society through the struggle against feudalism, capitalism, and imperialism; and the concept of a vanguard party or organization of dedicated, disciplined cadres bound together by a revolutionary ideology and programs with which to lead the masses in struggle. In order to appreciate the practical importance of these ideas to the Chinese intellectuals, we must remember that until 1919 their political activity had assumed only two forms; either spontaneous actions, as in the May 4 demonstrations, or study groups and journals containing new ideas for stimulating but essentially endless discussion.

The Chinese Communist (literally *Share Production*) Party held its first congress in 1921 with thirteen people in attendance, representing some sixty members distributed in six centers of activity, mainly large cities like Canton, Shanghai, Peking, Changsha and Wuhan. By the beginning of the 1925–1927 revolution, known as the First Revolutionary Civil War, these cadres had grown in numbers to approximately 950; two years later, at the height of the revolution in April 1927, they had multiplied nearly sixty times to sixty thousand. To the young people in the leadership and ranks of the party, this spectacular growth must have seemed very encouraging. Only later would they discover its dangers.

During the early 1920s the Chinese Communist Party received from Stalin and the Third International intensive ideological indoctrination, political advice and cadre training in methods of organizing and mobilizing the masses. The political advice included the recommendation that the Communists form a United Front with the Chinese Nationalist Party (*Kuomintang*) which had been organized by Dr. Sun Yat-sen. But Dr. Sun and his military leader Chiang Kai-shek, who took over after Sun's death in 1925, had also been impressed with the success of the Russian Revolution and were also seeking and receiving assistance from the Third International in the organization of a party. As a result, the Nationalists, who had close ties to the capitalists and landlords, were also experiencing substantial success in recruiting intellectuals and winning popular support on a general program of national unification, popular government, and social and economic reform.

The rationale behind Moscow's advice to the Chinese Communists was complex. But there is no doubt that at its core was the general Marxist-Leninist conviction of the inevitability of proletarian victory under a disciplined, dedicated revolutionary party, and the still-vivid experience of the powerlessness of the Russian middle classes and capitalists to check proletarian revolution in 1917.

On a world scale it should be added that the struggles in the 1920s in China were the first experience on any significant scale of revolutionary anti-imperialist struggle by any colonial or semi-colonial country. In 1919, at the Second Congress of the Communist International, Lenin had for the first time projected the revolutionary potential of anti-imperialist struggle (the so-called national question). In so doing, he had left open the question as to whether the entire nation, race, or people oppressed by imperialism constituted the equivalent of an oppressed class. It would take the actions of the Kuomintang in 1927 to make unmistakably clear the counter-revolutionary and revolutionary opposites inside the unity of nationalism.

Meanwhile, armed with the model of the Russian Revolution and their training by the Third International, the Chinese Communists proceeded to organize militant workers' unions in the major cities and farmers' associations in the countryside, particularly between Canton and Shanghai. With considerable success they called on the workers and peasants to mobilize on behalf of their own social and economic needs, while preparing to welcome the Nationalist Army which was marching north to unify the country under Chiang Kai-shek.

However, when a half-million Shanghai workers under Communist leadership, backed by a militia of some five thousand men, went on strike in April 1927, Chiang did not turn out to be the weakling that Kerensky, Tsereteli and others had proved to be in 1917 Russia. Instead, with the aid of the financial élite, the big gangsters, and the Western powers, Chiang was able to massacre tens of thousands of workers, and at least five thousand Communists.

Thus what happened in 1927 China turned out to be a replay not of 1917 Russia but of the drama that had been enacted in previous Chinese peasant rebellions. As the Northern Expeditionary Army approached each city or village, following the same route as the Taipings had traveled some seventy-five years earlier, the peasants and workers, organized and encouraged by the Communists, had prepared to welcome them not only with massive demonstrations, but by making militant demands on local capitalists for higher wages and better working conditions, by refusing to turn over crops to the landlords, by taking over mission schools and hospitals from the foreigners. Threatened with destruction, these landlords, capitalists, and foreign missionaries turned to Chiang, the warlord now leading a national army, to crush the workers and peasants and to destroy their leaders as earlier the Manchu rulers had turned to regional warlords and armies.

Many commentators, particularly those sympathetic to Trotsky, have blamed Stalin and the Third International for the catastrophic defeat of the Chinese Communists in 1927. Factual evidence of Stalin's role in guiding Chinese Communist policy during those crucial years is pretty convincing. But to us today, two things are much more important. First, Stalin and Moscow did not force their advice on the Chinese Communist Party; the Chinese themselves had been eager for advice and aid. Secondly, Mao himself did not blame Stalin but instead saw the disaster as a result of the theoretical and practical weaknesses and inexperience of the Chinese Communists themselves. He thereby established some very important theoretical and practical principles for any revolutionary leadership, which he first summed up in his lecture "On Practice" to the cadres preparing for a new stage of struggle at the Anti-Japanese Political and Military Academy in Yenan in 1937.

> Theory can only be tested in practice. In the practice of changing nature or changing society, ideas, theories, plans or programs may turn

out to be partially or entirely incorrect. . . . not only must a true revolutionary leader be adept at correcting his ideas, theories, plans or programs . . . but he must also, when a certain objective process has already advanced and changed from one stage of development to another, be adept at making himself and all his fellow revolutionaries advance and revise their subjective ideas accordingly; that is to say, he must propose new revolutionary tasks and new working programs corresponding to the changes in the new situation. Situations change very rapidly in a revolutionary period; if the knowledge of revolutionaries does not change rapidly in accordance with the changed situation, they cannot lead the revolution towards victory.

To some people what Mao says here may seem so self-evident as to scarcely merit emphasis. Yet if it were so simple, we should find fewer radicals continuing to accept ideologies and programs which have proved counter-productive; *or* wasting so much political energy in blaming others for failure that they have none left to evaluate and struggle against their own internal errors and contradictions; *or* failing to recognize at a glance that those professed political leaders who are always blaming others for defeat are in fact already convinced that they cannot win, and are preparing their alibis in advance.

Writing in October 1939, Mao summed up the failure of the First Revolutionary Civil War in these words: ". . . the party at that time was after all still in its infancy, a party inexperienced in the three basic problems of the United Front, the armed struggle, and party building, a party without much knowledge about China's historical and social conditions, about the characteristics and laws of the Chinese revolution, and a party which had yet no complete understanding of the union between the theory of Marxist-Leninism and the practice of the Chinese Revolution." Significantly, this passage appears in Mao's speech introducing the party's first internal theoretical journal, which had been launched for the express purpose of helping the rapidly growing membership to understand and hence avoid the mistakes of the first United Front with the Kuomintang in the 1920s.

Earlier we said that the events of 1927 had been a re-enactment of the earlier defeats of peasant rebellions in China. But the above passage from Mao brings to our attention the new and crucial ingredient present in 1927 and lacking theretofore. That ingredient was the party—that is, living human beings, cadres who had dedicated their entire selves, not only their arms, legs, and hearts but also their minds to revolutionary change, who had consciously and responsibly accepted a theory and tried to implement programs based upon that theory, and who were now ready as disciplined, dedicated, reflective human beings to accept the responsibility of developing and struggling over new theories and programs derived from evaluating the practice of earlier ones.

Mao never seems to tire of reminding the Chinese people of the distinctively human capacity to learn from experience. The continuing, committed, self-critical and organized way in which a group of people assumes responsibility for exercising this distinctively human capacity in a continuing relation "from the masses, to the masses" is what Mao calls the Marxist theory of knowledge, of which the party is the highest expression. Whether in defeat or in victory, or in that interim state of neither defeat nor victory (which is the most usual for the revolutionist), the dominant theme of Mao is the need for the party to learn by a dialectical process, from practice to theory to practice, in an organized interaction with the masses. In Mao's speech to the party as it prepared to take power in 1949, the phrase "we must learn" occurs at least eight times. This humility is reminiscent of the Lenin of 1923 and markedly different from the Lenin of 1917 who was so confident that "we will build socialism."

Not all the Chinese Communists who survived the 1927 massacre were ready to make the necessary reassessment. Unfortunately but inevitably, there were many who felt that the ferocity of the counter-revolution left no time to think or to re-evaluate, and who therefore allowed themselves to be provoked to increasingly desperate efforts to implement theories and programs which had already proved disastrous, as in the Canton uprising.

On the other hand, Mao and a few others retreated to the countryside, where first they led the peasants in armed struggles to seize land and set up revolutionary Soviets; then they became engaged in see-saw battles with Chiang's armies, which were out to crush them, and therefore undertook the fantastic six-thousand-mile Long March into the Northwest Provinces in 1934–1935. There, relatively isolated from the powerful ideological influence both of the Soviet Union and the West, they were finally able, in 1936, to begin establishing the Yenan base from which to develop the new philosophy, the new strategies, and the new programs, and therewith the cadres and the army to launch a new political offensive based on rallying the whole nation in a Second United Front with the Kuomintang, for a struggle against the Japanese invaders and to build a new China.

Meanwhile, Chiang Kai-shek and the Kuomintang in the cities were becoming completely dependent on the military and technological power of planes and weapons from the United States. With no base in the people, they became increasingly desperate and therefore resorted increasingly to the kind of terrorism against the people which we have since seen practiced by successive South Vietnamese regimes. Chiang passed antisubversive laws, put thought police into the schools, tortured youthful political dissidents, endlessly escalating the state police, the party police, the secret police. Thus step by step, he alienated all but the most corrupt and self-seeking elements in Chinese society until he had destroyed any kind of functioning army, functioning economy, or social order.

The result was that in October 1949 the Communist Party and the Red Army, which had fought its way under Mao's leadership from the surrounding countryside to the coastal cities, was able to take over the whole country, while the completely discredited Chiang could only flee to Taiwan with his henchmen and all the loot they could plunder.

It was only after intense debate and heated ideological struggles inside the party that Mao was able to win support, first for the Long March to Yenan, and then for the Second United Front with the Kuomintang. This cannot be too strongly emphasized, since it is impossible to understand the revolutionary politics of China, or indeed of any country, if one believes that all Mao had to do was give the word for the rest of the party to fall into line. This is the kind of myth which usually develops after a particular policy or individual leader has been spectacularly successful, becoming entrenched with the lapse of time. Whether in the beatific form of hero-worship, or the horrific form of faceless, passive masses obeying ruthless single-minded leaders, this myth is the opiate of the masses because it destroys their zeal for the political struggles without which political development is impossible.

Like any revolutionary leader worthy of the name, Mao knew that *a sentence that reveals the cultural rigidity of the received tradition of the Left the prose itself, to be ideologically "sanctioned" become wooden.*

differences exist within every situation and that new differences are always emerging after old ones have been resolved. This dialectical process of duality emerging within unity is especially marked in a vanguard organization which has been formed on the basis of a common ideology. It accelerates as the organization moves from the abstract to the concrete, from theory to practice, from agreement in words to devising programs of action, and especially as an organization grows in size and effectiveness.

Therefore a revolutionary leader must not only project directions, but also encourage democratic discussion of these projections, knowing that, in the course of discussion and debate, the differences will become clearer and eventually polarize. Then individual members must choose between the opposing roads, since without a choice there cannot be forward movement but only mutually canceling motions in all directions or up and down in one place. Extensive discussion ensures that after a decision has been reached by majority vote, not only the membership but the original proposer will understand its implications and the practical difficulties involved in carrying it out. Once the decision has been reached, everybody is bound by it, including those whose proposals are defeated. Both sides must expect to remain in the same organization. Otherwise the discussion has just been discussion for the sake of interesting (and endless) discussion, democracy for the sake of democracy. — *Hmm!*

Without the party Mao would have had no cadre (framework) for this process of proposing, discussion, polarization, and choice between opposing roads. In other words, without the party the world today would not have Mao's voluminous "writings," which are actually party documents for party discussion, party debate, party conferences, party schools, at critical moments in the development of the struggle, when differences or contradictions were emerging over policy. The continuing debates throughout the period leading to and after the formation of the Yenan government provided the Chinese party with valuable experiences in political struggle and the process of democratic discussion and decision-making. One of the important reasons for the bureaucratic degeneration of the Bolshevik Party after the seizure of power in 1917 was that underground life and continuing provocation by the Tsarist secret police had deprived the Russian revolutionaries of this practice in democratic processes. Traditional Chinese society had not provided the Chinese with political experiences of this kind any more than traditional Russian society had provided them for the Bolsheviks. Hence the continuing importance of ideological struggles to the Chinese revolution.

Equally important was the issue around which the ideological struggles in the Chinese party centered throughout the 1930s. It is one over which every revolutionary organization in every country must struggle before a serious struggle for power can take place.

Throughout the 1930s there were a number of Chinese Communists (particularly among those who had studied in the Soviet Union or in Europe) who were still trying to adapt the ideas of Marx and Lenin on class struggle and revolution to the revolutionary struggle in China. Some of these Communists regarded the retreat to the countryside as only a temporary interlude, and were impatiently awaiting a return to what they regarded as the real revolutionary struggle in the cities between the proletariat and the capitalists. Others simply wanted to transfer to the peasant struggle what they regarded as the proletarian model of class struggle, i.e., a constantly escalating antagonism over the distribution of land between peasants and landlords, or between poor peasants and rich peasants. There were also those whose only perspective for revolution was continuing armed confrontations between the Red Army and the Kuomintang Army which would hopefully culminate one D-Day in a decisive victory for the former.

Mao, on the other hand, was beginning to make a sober evaluation of the defeats of the 1920s and the ensuing see-saw battles with Chiang Kai-shek. Out of the catastrophic experiences with Chinese nationalism, he was beginning to gain a new appreciation of the national realities of China. Swimming about in a sea of peasants, he began to acquire that intellectual freedom and boldness inseparable from great revolutionary leadership. Slowly it began to dawn on him how relatively insignificant were the Eastern seaboard cities, the tiny Chinese bourgeoisie and the tiny Chinese proletariat, compared to the huge Chinese hinterland, the hundreds of millions of Chinese peasants, and the long cultural tradition of the Chinese. If the Chinese Communist Party was seriously struggling for power, it would have to quit trying to adapt the ideas of Marx and Lenin, and the scenario of the Russian Revolution to the Chinese scene. Instead it now had the awesome responsibility for devising a new revolutionary scenario or strategy which would both break with and take advantage of the long Chinese past. It would have to create its own vision of the goal of a Chinese revolution, its own definition of revolutionary class struggle. In short, if there was ever going to be a revolution in China, it would have to be a Chinese revolution. Quantitatively, it would have to embrace the great majority of the Chinese people and the entire country. Qualitatively, it would have to project goals and methods which the whole nation could recognize as advancing and enriching the values which the Chinese people had already contributed to the development of all humankind.

From the moment that Mao had retreated to the countryside in the late 1920s, he had been wondering how the peasants could be transformed into a revolutionary social force. He knew that there was no point in his even thinking about Marx's concept of the working class organized and disciplined by the process of capitalist production itself. Given China's state of industrial development as a semicolonial country, his problem was not a virtually nonexistent working class. It was the seemingly inexhaustible supply of youthful bandits and rebels roving the countryside. How could they be transformed into revolutionary soldiers? If they were recruited into the party, how would the party escape being infected with the military viewpoint, the ideology of roving rebel bands, the remnants of putschism, the lack of discipline, the subjectivism, and the illusion of absolute egalitarianism which distinguish such people in any country in which young people have become expendable in the existing mode of production?

Mao's December 1929 resolution, published under the title "Correcting Mistaken Ideas in the Party," shows how he was even then thinking of the political remolding or rectification of people which the party would have to undertake.

As both the military struggles against Chiang's encirclement campaigns and the debate over political direction within the party became more heated during the early 1930s, the national revolutionary strategy necessary for the conquest of power began to take shape in Mao's mind. The Communists, he realized, could not possibly come to power if they concentrated on increasing the bitterness of the different sections of the population against one another. Victory was possible only if they could unite the largest possible number behind them in armed struggle around a progressive issue of common concern.

Furthermore, the armed struggle could not possibly take the form of continuing confrontation with the hope of a D-Day kind of victory. It was necessary to develop the form of protracted guerrilla warfare from gradually expanding rural bases. This guerrilla warfare must not only have military purposes. The Red Army must see itself as "an armed group for carrying out political tasks of a class nature." In other words, protracted guerrilla warfare depended upon, and could be used as a means for, the most rapid political development of the peasant masses. Under the circumstances, it was the best means to expand their concern and their capacity for social and political decision-making beyond their previous narrow preoccupation with material survival.

In every class society, the masses live restricted lives dominated by economic considerations, while politics remains the province of the ruling class or its agents, the politicians. Nowhere had this class restriction on the masses been so institutionalized as in China, where for thousands of years the masses had been considered capable only of partial or small interests, while the intellectuals or "gentlemen" were responsible for the general or social interest. Hence in China the essence of revolutionary class struggle meant protracted struggle by the party to challenge the peasant masses to "Put Politics in Command of Economics," i.e., to assume the rights and responsibilities for social decision-making which had theretofore been the exclusive responsibility of the intellectuals. At the end of a combined struggle, both against the external enemy which rested upon this class relationship and against the political backwardness of the masses, the revolutionary party would be able to capture the total power necessary to transform the whole society.

In this concept of transformation or remolding of the masses, Mao was drawing on the centuries-old Chinese cultural tradition which, since the time of Confucius, has stressed moral rather than legal force as the foundation of political authority and legitimacy, and conceives goodness in terms of a relation between people rather than as a moral quality which an individual can have on his/her own. For example, "politics" is conveyed in the Chinese language by two characters, pronounced *zheng zhi*. *Zheng* means "to straighten or correct" while *zhi* means "to heal or cure." The character for humanity or benevolence is made up of two radicals, the radical for *ren*, meaning "man" or "human being," and the radical for *er*, meaning "two," i.e., more than one.

But the revolutionary class difference between the Chinese cultural tradition and Mao's concept of cultural transformation is equally sharp. In Chinese tradition, the goodness of ordinary people involved their acceptance of the limitations of their position in the social hierarchy and the judgment or direction of those above them in this hierarchy. In the family, the son was subordinate to the father and the wife to the husband. In the political realm, the Mandarins or intellectuals were responsible for defining wisdom and moral principle, while the masses at the bottom were deemed capable of acting only by ritual. On the other hand, in Mao's new concept of transformation, goodness or responsibility to society requires *everybody*, intellectuals and masses, men and women, young and old alike, to *fanshen*, i.e., to struggle both against the internal limitations stemming from their position in the social structure, and against those who try to maintain the structure which limits them in this way. Thus the class struggle is the struggle to transcend the limitations of class society.

This is well put.

The political struggle for state power can be effective only after the great majority of a society, beginning with the most oppressed, have been set into motion to struggle against their old habits of individualism and self-interest, their old social ties to family and clan, their old ideas of right and wrong in terms of hierarchy—in short, to *fanshen* or overturn themselves. Thus, in Mao's concept of class struggle, economic struggle has not only become subordinate to political struggle but is recognized as implicitly, and eventually explicitly, contradictory to political struggle.

In this concept of transformation the basis has also been laid for going beyond the traditional Leninist or mechanical concept of the relation between party and mass which suggests that the party, a relatively small physical entity or apparatus, sets into motion the masses, a much larger physical entity, in escalating struggles for economic or material needs. Physical combat with the external enemy and the violent struggle for state power are still necessary, but they become episodes within the context of the fundamental ongoing struggle to enlarge the political consciousness and sense of social responsibility in the people. Moreover, after every physical or military victory, the battle to expand the political activities of the masses must begin again on a higher level because the aim has never been just to gain power but has essentially been the continuing transformation of the great masses of men and women and children into politically conscious, socially responsible, independently creative, and unashamedly self-critical human beings.

By grappling with the concrete contradictions of the Chinese reality and by using the contributions of the Chinese past to serve the China present and future, Mao began to create a new strategy and new goals for revolutionary struggle completely different from those which had developed in Russia. Instead of trying to capture state power abruptly or with one audacious blow, he conceived the struggle for power as a protracted struggle, in the course of which the mass revolutionary forces would not only defeat the class enemy but would steadily increase their own zeal as well as their practical capacity and power for political decision-making. Instead of the oppressed struggling against the oppressor to obtain a bigger slice of a pie which already exists (land, means of production, profits, state power), the oppressed are mobilized through concrete struggles to increase their capacity and power to govern, while the oppressors are welcomed back if they are ready to accept the new situation created by the decisions of politically conscious masses. At the end of such a protracted struggle, the new revolutionary government would be in a much better position to prevent the bureaucratic degeneration which in Russia had been encouraged by the masses' own political apathy and preoccupation with questions of economic survival.

Mao did not win the political support of the party for his new revolutionary strategy until the Tsunyi Conference, held in January 1935 during the Long March. It is only at this Conference that he assumed the newly created posts of Chairman of the Political Committee and also head of the party's Military Committee. And it was not until December 1935, nearly a year later, when the Central Soviet Government had been established at Yenan, that he was able to convince the party to adopt the policy of joining with the Kuomintang in a Second United Front to fight the Japanese invaders.

Heated debate was necessary to persuade the majority of the Political Committee that the disasters of the First United Front with the Kuomintang could not recur. The Communist Party had now been seasoned by political and armed struggle and the Long March, Mao explained patiently. It had a clear political strategy, its own government, its own army, and its own territorial base, whereas Chiang Kai-shek was supported only by a thin upper crust and was becoming increasingly dependent upon the United States for arms and money. Hence only those comrades still dominated either by dogmatic formulae of class struggle or instant revolution borrowed from the Russian Revolution, or by subjective hatreds lingering from the bitter experiences of the 1920s, could fail to see the long-run advantages to the Communists of a new United Front with the Kuomintang.

Through this debate the party members began to learn that in revolutionary politics one cannot afford to make policy based on resentments stored up from past grievances. In the historical development of any movement or any society, many wrongs are done, many mistakes made. A revolutionary leadership must, of course, try to ensure the objective conditions which prevent these wrongs from being repeated. But if all those who have wronged an individual, a movement, or a people are never given an opportunity to conduct themselves differently, where are they to go? Moreover, only sectarians confuse their conviction that the enemy cannot be redeemed, which they have gained from their own experiences, with the awareness of the masses who have not undergone these same experiences and who, except in the heat of battle, are usually ready to give their oppressors another chance if only because it puts off the time when they must themselves assume the responsibility for governing.

In the summer of 1937, speaking to the cadres at the Anti-Japanese Military and Political College at Yenan, Mao explained in his famous lectures "On Practice" and "On Contradiction" the process by which he had arrived at the new concepts of revolutionary struggle which were now guiding the activities of the party. Mao was now ready to generalize this process into a set of philosophical principles. But he also left no doubt that his aim was not just abstract philosophy but the continuing struggle against the erroneous tendencies which remained in the party and which exist in one form or another in any vanguard party. These are the tendencies to *dogmatism*, i.e., to turn the successful ideas of the past or ideas in books into formulae which one simply applies or tries to prove in the present, without grappling with the concrete contradictions of the new situation; and to *empiricism*, i.e., the tendency simply to react to the present concrete situation without the guidance of general conceptions drawn from past experiences.

In "On Practice" Mao outlines the process by which knowledge in fact develops, from the *perceptions* of concrete reality which arise in the course of practical experiences, to the *conceptions* which penetrate into the essence, the totality, and the internal relations of these concrete phenomena. It was through this process that Mao himself had arrived at the realization that the Chinese revolution would have to be a *Chinese* revolution, and at concepts and goals for the revolutionary struggle far beyond those of the Russian Revolution. How advanced these new concepts were can be seen by his statement in "On Practice" that "when the whole of Mankind consciously remolds itself and changes the world, the era of world communism will dawn."

Note the way in which Mao joins mankind's task of "consciously remolding itself" with that of "changing the world." Many radicals, consciously ignoring the profound questions raised by Lenin after the Russian Revolution, still believe that all one has to do is eliminate oppressive institutions with one audacious blow and the oppressed masses will automatically change. Many people still continue to believe that human behavior is completely determined by objective conditions. Through the practice of revolutionary struggle, however, the Chinese have developed the strategy of struggling simultaneously to transform both institutions and people. Institutions which promote hierarchy and exploitation must be eliminated, but institutions are not rubbed out like marks on a blackboard. The oppressed are an integral part of the system which oppresses them, unless they break loose from that system. Therefore until they begin to change themselves, i.e., to become self-determining rather than determined, they cannot get rid of oppressive institutions. Moreover, eliminating oppressive institutions only provides the external conditions for the transformation of people; it does not guarantee that people will change. The change in people has to be made by people themselves.

Note also that Mao is not defining communism within the traditional distributive-productive (economic) framework of "To each according to his needs, from each according to his abilities." His framework is rather the distinctively political one of "Mankind consciously transforming itself and changing the world."

A month later Mao returned to the attack on the dogmatists in his lecture "On Contradiction." Contradiction is a universal phenomenon, but this universal phenomenon can only exist in a particular form and development can only take place through the struggle to resolve the internal contradictions of a particular reality. Mao was still trying to get the cadres to recognize the Chinese-ness of the Chinese revolution. "Some people," he said, are still trying to introduce into the Chinese revolution the Marxist formula that "the productive forces and the economic basis always play the decisive role. . . . This is the mechanistic materialist conception."

In concrete practice, Mao had realized that to apply this mechanistic materialistic formula to a Chinese revolution would preclude the possibility of a Chinese revolution, since a semicolonial country like China can never achieve more than the most insignificant development of productive forces. Mao had already won support for his revolutionary strategy to remold the Chinese masses through political struggles. Now he was laying a philosophic foundation so that in the future development of the Chinese revolution (and indeed in all future revolutions), the revolutionists would be able to recognize that economic development is not a prerequisite for political development, and can even become an obstacle to it. "When a task, no matter which, has to be performed," he says,

> but there is yet no guiding line, method, plan or policy, the principal and decisive thing is to decide on a guiding line, method, plan or policy. When the superstructure (politics, culture, etc.) obstructs the development of the economic base, political and cultural changes become principal and decisive. Are we going against materialism when we say this? No. The reason is that while we recognize that in the general development of history, the material determines the mental and social being determines social consciousness, we also—and indeed must—recognize the reaction of mental on material things, of social consciousness on social being and of the superstructure on the economic base. This does not go against materialism, on the contrary, it avoids mechanical materialism and firmly upholds dialectical materialism.

In this lecture Mao also lays the philosophic basis by which revolutionary leadership can avoid freezing any struggle between opposing classes into an antagonistic relationship.

Antagonism is one form, but not the only form, of the struggle of opposites.

We must make a concrete study of the circumstances of each specific struggles of opposites and should not arbitrarily apply the formula [of antagonistic contradiction] discussed above to everything. Contradiction and struggle are universal and absolute, but the methods of resolving contradictions, that is, the forms of struggle, differ according to the differences in the nature of the contradictions. Some contradictions are characterized by open antagonism, others are not. In accordance with the concrete development of things, some contradictions which were originally non-antagonistic develop into antagonistic ones, while others which were originally antagonistic develop into non-antagonistic ones.

These statements must also be seen both as guides to the concrete problems faced by the party in furthering the Chinese revolution and as guides to general revolutionary practice. Concretely, Mao was searching for the methods that would unite the landlords and the peasants in a struggle to oust the Japanese imperialists, and at the same time improve the conditions and the strength of the peasants relative to that of the landlords. Out of this search has come the distinctive style of the Chinese revolution which involves the most aggressive struggle against the antihuman or antisocial behavior of the class enemy, while always leaving the door open for the individual member of the enemy class to re-enter the social and moral universe. The key to this style lies in first arousing the oppressed out of their lethargy to carry out struggles based on what is right, to the point that the humanity within the oppressors is itself stirred to revulsion against their past behavior and to a desire for reform. In this way, it is only the most diehard reactionaries who become isolated while the revolutionary forces grow in strength and numbers.

It is important to note that Mao originally presented these new philosophical concepts to the cadre training school. First, he was concerned that the cadres themselves, many of whom were students from the cities, understand the need to struggle against their own internal contradictions, and especially the tendency of intellectuals to dogmatism, before going among the masses to develop them in struggle. Second, as anyone who has trained cadres soon learns, you cannot build continuing commitment simply on the basis of compas-

i.e. the illus in that "the people "can and should "write their own history."

sion for the oppressed or on the romantic myth that the oppressed already have the answers to the building of a new society. All you can build on compassion and myth is continuing disappointment which in turn leads to either careerism or to desperate acts of adventurism. For continuing commitment to protracted struggle, cadres must first internalize a profoundly human vision of the goals toward which a revolution is moving. Then the party must provide them with concrete programs for the systematic transformation, stage by stage, of the most oppressed masses through collective struggles, or what the Chinese call "a mass line." Without cadres committed to such a vision and to such concrete programs among the masses, leadership of the masses quickly turns into community organization or community projects. The concept of transformation itself quickly turns into another form of idealism, i.e., of religious conversion or individual therapy inside a room. This is true no matter how large the group which is engaged in this "behind closed doors" transformation. Without such programs the individual begins to believe that there is a final answer or state of beatitude toward which he/she is striving and hence to compare him/herself with others who seem to be further advanced toward this goal. The latter in turn begin to use their more elevated position on this ladder to manipulate those below.

On the other hand, through the practical programs of a party, the cadres have a practical and objective way to develop and evaluate both their own development and that of the masses, knowing that in the course of practice they will discover new problems or contradictions which will require new programs.

How this strategy was applied in practice can be seen from the way cadres mobilized the peasants of Ten Mile Inn to fight the Japanese, as described by David and Isabel Crook in *Revolution in a Chinese Village* (New York: Humanities Press, 1959). As the Japanese army approached a village, it would send word ahead for the villagers to set up a structure to levy taxes and to procure grain and women for their use. In many villages the peasants, having experienced the plundering by Chiang's troops, were apathetic, because they could not see how the Japanese could be any worse. To arouse the peasants to political action and heighten their social consciousness, small units of Chinese cadres would begin a heated debate around the question of how the levies should be paid, whether on the

i.e. cease to be cultural transformation.

H. L.

basis of a flat rate per capita, or by a bigger burden on the rich and the exemption of the poorest. The landlords, of course, preferred the flat rate, and since they knew that the Japanese would enforce it, were ready to welcome the enemy. The poor peasants, on the other hand, having been exposed to a vision of a more just apportionment of the burden, began to act on the Communist proposal to evacuate the villagers with all their belongings and to hide in the hills until the Japanese had left. This forced the landlords to follow the peasants' example since if they remained behind, they would be the only ones available for the Japanese to tax. The landlords were still acting on the basis of self-interest, while the peasants' political consciousness had been enlarged to include new concepts of justice and equity through debate and action. Thus, in terms of political consciousness and social responsibility, the positions of the rulers and the ruled had been reversed.

Particularly moving and instructive are the cases of *fanshen* by Chinese women, the majority of whom had been for centuries in much the same position within Chinese society as the blacks inside U.S. society—enslaved, raped, and beaten by men, forced to marry against their will, waiting hand and foot on their husbands and in-laws, thrown only scraps for food and rags for clothing.

To convince these women that they would have some support when they decided to rebel, a unit of the Chinese Red Army would first pass through a village. Shortly after it had left, one or two Communist cadres would come into the village, call a meeting of the women, declare that the Communists stood for the equality of women and the right of divorce, and then urge those women with particular grievances to meet with them secretly. By patient and continuous work of this kind, a women's association would eventually be formed. On the invitation of an especially abused woman, the group would then visit her husband or father-in-law, take him prisoner and expose him to a small group "Speak Bitterness" meeting at which the aggrieved woman would pour out her complaints. Sometimes the assembled women would be so moved by the tale of abuse that they would beat the offender mercilessly, particularly if he remained unrepentant. But in many cases the public shaming was enough to force the recalcitrant man to reform and to seek readmission to the moral and social universe.

The dialectical movement here is what the Chinese Communists call "unity-criticism-unity," that is, from an old outworn unity, through struggle, to a new and more righteous one. The strategy has the enormous advantage of stabilizing rather than tearing apart a society through struggle. For example, as Jan Myrdal observed in *Report from a Chinese Village* (New York: Signet, 1965), women who had exercised their new freedom to divorce their husbands and remarry men of their own choice, then felt a moral obligation to struggle to make their new marriages work. Freedom had become responsibility. This is an example of the dialectical approach to abstract concepts which is becoming a part of the Chinese way of thinking as a result of the actual struggles of the Chinese revolution. Nothing is an end in itself except the continuing struggle to advance, to enlarge one's humanity. Freedom is not for the sake of freedom, democracy is not for the sake of democracy, organization is not for the sake of organization. Each of these is only a means to the evolutionary human goal. Any other way of thinking or acting about a result which has been achieved leads one into the defense of abstractions even when these abstractions have become fetters on further development.

It cannot be repeated too often that none of these struggles was an isolated event, either in time or in space, because cadres of the party had already been organized. New ones were constantly being recruited and developed to carry on the continuous evaluation of each step of the struggle "from the masses, to the masses"; to relate the struggles within one community to those in another; and to assume the responsibility within each community for encouraging the downtrodden to begin organizing new structures in which they could learn through trial and error the responsibilities of self-government, thus constantly increasing not only the momentum but the vision of the masses relative to that of the upper classes.

The policy of uniting members from opposing classes in a common struggle entailed great risks, as indeed any bold step forward always does. In particular, by encouraging intellectuals and members of the landlord class to join in the anti-Japanese resistance and help in the administration of the many new areas coming under Communist control, the party ran the risk of crowding out the often illiterate peasant cadres by those with superior literary and technical skills.

There was a real danger that the traditional Chinese class division between the politically active intellectuals and the politically passive masses might be restored.

By this time Mao had begun to realize the practical importance for revolutionary struggle and the tremendous historical significance of the new unity of intellectuals and peasants which the party was forging. Peasant rebellions over economic grievances had been a continuing part of the Chinese landscape for thousands of years—indeed, an old Chinese saying refers to "a small rebellion every thirty years, a big one every hundred years." At the opposite pole, a substantial section of the intellectual class had always been concerned with political philosophy. But they had seen this philosophy chiefly as a way to remold bad rulers into good ones and even in some cases to get rid of those rulers who were behaving so badly that they could not be regarded as rulers at all. Hitherto, the Chinese peasants and the Chinese intellectuals had never gotten together politically, with the result that Chinese society had remained practically the same for thousands of years. Moreover, because the Chinese intellectuals had never made a serious critique of the Chinese intellectual tradition or their own role in it, they had for centuries wavered between the Taoist outlook, which views movement forward in history as movement towards disintegration, and the Confucian outlook, which views the intellectual as responsible for giving political guidance to the ruler. Only after they had adopted the philosophy of Marxist-Leninism were the Chinese intellectuals able to break loose from this dilemma. Since then, the anti-Japanese struggle had given them the opportunity to practice their new political relationship with the masses. Now this new unity was giving rise to new contradictions.

In *The Yenan Way in Revolutionary China* (Cambridge: Harvard University Press, 1971), Mark Selden has described some of the forms assumed by this new contradiction and the way that the party dealt with these.

Between 1937 and 1941 two distinct types of cadres began to form: the bureaucracy centered at the regional level in Yenan and made up of educated officials capable of handling the growing volume of paper work and reports; and the local cadres who had been elected to the councils running local districts by the people of that district. The first was beginning to send down orders to the second, in much the way that the Chinese bureaucracy always had, but now they were doing it in the name of the revolution.

To meet this new contradiction, Mao launched the Rectification Campaign of 1942, mobilizing both the intellectual cadres and the local cadres to undergo intensive criticism and self-criticism in order that each might overcome its partial or subjective viewpoint and develop a wider view. In this campaign Mao showed how to pose criticism and self-criticism in objective historical terms rather than in individualistic or personal ones. The cadres of peasant origin who were experienced in work, Mao directed, "must take up the study of theory and must read seriously; only then will they be able to systematize and synthesize their experience and raise it to the level of theory; only then will they not mistake their partial experience for universal truth and not commit empiricist errors."

On the other hand, the intellectuals must struggle against "the greater danger," their tendency to dogmatism, their habit of "fancying themselves as learned" and their tendency to use "odd quotations from Marxist-Leninist works as a ready-made panacea which, once acquired, can easily cure all maladies." In other words, the Chinese revolution could not succeed if, at one pole, the workers and peasants did not strive to develop their minds and their political capacities or if, at the other pole, the Chinese intellectuals used the writings of Marx and Lenin in the same dogmatic way that Chinese intellectuals had been using the Analects of Confucius for thousands of years.

Anticipating the Cultural Revolution by two decades, the Rectification Campaign was conducted through intensive meetings taking the place of regular schooling, which was suspended for more than a year throughout the organization. To meet a pressing practical need of the revolution, the party had to break down leadership concepts reappearing like ghosts from the Chinese past. In order to do so, they were introducing into and making a normal part of Chinese political life, the objective and historical method of criticism and self-criticism.

In June 1943, as the Rectification Campaign continued, Mao returned to the fundamental problems involved in uniting the intellectual leadership with the peasant masses. In "Some Questions Concerning Methods of Leadership" he says that the question is fundamentally one of combining the "general with the particular."

"Subjectivists and bureaucrats do not understand the principle of combining the leadership with the masses and the general with the particular," he says. "They clearly impede the work of the Party." It is in this document that the famous passage on "From the masses, to the masses" appears. In it Mao also deals very concretely with how a leader gives direction on specific tasks to the rank and file and how he/she draws workers and peasants into the leadership.

Meanwhile the party had begun concrete measures to reorganize the actual structure of government so as to achieve both the advantages of centralization without the disadvantages of bureaucracy, and the advantages of self-reliance and popular participation from below without the disadvantages of anarchy. Previously the regional administration had been sending down directives on a vertical basis to the district administrations which in turn sent them down to the individual district. Now policies from the regional administration had first to be approved by a district magistrate and a district affairs committee, mostly composed of local cadres and elected by the people of the local area. This early experience in reorganizing the channels of responsibility and communication in order to combine the advantages of centralization and decentralization would be called upon again and again after the Communists came to power in 1949. Through the effort to resolve a concrete contradiction, which was at the same time a historical contradiction reappearing from the Chinese past, the party was learning that all organizational structures contain the danger of bureaucracy and therefore no organizational structure should be considered immune from drastic reorganization.

It is only by keeping vividly in mind the struggles within the party and in the party's relationship with the masses during the period before the conquest of power that we can understand the dramatic developments that have been taking place in China since 1949.

When the Chinese Communists took power, they faced the first two tasks of every revolutionary government, namely, to defend the new socialist state against the imperialist enemies; and to increase or maintain production and services on a level that would assure the economic welfare of the masses. By 1952 the Communists had demonstrated in the Korean War that they could take care of the first of these tasks, and by 1955 they were well on their way to achievement of the second. Mao concluded therefore that the time had come to make another big jump toward the fundamental goal of developing the masses politically. Conscious of the traditional preoccupation of the Chinese masses with economics, whether their material conditions were worsening or improving, aware also of the steady depoliticization taking place in Russia in the wake of economic development, he set out to jolt the masses into the kind of political discussion and ideological struggle which had helped the party make the revolution before 1949.

The politics of this period, known as the Let a Hundred Flowers Bloom period, is set forth in "On the Correct Way to Handle Contradictions Among the People." In this document Mao makes clear that democracy must not be regarded as an end in itself or as a symbol which moves some people to cheers and others to jeers. It is a political process, a procedure in which people engage in discussion, debate, and controversy and thus arrive at political understanding and the capacity to make political decisions. The time had come, Mao felt, for the Chinese people to begin to engage in this essential political activity so as not to drift back into preoccupation with economic activities.

As it turned out, Mao was premature in his expectation that the Chinese masses were ready for this kind of political discussion and ideological controversy. Mao had assumed that the six years of material security and improvements which socialism had made possible for the Chinese masses meant that they would be ready to defend socialism politically. Instead, when the intellectuals launched a barrage of reactionary attacks against socialism, the masses did not come forward. Mao was therefore forced to clamp down on the intellectuals.

Most Western observers find it inconceivable that in the midst of a period of economic progress, Mao should have deliberately precipitated an ideological crisis. One observer has even called this practice "a vicious circle." It is inconceivable to him, as to other Western social scientists, that it might be virtuous rather than vicious to intervene politically, when economic development is progressing smoothly, for the specific purpose of keeping people from becoming obsessed with the pursuit of material comforts and to remind them that the chief aim of a new society in this day and age is to create not gluttons but politically and socially responsible human beings. For them the idea that economics should command politics is as normal as breathing. They do not stop to question whether constantly expanding production and constantly expanding consumption are good for human beings. They simply assume that because constantly expanding production and constantly expanding consumption have become the way of life in the United States, it has always been and should always be the goal of all societies and all countries.

On the other hand, during the protracted struggles leading to the conquest of power, Mao had conceived the goal of revolution to be "Mankind consciously remolding itself and changing the world." His retreat from the Hundred Flowers campaign was therefore only temporary, for the purpose of asking himself why the peasants and intellectuals were still so bourgeois, so individualistic, so preoccupied with their own self-interest. His conclusion was that the peasant masses had not yet had sufficient experience in the collective practices and structures of modern production. Hence in 1958 he launched the campaign known as the Great Leap Forward, calling for the formation of communes all over the country and a rapid expansion of industrial production which would educate the peasants to behave more collectively.

Economically the Great Leap Forward was a failure. The emphasis on heavy industry was disproportionate and light industries as well as agriculture suffered. To make things worse, the Russians pulled out their technicians in 1960, leaving many Chinese factories stranded for parts and skills. Nature was also unfriendly, and one of the worst droughts in years resulted in crop failure and famine. Consequently, Mao was forced to step down as head of government and was replaced by Liu Shao-ch'i.

But at the same time the peasants were making gains in collective political and scientific consciousness. Through the involvement of everybody in collective production in the communes, the rural population was given the opportunity to approach fundamental problems in collective practice rather than as individuals. A new concept of equality began to emerge, one which avoids both the myth that everybody is equal and the concept of equal opportunity which encourages everybody to rise above everybody else and thereby creates competition and envy between individuals. David and Isabel Crook have given an account of how this new concept of equality was developed through practice at one commune. In the chapter on "Mass Line Leadership and Leaders in Rural China" in their book on *The First Years of the Yangyi Commune* (New York: Humanities Press, 1966), they write: "The county cadres went by the principle of 'grasp each end to pull forward the middle.' This meant, on the one hand, spending time with units which had achieved conspicuous successes, mastering their methods and helping them to advance still further; and on the other hand, working with units where failures had occurred, giving them guidance and help. After the experience of both the backward and advanced had been summed up, lessons were drawn and publicized for the benefit of the mass of average units—'the middle'—so that similar mistakes might be avoided and successes achieved on the broadest possible front." Thus equality in China has come to mean very practical struggles to break down traditional class divisions. The basic aim is that no individual or group should be left behind economically or culturally and that society should not become a pyramid with all the knowledge and skills at the top and the masses doomed to ignorance and backwardness at the bottom. But at the same time it is also a struggle against reducing everybody to homogeneity or the least common denominator. Rather, using the means of "grasping each end to pull forward the middle," it aims at constantly raising the level of the whole society.

One of the main aims of the Great Leap Forward can be seen in the story of the backyard furnaces. During this period the rural population was mobilized to build the apparatus for making steel. Most Westerners, concerned more with the product than with the evolution of people, heaped scorn on these backyard furnaces because the steel they produced was of poor quality. But the backyard furnaces introduced hundreds of millions of Chinese peasants to new scientific methods of production. Once the peasants had gone through the essential steps of making steel, the huge steel mills then being planned would not be a mystery to them, so that when they went to work in modern plants, they would not be just robots or button pushers.

Under Liu Shao-ch'i the Chinese economy not only recovered but began to develop rapidly again. As a result, a marked tendency began to manifest itself among high-ranking members of the party to emphasize technical efficiency, specialization, urbanization, and development of the economic forces at the expense of continuing technical, political, and social development of the masses and the countryside. A real danger arose that the Chinese revolution might go down the same road as the Russian, toward the consolidation of a technical, intellectual, and political élite managing the economy and the country, while the masses became more and more depoliticized and consumer-oriented. This would have countered the entire process and purpose of the Chinese revolution as it had been developing for many decades.

It was to defeat this counter-revolutionary tendency that in 1966 Mao launched the Chinese Cultural Revolution, mobilizing the ranks for a struggle against élitism in every institution, every factory, every school, every hospital, every cultural unit, every party unit, as well as the party and the society as a whole. With a boldness without parallel in human history, Mao encouraged the ranks to criticize the highest officials in the party, the government, the schools, etc., no matter how that criticism disrupted society and the party. In fact, the Cultural Revolution was an invitation to disrupt and to shake up a society and a party that were threatening to settle back into the traditional Chinese division between the élite and the masses.

The Cultural Revolution has produced political, productive, and intellectual activity at the bottom of Chinese society on a scale and with a zest such as even the most visionary prophet could never have imagined ten years ago. But it was able to get off the ground only because a spontaneous rebellion had already erupted among the youth at Tsinghua University against an educational system which was still organized on the élitist principles of pre-revolutionary China. Mao's famous endorsement of the Tsinghua student rebellion with the statement "It is right to rebel" reflects his joyful recognition that, with the uprising of the students, the two factors necessary for successful revolutionary advance in China—the *particular* spontaneous rebellion from below and the *general* vision from above—were now present together as they had not been in 1955.

For us the most important thing to understand about the Chinese Cultural Revolution is that it was not something that just happened, not just "a happening." Essentially it was a bold continuation of the struggles which Mao and the Chinese Communists have been conducting for nearly forty years to get rid of the class division between the élite and the masses and to involve every person at both poles of society in responsibility both for politics, or the affairs of state, and for production, or the affairs of the economy, the two main forms of human activity.

From the years of ideological struggle that led to the seizure of power in 1949, Mao had realized that raising the political consciousness of the masses could not be simply a matter of political indoctrination or book learning. He had no illusion that the masses could become political by studying the history of revolution or the theoretical writings of leading revolutionists as the Chinese intellectuals once studied Chinese history and the Analects of Confucius.

If the masses were to become politically developed, they would have to engage in the kind of political struggle, linking theory with practice, that the party had pioneered and in which it was still engaged. The path of political development could not be a smooth one of increasing enlightenment toward the mythical ideal of a philosopher-king, any more than the path of economic development could be a smooth one toward an increasing Gross National Product.

So today Chinese society is like one vast school in every sphere—the plants, the schools, the hospitals, the theater, the neighborhood, the city, the countryside, the party—with everybody teaching everybody else. Everybody is responsible for analyzing, struggling over and arriving at the most socially responsible decisions in every sphere, in every group of which he/she is a part as well as in society as a whole. No realm of human endeavor is immune from the struggle to abolish the traditional division of labor between the political élite and the apolitical masses. Everybody has to prepare him/herself to make the right political choices that serve the people and avoid the twin dangers of right-wing opportunism or careerism, and left-wing opportunism or adventurism. Every practical task, every political issue, demands the most creative application by every individual of the principles of dialectical philosophy, of scientific experiment, and of class struggle. In other societies these were considered the province of the intellectual or politician. Political and practical mistakes are not evaluated subjectively or in terms of individual personality but in terms of the old ways of thinking and the old divisions which everyone must leave behind if the entire society is to advance. Everybody is continuously involved in getting rid of the old ways and the old divisions in the same way that a healthy body works continuously to rid itself of poisons and disease.

Hence what is most impressive in China today is not what you can see with your eyes but the process that you sense is taking place within people, the process of millions of human beings consciously and deliberately transforming themselves into more developed, more creative, more critical, more responsible, in short, more human human beings.

It would be easy to regard such a fantastic leap forward in human evolution as a miracle. But what is happening today in China is not a miracle. It is the result of many difficult struggles over many years and the beginning of many more difficult struggles in the future. That is why we have concentrated in this chapter so much on the conflicts, the debates, the mistakes, the bold leaps forward and the retreats, the emergence of new contradictions as soon as the old ones were resolved.

What is happening in China today appeals to the noblest aspirations in the Chinese people and the people of the world. But it is not idealistic because it involves the great masses of the people at the bottom of the society struggling to put the most advanced ideas into practice in their daily lives. It is not idealistic because it involves and is constantly seeking to involve the masses of people in solving their own problems through collective theoretical and practical struggles, in a conscious effort to develop maximum self-reliance and to rid themselves of the slavish dependence upon gods and messiahs which has been the way of oppressed people the world over since the beginning of class society. It is not idealistic because it consciously struggles against the very human tendency to believe that there is some final struggle or some simple solution.

Twenty-four years after the victory of the socialist revolution, the Chinese people, by continuing, conscious, and collective struggles, have been able to create hundreds of millions of unselfish and committed men, women and children who are the marvel of all observers—something which all the preachings of the Ten Commandments, the Sermon on the Mount, and "the Brotherhood of Man" have not been able to accomplish in thousands of years. They have not done this through the use of force. The Red Army had all the power it needed to take Liu Shao-ch'i and cut his head off. Instead Mao used Liu as an example to show the people the difference between the capitalist road and the socialist road, to show that new socialist men, women and children could be created at a running pace by recognizing and solving contradictions and by holding fast to the philosophy that rapid human development is a product not of rapid economic development, as the Russian leaders claim, but of political struggles.

In China today everybody feels useful, the old as well as the young, women as well as men, children as well as adults. Even in mental hospitals those who are making more progress help those who are not doing so well. No one is wasted, everyone has something to teach and something to learn. People who are different are not pitted against one another; instead they work together to combine their good qualities and overcome their bad ones.

In every field the divisions between intellectual and worker, between professional and layperson, are being broken down. For thousands of years philosophy had been considered a mystery, something only geniuses could understand. Now Chinese peasants in remote villages are consciously using the fundamental laws of dialectics to meet challenges in their daily lives, e.g., to grow sugar beets where they have never been grown before or to resolve family problems. Their minds have been freed to practice the most advanced ideas. The whole society is mobilized to develop all-sided human beings, individuals who are not only farmers but philosophers, not only machinists but artists, not only patients but medics, all coming out of the people, committed to and able to serve the people because they are not trying to climb some individual ladder of success or specialization to get away from the people.

All over the world capitalist societies create monstrous cities in which millions of people are so jammed up against one another that they cannot even enjoy the advanced technology, specialized skills, and sophisticated culture which have been centralized in these cities, while rural communities are turned into ghost towns. Between the farmers and housewives, there are dozens of intermediaries, each of which gets a cut at the expense of the producer at one end and the consumer at the other. Between the people and the services they need is a great wall of bureaucrats and specialists who use their superior position or education to maintain the rest of the population in ignorance and dependence. In every factory men and women are slaves rather than masters of the technology they have created.

In China today, on the other hand, the great majority of the people live and work in factories near the source of their food, and at the same time enjoy easy access to modern doctors as well as traditional medicine, electric power as well as cultural events. The factories in which they work are under the control of those who work in them. Living and working in decentralized communes, large enough to be self-sufficient in basic necessities and yet small enough to be managed by those who live and work in them, the Chinese people are today masters of their fate to a degree beyond the most visionary imagination of socialists only a decade ago.

Future revolutions in other countries will, indeed must, go beyond the Chinese revolution. But henceforth any struggles which aim at less than the Chinese have attempted can at best be reformist and will more likely be reactionary. They will at best be efforts to maintain the status quo or to push humanity back from reaching a mountain top which has already been sighted.

For five hundred years, in the wake of the tremendous progress made by the West in science, technology, and the arts, people the world over have thought that the only way for any society to advance was by encouraging individualism and putting human greed, profits, and economics in command. Now the Chinese revolution has demonstrated that a society built on unselfishness, on serving the people, the country, and oppressed peoples all over the world, is the key not only to social and technical advance but to personal happiness. In every Third World nation the Chinese revolution is now providing the inspiration once provided by the Declaration of Independence and then by the October Revolution.

The Chinese have been able to extend the revolutionary vision of the whole world only because they grappled with the internal contradictions of Chinese society. Revolutionists in other countries can learn much from the Chinese revolution, but they will never be able to make a revolution in their own countries until they begin to grapple with the internal contradictions of their own countries.

4

THE LIBERATION OF GUINE: BUILDING AS WE FIGHT

We have chosen to discuss next the revolutionary struggle now going on in Guinea-Bissau, or Guiné, because it has opened the minds of a whole generation of African revolutionaries to the new kind of revolutionary struggle which they must develop if they are to liberate Africa from colonialism and neocolonialism.

The African people have been exploited for the benefit of the economic development of the Western imperialist countries more savagely, more systematically, and for a much longer period than any other people in the world. The material condition of the overwhelming majority of Africans is still far below that recognized to be the minimum necessary for physical survival. Under these circumstances it might seem to many that the revolutionary struggle should concentrate on the mobilization of the African masses to make escalating demands upon their oppressors for higher wages for their work or higher prices for their commodities. In fact, the revolutionary struggle in Guinea-Bissau began when the leadership recognized that such economic struggles, no matter how militant, would only increase the dependence of the masses upon their oppressors and therefore should not be organized by a leadership which purports to be revolutionary.

Guiné is a territory on the West Coast of Africa, approximately one-half the size of Maine, with a population of some 800,000 people—smaller than the black population of New York. Since 1886, when the European powers met in Berlin to divide Africa up among themselves, it has been claimed by Portugal. For the past eleven years the people of Guiné have been carrying on an armed struggle under the leadership of the African Party for the Independence of Guiné and Cape Verde (PAIGC) and have succeeded in liberating two-thirds of their country from Portuguese control. The PAIGC was founded in 1956 by only six people, but did not initiate armed struggle until 1960.

Behind these bare facts is not only the mass struggle of the peasants of Guiné but the reflections and creative thinking of a small group of intellectuals, and particularly of Amilcar Cabral, who built the PAIGC on such solid foundations that it is capable of continuing the struggle for liberation despite his tragic assassination in the spring of 1973. Cabral's abhorrence of revolutionary rhetoric, his methodical thinking, his deep appreciation of the fact that the human being has needs not only of the body but of the mind, his persistence in tying the most profound theories of human nature to concrete programs, his straightforward appeals to the people of Guiné to take on the responsibilities of building a new society, his insistence that oppressed people must struggle simultaneously against their own weaknesses and the external enemy, have raised revolutionary politics to a new level. In the future the revolutionary movement in Africa may advance beyond Cabral, but any retreat from the high standards he set can only be temporary.

Fortunately, the story of the PAIGC is available to us both in Cabral's own writings and speeches and in two remarkable books, *The Liberation of Guiné* by Basil Davidson (London and New York: Penguin, 1969) and *Armed Struggle in Africa* by Gérard Chaliand (New York: Monthly Review Press, 1969). Anyone reading Cabral and these two books should feel fortified for the struggle still to be waged and won against the anti-intellectualism of much of the U.S. left, which somehow makes it appear undemocratic to recognize the indispensability of the creative intellectual in making a revolution, and more revolutionary to depend upon impersonal or humanly uncontrolled forces of economic development.

The revolutionary struggle now going on in Guiné demonstrates that revolutions are *made*. They don't just happen by accident or spontaneously. Nor do they take place because of some divine law which decrees that the first shall be last and the last first. Nor because of some economic law "discovered" by some social scientists as Newton discovered the law of gravity. Revolutions are made by human beings whose imaginations have been fired by a vision, an ideal of a new and better life and a new and better society, and who then begin to organize themselves so that they can organize and mobilize others to struggle for that new and better life and society.

New ideas are not just born. As we emphasized in the first chapter, they are created by actual living individuals, with a very few pioneering for the great majority. That these ideas then have to be projected to the masses is nothing new. That has always and will always be a concrete problem. But for anything new and original—and there is nothing *newer or more original* than a revolution—the new thoughts, the new ideas have to come first. Where do they come from? They come from creative, thoughtful individuals, reflecting upon a specific historical reality which they recognize must be changed, and upon what others have done in the past to try to change that reality. Out of that reflection, and in a close and continuing dialogue with their own masses, they must create a new conception of the new social tasks which their people are to accomplish if they hope to participate in the evolution of humanity. This conception is the essence of *ideology*.

To some readers all these concepts may seem elementary. But they are repugnant to many people and much more difficult to hold fast to than most people realize. That is because remnants of other ideas or myths by which men and women have lived in the past persist in most of us. For example, the myth of a god who is the guarantor of a day of reckoning when the oppressors will be destroyed or will destroy themselves is a very prevalent myth, particularly among the *uneducated masses* because they don't know any better and because they have no other basis for hope. As many people know, it is also a very dangerous myth because it creates the illusion that the future is in God's hands and therefore it is unnecessary or futile for mortals to struggle.

But there is an equally dangerous myth which prevails among educated people. This is the myth that the spontaneous revolt or rebellion of the oppressed is not only inevitable but revolutionary, i.e., it brings with it the ingredients for a new society. This myth (which can be characterized as a form of economic determinism or mechanistic materialism) prevails chiefly among radical intellectuals and social scientists who are either unwilling or unable, because of various objective circumstances (including the absence of masses who can be easily organized), to go among the masses and transform them through revolutionary struggle. It is a myth that serves to justify continuing faith during a period of repression or to rationalize an ivory tower existence under any circumstances.

These myths are forms of fatalism. Religion is the fatalism of the uneducated. Economic determinism or mechanistic materialism is the fatalism of the educated. The revolutionist must systematically rid him/herself of both forms of fatalism.

The first task faced by Cabral and his colleagues was the evaluation of the struggles of their predecessors. This identification with the aspirations of one's predecessors, reviewing their experiences and learning from them, is a capacity unique to human beings. Through such an identification a new generation acquires both the momentum of past struggles and the need to transcend their limitations. The average American radical wastes this distinctively human capacity to an incredible degree. The revolutionist must exercise it consciously and conscientiously. To do so requires the criticism not only of the practices but of the thoughts, the ideologies of one's predecessors.

Like most African liberation fighters of this generation, Cabral was aware that for over five centuries Africans have been engaged in continuing struggles to resist European aggression. But all these struggles have been ruthlessly crushed or subverted. Why? Was there something lacking in their ideology and organization?

Until the end of World War I, the idea governing the resistance struggles of the African people had been that the gods had given the land to their ancestors, and that their ancestors, guardians of the living and the yet unborn, had been dishonored by European intrusion. Inspired by this religious conviction, famous wars had been fought, usually by highly structured societies under the leadership of hero-kings. Perhaps the best-known of these wars were the ones fought by the Ashanti in northern Ghana and the Zulus in southern Africa. When these hero-kings were finally defeated at the end of the nineteenth century, smaller, less structured societies continued the resistance in the form of periodic revolts and attacks on the white invaders. The European view of these resistance struggles has been memorialized in the old movies depicting the dangers facing white hunters and explorers in Africa.

In the early twentieth century the religious inspiration of this resistance movement began to become more Westernized, as African Christian preachers formed independent Christian churches dedicated to the idea that the Christian God was also the African God who would give back Africa to the Africans. These dissident churches were also repressed, usually by the jailing of the more militant leaders. In some cases, the congregations put their convictions into practice and occupied European land, whereupon the colonialists sent troops against them.

Not until after World War I did the African struggles begin to take on clearly secular form, based on the ideology of nationalism or self-determination, and seeking to form political parties that would take political power away from the European imperialists and establish government by the African peoples themselves. In the 1930s and 1940s, men like Jomo Kenyatta of Kenya and Kwame Nkrumah of the Gold Coast, educated in the West and under the political tutelage of such West Indian Marxists as George Padmore and C. L. R. James in London, prepared themselves to return to their countries in order to lead their people in struggle for what Nkrumah called "the political kingdom." The ideology of this new generation of nationalist leaders was a mixture of Marxist-Leninism (which gave them the economic analysis of imperialism, the perspective of socialism, the general concept of a revolutionary party) *and* of political independence, strongly reminiscent of the Founding Fathers of the United States.

By the end of the 1940s, both Kenyatta and Nkrumah had returned to their respective countries with this general ideology and were soon addressing mammoth mass rallies of 50,000 to 100,000 people, denouncing the imperialists and inspiring in their audiences expectations of the new millennium which would come with freedom (*Uhuru*). On March 6, 1957, the first breakthrough in this stage of struggle for African national liberation came with the celebration of the political independence of Ghana under the leadership of Nkrumah. Thereafter France, England, and Belgium granted political independence to dozens of other African nations at such a rate that modern African history might well be divided into Before Ghana (B.G.) and After Ghana (A.G.).

A few highlights about the struggle in Ghana and Kenya will help us appreciate the achievements and the limitations of the nationalist leadership of the post-World-War-II period.

Nkrumah returned to Ghana from the United States and England in 1947 and almost immediately began to clash with the more conservative black intellectuals who were chiefly interested in a legalistic struggle for independence without stirring up the masses. Nkrumah, on the other hand, believed in appealing to the militant young and to women. In 1949, just as he was beginning to build the Convention People's Party on the basis of these forces, the British put him in prison. Two years later, in 1951, after nearly 100 percent of the voters in Accra had elected him their representative to the Legislative Assembly, the British took Nkrumah out of prison and made him leader of Government Business. This placed upon Nkrumah numerous administrative responsibilities along with the burden of negotiations with the Colonial Office for the political independence of Ghana. Thus, the British effectively cut Nkrumah off from the political task of developing party cadres who could go among the people in order to organize them in struggle and preparation for the responsibilities of independence. In consequence, when Ghana was finally granted independence in 1957, the new government was plagued with virtually insoluble problems.

Without political cadres who had acquired deep roots in the masses and the habit of selfless dedication, without a politicized army built in the course of carrying out "political tasks of a class nature" among the masses, with the masses in Ghana expecting that independence would automatically bring with it the satisfaction of all their wants and needs, and with the world powers continuing to control the economic life of the country, Nkrumah in power was a leader without power. The first African to lead his people to political independence, the Pan-Africanist Nkrumah continued to act as a beacon and a resource for other liberation fighters who hoped for a socialist United States of Africa. But in his own country he had not developed a vanguard party seasoned in criticism and self-criticism and hence able to struggle against the greed and petty ambitions of the new caste of African administrators. He had no cadres to work among the masses, helping them to understand the self-reliance and the sacrifices necessary to overcome imperialism and their own messianic tendencies. He could not get rid of the army officers who had been trained in the British élitist tradition because he had not built a people's political army to take their place. As a result, he became trapped in the problems which await the most able and dedicated leaders of any new nation. In desperate need of politically conscious aides, he became increasingly dependent upon Afro-Americans, Afro-West Indians and Afro-South Americans. Unable to satisfy the demands of striking workers, he resorted to force. At home he became engulfed in administration, while internationally he tried to exercise moral influence, until he was finally overthrown by a military coup in 1966.

Meanwhile, in Kenya, Jomo Kenyatta, an anthropologist with an affinity for cultural nationalism, had introduced into the independence movement of his country the ritual practices of the Kikuyu, the largest tribe in Kenya. Fired by warrior oaths and the rhetoric of independence, young Kenyans began organizing into fighting groups which in turn led to isolated acts of violence. These acts of violence were not numerous, but they helped precipitate a counter-revolutionary situation for which the movement was almost totally unprepared. Using these acts of violence as an excuse, the British government declared an "Emergency" which they said had been created by the Mau Mau. The declaration of the Emergency provided the legal cover for a three-year campaign of savage counter-revolutionary violence against the militant youth of Kenya on a genocidal scale which has been equalled in modern times only by the United States in Vietnam. The youth fled into the forest, forming the Land and Freedom Army. The British followed overhead with their bombers. The leaders of the young Kenyans, particularly Generals Kimathi and China, tried desperately, but were unable under these impossible circumstances, to put together an overall strategy and the coordinating structures necessary to regain the political offensive. Following the death and capture of Kimathi and China, the war finally came to an end in 1955, and after years of negotiation the British granted independence to Kenya under Kenyatta in 1963.

During the Emergency and for several years thereafter the British had kept Kenyatta in a remote prison, completely out of touch with the movement. In the murderous repression, they had killed off the cream of Kenya's militant youth. Meanwhile, they had taken the opportunity to build up a base among the Kenya Africans who were willing to collaborate.

In consequence, the government of Kenya since independence has moved steadily to the right, supported by a new middle class of African businessmen and administrators, which the British had been grooming during the Emergency, and crushing all efforts to struggle against the continuing economic domination of Kenya by British neocolonialism.

In the final analysis, responsibility for the desperate problems of Ghana, Kenya, and indeed all the new nations in Africa, lies with imperialism, which maintains economic control behind the facade of political independence, through what is now known as neocolonialism. But having identified the enemy, it is not enough to indict or denounce it for its crimes as if what it is doing is somehow to be altered by rhetoric or revolutionary verbalism.

Rather, we must ask what we can learn from the fate of the independence struggles in Ghana and Kenya that would enable us to transcend their limitations. Is there anything that the liberation movements can do about the fundamental ingredients of revolutionary struggle which are under their *control*—that is to say, ideology, organization and the forms mass struggle should take? These are the questions which Cabral and the PAIGC have tried to answer. In so doing they have faced, with unprecedented candor, one of the basic principles of revolutionary struggle, namely, *the need to struggle against our own weaknesses.* As Cabral put it many years later in his speech to the First Tricontinental Congress of Asia, Africa, and Latin America, held in Havana in January 1966:

> Our agenda includes subjects whose meaning and importance are beyond question and which show a fundamental preoccupation with *struggle.* We note, however, that one form of struggle which we consider to be fundamental has not been explicitly mentioned in this programme, although we are certain that it was present in the minds of those who drew up the programme. We refer here to *the struggle against our own weaknesses.* Obviously, other cases differ from that of Guiné; but our experience has shown us that in the general framework

of daily struggle this battle against ourselves—no matter what difficulties the enemy may create—is the most difficult of all, whether for the present or the future of our peoples. This battle is the expression of the internal contradictions in the economic, social, cultural (and therefore) historical reality of each of our countries. We are convinced that any national or social revolution which is not based on knowledge of this fundamental reality runs grave risk of being condemned to failure.

In the late 1940s and early 1950s, when Nkrumah and Kenyatta were rallying the masses in Ghana and Kenya, Cabral was still an engineering student in Lisbon, where the less than one-half of one percent of Africans for whom the Portuguese provided a higher education had traditionally spent their student years preparing for assimilation into the administrative apparatus of Portuguese imperialism. By the end of World War II, however, some African students were beginning to think in terms of Re-Africanization. Among these were Agostinho Neto and Mario deAndrade from Angola, and Cabral from Guiné. Using the study of African languages as a cover, the three began discussing what they must do to liberate their countries from Portuguese domination. By 1950 they had arrived at much the same views of imperialism and the need for political independence as Nkrumah and Kenyatta. Unlike the latter, however, they did not go back immediately to organize and mobilize the masses behind ideas which had been arrived at in an environment remote from the masses. The fascistic conditions in the Portuguese territories prevented them from taking this course.

Instead, Cabral took a job with the colonial administration as an agricultural engineer, and spent several years traveling through the countryside, getting to know the needs of the people and the very specific effects Portuguese colonialism had had on them. He learned that the chief problem in Guiné is not land, since European settlers did not monopolize the best land as they had in Kenya. Nor is it wages, since there were not the kind of European-owned mines and plantations on which Africans are forced to work at starvation wages as in other African colonies. The chief form of exploitation in Guiné has been the exclusive use of the population for growing cash crops—rice and peanuts—for export at minimal prices. No concern had been shown for the development of the social productive forces of the people through political participation, the introduction of more advanced techniques, or the establishment of the elementary institutions of education and health care facilities which have become a normal and natural part of social existence in the European countries.

From his travels throughout Guiné, which brought him into intimate contact with the masses of people in the most remote villages, Cabral derived a profound appreciation of the cultural underdevelopment and the exclusion from the general course of human history to which the Portuguese imperialists had systematically damned the people of Guiné.

What Cabral did *not* do at this point is crucial to the development of the African liberation struggle. He did *not* try to find ways and means by which he could immediately bring to his people the message of the wrongs which had been done them by the oppressor and their *right* to independence and to self-government. Instead, based upon this concrete experience and reinforced by his observations of the new African nations, he began to develop a new ideology based upon a fundamental distinction between political independence and national liberation. National liberation, he said, cannot come only from political independence with its celebration of the symbols of independence—the raising of the flag, the singing of the national anthem, and political heroes in the tradition of Africa's hero-kings. National liberation must put an end not only to suffering, but to backwardness. It must enable Africans to rejoin the mainstream of human history and human evolution from which they have been excluded by imperialism. The struggle for national liberation must *transform* the masses from their present passivity and dependence on others. It must develop *in them* and *through them* the power, the will, the capacity, and the structures to govern their own accelerated development. The masses must begin to see themselves as making their own history. Only through this fundamental transformation in attitudes, and through the creation of new infrastructures by the people themselves, can the social productive forces of the people be liberated.

Such a cultural change can only be accomplished by reversing the present course of affairs, i.e., by revolution. But revolution must have as its goal and its modus operandi not only the elimination of the oppressor but the most rapid development and transformation of the oppressed as well. It must involve the people both in struggle against their oppressors and in a cultural revolution against their own weaknesses, their own traditional attitudes. The people must be mobilized to fight *mental battles* as well as *physical* ones, so that not only their physical courage but also their *intelligence,* their *daily participation,* their capacity for confronting new problems in new ways, their ability to think for themselves can be expanded. Any movement which fails to meet these requirements will remain a movement without roots, ripe for manipulation by charismatic leaders or bureaucrats and unable to endure and expand.

In 1956, Cabral and a handful of associates, including his brother Luis, formed the PAIGC. Their program called for immediate national independence for Guiné and the Cape Verde Islands; emancipation and democratization of the African population of those countries, which had been exploited for centuries under Portuguese colonialism; and rapid economic progress and true social and cultural advancement for the peoples of Guiné and the Cape Verde Islands.

There was nothing particularly startling or striking about this program as compared with other programs for national independence.

Two years later, encouraged by the achievement of national independence in neighboring Guinea under Sekou Touré, the PAIGC began organizing the workers in the urban areas. The next year, following the ruthless massacre of dock strikers at Pidjiquiti, the party recognized that it had made a fundamental mistake in concentrating its activities on the urban masses, and that the urban centers were, in fact, the stronghold of colonialism.

The unhesitating way in which the PAIGC at once admitted its mistake marks one of the great strengths of Guiné's revolutionary leadership. It suggests that on the wall of every revolutionist should be a poster saying "What really helps the enemy is not the recognition and acknowledgment of errors—but the errors themselves." The recognition of errors must lead to a fundamental analysis of the political premises behind them—this process provides one of the richest sources of the creative energy required for political redirection. That admission and analysis is a far cry from the typically American habit of saying "I'm sorry," as if an error were a sin or crime for which one must apologize or do penance.

A month after the Pidjiquiti massacre, the PAIGC held a secret meeting to draw the conclusions from their self-criticism. Henceforth the only dialogue with the imperialists would be armed struggle, and the peasant masses would have to provide the main physical force of the revolution.

Having arrived at these conclusions, the party did not rush into armed struggle. First it was necessary to develop the peasants into a revolutionary force. To do this political cadres from a background similar to that of the peasants but more advanced politically had to be recruited.

These cadres had to come from the urban areas, since that is the only place where one might find people who are literate and who have had the direct contact with Europeans from which average Africans derive their beginning consciousness of economic, political, and social deprivation. Then through a process of careful examination, the PAIGC leaders systematically *eliminated* various sections of the urban Africans: the *upper officials* with their assimilationist tendencies; *the lower middle class* of employees, clerks, and merchants because of their timidity; and the *lumpenproletariat* of prostitutes, petty criminals, and loafers, who actually provided the secret police with their best recruits. The PAIGC then decided to concentrate its cadre recruitment drive among the day-to-day wage laborers and among the youth who worked occasionally and were not disposed to petty crimes. By 1960 it had recruited enough of these cadres so that Cabral could begin their training in the cadre school established in nearby Conakry, the capital of the Republic of Guinea.

The PAIGC was equally systematic in determining which sections of the peasantry should be mobilized first for the armed struggle. Out of the 800,000 people in Guiné, the four largest ethnic groups are: first, the Balantes who number 250,000; then the Manjaks numbering 140,000; then the Fulahs with 100,000; and finally the Mandingos with 80,000. The PAIGC chose the Balantes to work among first, not only because they were the most numerous but also because their social and political organization was the least structured and most democratic, and therefore the most susceptible to reformation.

The Fulahs and the Mandingos, on the other hand, athough somewhat more advanced culturally, were Muslims, living in highly structured societies, with chiefs, a religious clergy and relatively sharp differences between classes. The people in these groups showed a tendency to follow their chiefs and religious leaders.

Not until 1962, three years after the shift to work among the peasantry and the beginning of cadre training, was the PAIGC convinced that it had developed enough cadres and implanted the fundamental ideas of liberation deeply and concretely enough among the peasants to begin the armed struggle. They were determined to make the ideas so much a part of the people that the desire to struggle for these ideas would come from within the people themselves. Thus, even if and when the cadres were not there, the people would still want to struggle and would know what they were struggling for. Only in this way would the ideas, the politics, be in command of the weapons, making the combatants armed militants rather than militarists.

The tireless dialogue which the cadres carried on with the people is summed up in this 1965 Political Bureau directive on the responsibilities of PAIGC members:

> Oppose tendencies to militarism and make each fighter an exemplary militant of our party.
>
> Educate ourselves, educate other people, the population in general, to fight fear and ignorance, to eliminate little by little the subjection to nature and natural forces which our economy has not yet mastered. Fight without useless violence against all the negative aspects, prejudicial to mankind, which are still part of our beliefs and traditions. Convince little by little, and in particular the militants of the Party, that we shall end by conquering the fear of nature, and that *man* is the strongest force in nature.
>
> Demand from responsible Party members that they dedicate themselves seriously to *study*, that they interest themselves in the things and problems of our daily life and struggle in their *fundamental* and *essential* aspect, and not simply in their appearance. . . .
>
> Learn from life, learn from our people, learn from books, learn from the experience of others. Never stop learning.
>
> Responsible members must . . . take life seriously, conscious of their responsibilities, thoughtful about carrying them out, and with a comradeship based on work and duty done. . . . Nothing of this is incompatible with the joy of life, or with love for life and its amusements, or with confidence in the future and in our work.

The directive goes on to encourage cadres to exercise audacity and great initiative in helping enemy soldiers to desert and to carry out political work among Africans still in enemy service.

Finally, the directive calls upon the members to practice "Revolutionary democracy in every aspect of our Party life," and spells out its meaning:

Every responsible member must have the courage of his responsibilities, exacting from others a proper respect for his work and properly respecting the work of others. Hide nothing from the masses of our people. Tell no lies. Expose lies whenever they are told. Mask no difficulties, mistakes, failures. Claim no easy victories. . . .

Collectively to control, in a given group, means to study problems together so as to find the best solutions; means to take decisions together; means to profit from the experience and intelligence of each member, and thus of all members, so as better to direct, to instruct, to command.

Note the tremendous advance, the evolution, the development that has taken place in the concept of the responsibilities and the activities of party members since Lenin. We are no longer talking about such *minimum* prerequisites as acceptance of the party program, payment of dues, and working under the discipline of a party unit, which Lenin had to struggle for nearly seventy years ago. Propaganda and agitation, organizing study circles, establishing connection with the centers, publishing and distributing literature, and training others, all these are essential. But it is now clear that these must be infused with the theory and practice of new human values in the political relations between leaders and masses, between members and members, between human beings.

The center, the heart, the key to the success of the struggle in Guiné is the day-to-day political work of the cadres among the masses, their tireless work of listening and talking, explaining, watching, correcting, suggesting, guiding, taking the message of the party to the masses and not only getting but also evaluating their responses. This process of communication has been the difference between success and failure. The cadres who have been the transmission belt between the top leadership of the party and the people in the revolutionary struggle prior to the taking of power are also the key to the continuing participation of the people after the taking of power.

To get an idea of how these cadres function, you have to read, in Davidson's and Chaliand's books, the accounts of men like Chico, who at the age of twenty-seven is political commissar for the northern inter-region; or Oswaldo, also twenty-seven, who is military commander of the entire northern region. It is only from their own words that you can get a real appreciation of the energy and patience required to ensure, for example, that one-half the members of the village committees are *women;* that the *elders* are respected at the same time that the *young* are encouraged to take the initiative; that each village sees its struggle as extending beyond its own borders to the whole country; that each village committee has the opportunity to learn from its own mistakes with all that this can often mean in decreased efficiency in the short run; that close relations are maintained between the fighters and the rest of the population; that complicated language problems are solved; that a new administrative and economic infrastructure is being built in the course of the fighting, so that when state power is finally taken there will be something substantial to take the place of the colonial infrastructure.

The PAIGC has been in no hurry to move from the countryside into the city or to take state power from the Portuguese. It has also sedulously avoided stirring up the people with the rhetoric of power. Acutely conscious of how all the African peoples have been systematically robbed of centuries of historical development by the slave trade, colonialism, and imperialism, acutely conscious also of the contradictions in which previous African nationalist leaders like Nkrumah were trapped because of the abruptness with which they assumed the responsibilities of government, confident that time can only multiply the internal contradictions on the side of the enemy, a colonial power without any of the objective prerequisites of power, and bearing in mind the lessons of the Chinese and Vietnamese revolutions, the PAIGC has used the armed struggle as much, if not more, to unite and develop their people economically, politically, and socially, as to defeat the Portuguese militarily.

The main point is that, from the first, the struggle for power was tied into the gradual realization of new socioeconomic structures, built by the people themselves. Without this frank acceptance of the obligation to "build the revolution as you fight," there could have been no means, except the very limited means of military action, of transforming the ideas of a very small, necessarily élite, grouping, into a movement of the masses, and so guarantee that revolution stood for something greater, more valuable, and more meaningful than a mere substitution of African for Portuguese rulers.

It is only this kind of struggle that can bring national liberation, and not just the facade of political independence, to those people everywhere who are still struggling to rid themselves of imperialism.

Today not only in Guinea-Bissau, but in Angola and Mozambique as well, African peoples are pursuing this kind of struggle. Their leaders have learned much from the struggles in China and in Vietnam, but essentially it is on the basis of the experiences of the African movement and of their own countries that they have arrived at the conclusion that one must build the revolution as one fights. It is from their own practice and their own history that they have derived their ideas. In the words of Cabral:

> No matter how close may be the similarity between cases and between the identities of our enemy, national liberation and social revolution are not for export. They are—and every day they become more so—the outcome of a local and national elaboration that is more or less influenced by external factors (favorable or not) but essentially determined and influenced by the historical reality of each people, and carried to success by right solutions to the internal contradictions which arise in this reality.

5
PEOPLE'S WAR
IN VIETNAM

The development of the Vietnamese revolution runs parallel to that of the Chinese revolution, both in time and in direction. Essentially both revolutions have been taking shape over most of this century. Both are based on the principle that the aim of revolution is not only the defeat of the oppressing classes, but the rapid and continuing development of the great masses of the people to assume total political responsibility for the direction of their society.

This parallel development is not surprising since both Vietnam and China were ancient feudal societies which, since their invasion by Western guns and goods in the middle of the nineteenth century, have been searching for a way to make the progressive ideas of the West a part of their own history. Moreover, both countries share a cultural background in Confucianism, a philosophy which has never made the division between politics and ethics which Christianity ("render unto Caesar that which is Caesar's") and Machiavelli (who originated the idea of value-free political "science") have made so integral a part of Western thinking. Finally, China and Vietnam are so close geographically that revolutionary (as well as counter-revolutionary) ideas and individuals can easily slip across the border.

Nevertheless it would be misleading to view the Vietnamese revolution as an imitation of the Chinese revolution or as controlled by it. Throughout this book we have insisted that every revolution has its own history, every revolution has its own national character. Every revolution is the effort to resolve the specific contradictions of a particular society, and can therefore only develop by its own dynamic, through a series of struggles, evaluation of struggles, and new projections for struggling along one road rather than another, by actual living individuals who emerge from but who also expand the social experiences and political perspectives of their people.

The unique importance of the Vietnamese revolution is that it has taken shape in the course of a people's war by a small and weak colonial country against the citadel of world capitalism. Hence, while the Vietnamese revolution has characteristics in common with the revolutions in Russia, China and Guinea-Bissau, it has been forced, both by the nature of its own reality and that of its enemy, to develop its own forms of struggle. In so doing, it has become a source of inspiration and instruction to others who are also threatened by the counter-revolutionary power of U.S. imperialism.

The lesson of Vietnam can be summed up in a single sentence. Under the leadership of a Marxist-Leninist party, seeking to resolve the specific contradictions of a particular society, a tiny technologically inferior revolutionary force can acquire in the course of protracted struggle, the political and moral superiority to defeat the most powerful counter-revolutionary force in the world.

That the building of such a party is itself a protracted struggle is demonstrated by the experience in Vietnam.

The Vietnamese repeatedly describe revolution as not only a science but an art, requiring not only courage but wisdom and imagination. The greatest artists usually first internalize the achievements of their great predecessors and only then find it possible to exercise their maximum creativity. That this can also be the method employed by a great revolutionist is revealed in the protracted development of Ho Chi Minh, whom the people of Vietnam appropriately honor as the "symbol both of our times and of our revolution."

Ho Chi Minh° was born in 1890 in Nghe Tinh, a region in Central

---

° The Vietnamese leader did not assume this name until he was nearly forty years old, but we use it because it is the one by which he is known to the world. His

Vietnam known for its rebellious intellectuals and courageous revolutionary fighters against foreign invaders. At the time of his birth, the French had just conquered Vietnam militarily and were beginning to introduce into the society the centralizing, fragmenting, and polarizing dynamics of capitalist development with the ruthlessness of a foreign imperialism. From Vietnam the French chiefly wanted rice and rubber for export. The establishment of rubber plantations necessitated removal of the peasants from large tracts of land. The peasants thus displaced were transformed into a labor force working to produce rubber and rice and to construct the roads and railroads to take these commodities to the ports. The sale of opium and alcohol was encouraged to help the police force control this labor force. To finance the new apparatus of transportation and control, taxes had to be collected, etc., etc.

By the time Ho was a young man, the French had succeeded in virtually destroying the ancient civilization of this tiny country, transforming it from a cohesive, relatively harmonious, village-centered society into a centralized, tax-collecting, policing state, whose only social support was a small group of landowners and administrators increasingly alienated from the great majority of the people.

The son of a peasant-born minor official, a provincial mandarin who had participated in the 1885 Scholars' Revolt against the French, and with an uncle and elder sister who were active supporters of the nationalist movement, Ho grew up in the countryside in an atmosphere of resentment and rebellion against French rule. Before he was old enough to have seen much for himself, he must have been exposed not only to tales of the heroic struggles his people had waged for two thousand years against the Mongol and Chinese invaders, but to lively debates on how to oust the French as well. In the tradition of his family and of his region, Ho, then a teenaged student, participated in the insurrectionary movement of 1908.

With the defeat of this movement, Ho was faced with a dilemma which many young Americans who have come to political consciousness in recent years should find familiar. What next? Should he

---

childhood name was Nguyen Tat Thanh, while the name by which he became known to his countrymen during his decades of exile was Nhuyen Ai Quoc, "the man who loves his country."

continue to participate in, and thereby encourage, the obviously futile rebellions against French rule that were led mostly by members of the old intellectual ruling classes and aimed chiefly at the restoration of the old society? Or should he, like others of his generation and class, give in and become an administrator for the French in the false hope that once in office he would be able to humanize or reform French rule?

Ho decided to reject both the road of continuing but hopeless confrontations with the French and that of cooperation in the destruction of his people. Instead he left Vietnam altogether, and in 1911 signed on as a mess boy on an ocean liner traveling between Haiphong and Marseilles.

During the next few years, Ho visited most of the chief ports of North Africa and the Mediterranean, discovering for himself the international character of colonial exploitation with the eyes not of a tourist but of a worker. The eruption of World War I revealed to him that the West was not monolithic: the more the colonial powers expanded into Asia and Africa, the more explosive the contradictions between them. After an overseas voyage which took him to Boston and New York, and a stint in London as a dishwasher, Ho finally ended up in a Paris garret on the eve of the October Revolution. Through these experiences Ho had come to realize that not only are there contradictions *between* Western imperialism and the colonial masses, and *among* the imperialists themselves, but also contradictions *within* the imperialist countries between the rich and poor as well. And all the while he could not but contrast the backwardness of his own country with the miracles of Western production, transportation, and communication, which offered such possibilities for the liberation of all man/womankind from bondage to external forces.

It is only when we try to put ourselves into the mind of Ho, now nearly thirty years old and striving to integrate the experiences of his childhood with those which he had been absorbing since he left home, that we can appreciate the joy with which he embraced Leninism in 1920. Lenin, the Marxist, had not only led a working-class revolution to overthrow feudalism and capitalism and to create a new socialist society. Living in the period of monopoly capitalism, Lenin had also been able to develop beyond Marx in his analysis of imperialism and his recognition of the revolutionary validity of the anti-imperialist struggles of colonial peoples. Furthermore, in originating the vanguard party, Lenin had created the political form for a protracted struggle by revolutionary leaders to mobilize the working masses. No wonder Ho found Leninism "food and drink to the hungry and thirsty traveler."

Ho had found a coherent doctrine, a political philosophy with which he could actively combine his love for his own country with love for all humanity, his struggle to liberate his own people with his struggle to advance their level of social and political development. Looking back at the decades of struggle by the Vietnamese against French and then U.S. imperialism, we can see how Ho embodied in himself and inspired in his people an indivisible unity of ardent patriotism with genuine internationalism, of the ideal of independence and freedom with that of socialism and communism. We can see how indispensable this unity of opposites has been to the Vietnamese people, how it has infused their strategy and tactics and enabled them to build a firm basis of support in the minds and hearts of their own people and of the people of the world. Revolutionists in the United States have yet to wrestle with the awesome challenge of uniting these opposites in a society which has been the beneficiary rather than the victim of imperialist exploitation. But it is a challenge they will have to meet, since it is impossible to lead the struggle to revolutionize any country unless you love and want to advance that country and its people.

For Ho, now committed to a lifetime of revolutionary struggle, the philosophy of Marxist-Leninism, like any revolutionary philosophy worthy of the name, was of immediate concrete value in understanding and struggling against other tendencies in the Vietnamese movement. In a revolutionary period when one's friends and family are likely to be engaged in some form of movement activity, a revolutionist cannot develop the confidence necessary for protracted struggle unless he/she is absolutely clear about the philosophical, historical, and social limitations of other proposals for action. Looking back, Ho could now understand how idealistic and static had been the thinking of his father, his uncle, and the rebellious scholars with whom they associated. They had failed to mobilize the masses in a struggle against the French because, as a part of the old society, they could not grasp the historical development from feudalism to capitalism to socialism.

Ho now had a theoretical basis for combating the narrow

nationalism and racialism of the new generation of Vietnamese militants. Mostly members of the middle class who had become aware of the backwardness of their homeland while studying in France or Japan, these nationalists hoped to get rid of the French so that they themselves could carry out the industrialization of Vietnam along capitalist lines. Hence they sought to rouse the masses of Vietnam against the French on racial rather than class grounds, while internationally they sought the support of the Chinese Kuomintang and the Japanese, whose rapid economic development seemed to them a proper model for an Asian people.

Ho remained in Paris until 1922 or 1923, functioning as a member of the French Communist Party, absorbing its basic training in Marxist theory while challenging the party's weakness on the colonial question. From there he went to Moscow, staying until 1924 or 1925, when he was sent by the Third International to China to assist in the revolutionary movement there. His exact movements during the next fifteen years are difficult to trace since, in order to evade the police, he changed his name as easily as most people change clothes. Some of the time he was in Moscow, at others in China or Thailand (then called Siam). Often his body was in prison but never his mind.

Yet we do not need exact details in order to discern a political pattern that is emerging. Ho did not waste his time devising schemes to get back to Vietnam. He did not bemoan his inability to get to the scene of "the action," as so many political exiles do. Nor did he try to give day-to-day direction to the struggles at home, as was Lenin's wont. Rather he continued to absorb every possible lesson from the revolutionary struggles of other countries and to develop his distinctive combination of international and national struggle. Throughout this period there is no indication that he saw anything in Soviet Russia to criticize, although we can be sure that, ever observant, he was learning both what to do and what not to do.

Internationally, during this period, his main efforts were devoted to implementing the Third International's official policy of support-ing national liberation struggles, especially in Asia. His activities brought him into close contact with both Chinese Communist and Kuomintang leaders (as well as with the Chinese police) and with revolutionary leaders from other Far Eastern countries. These international connections were invaluable later when the struggle to liberate his own country began.

In Hongkong, in Canton, in Shanghai, in Bangkok, in any city where there was a colony of Vietnamese, Ho sought out those individuals who could be developed into cadres to go back to Vietnam and awaken the minds of Vietnamese workers and peasants. Between 1925 and 1930, he is said to have trained between two and three hundred cadres, mostly young people, many of whom were militants who had been forced to flee Vietnam because of their political activities. As anyone who has done cadre training can testify, that is an astonishing number for a period of relative quiescence. It is evidence both of the hunger of young Vietnamese for a new philosophy and ideology, and Ho's extraordinary capacity to inspire others and to persevere in the course he had set himself. How many of these cadres remained a part of the continuing revolutionary leadership and how many faltered along the way, we do not know. However, experience has shown that those attracted to a revolutionary organization during a period of lull and evaluation are more likely to be good for the long haul than those who advance rapidly to revolutionary leadership in a period of mass upsurge.

Ho's lectures in the political training courses held in Canton (excerpts from which are reprinted in his *Official Biography*, published in Hanoi in 1970) show him enriching Lenin's concept of the vanguard party to incorporate into it the Vietnamese philosophical outlook. The Vietnamese have never separated ethics from politics. Therefore, Ho conceived the party as a source not only of theoretical and political clarity but also of spiritual and moral strength.

Ho began by setting forth "the spirit of radical revolution" which must combine a sense of historical urgency with the consciousness of historical continuity:

> To live one must wage revolution. Even a small undertaking would never succeed without the necessary effort. And so how could such an immense undertaking as freeing one's fellow-countryman, freeing mankind, from the fetters of servitude succeed without trying one's utmost? Some people are discouraged by difficulties. They don't realize that no matter how difficult an enterprise, it can always be achieved if one is resolved to do it. If it cannot be done because there are too few people, let many join their efforts. If it cannot be completed by the present generation, it can be finished by the next. To make revolution, one must have resolve, a spirit of sacrifice, perseverance and unity. To

this end everyone must first and foremost understand why revolutions should be made, why it could not be otherwise, why everyone should join in the effort and this immediately, without delay.

With this "spirit of radical revolution" must be united the qualities of "revolutionary morality." So the revolutionist must "display industry and thrift, total dedication to the public interest and complete selflessness, be resolved to correct his defects, abstain from vainglory and arrogance, conform his deeds to his words, hold firm to his revolutionary beliefs, be ready to endure sacrifices, not be influenced by material interests."

For Ho and the Vietnamese, education in Marxist theory and in the correct line and methods come only *after* a militant has demonstrated this kind of radical revolutionary spirit and revolutionary morality. For a Vietnamese revolutionist, dedication to humanity must always constitute the foundation for the politics or policies of struggle; know-why, or a sense of historical process, must precede know-how, or technique; principles must precede programs and plans.

Once enough cadres had been philosophically and politically developed, they were given systematic practice in the application of their politics through living contact with the masses and in the most varied types of struggle. The decade of the thirties provided this apprenticeship for the cadres in Vietnam.

Working in the factories, mines, and plantations during the early 1930s, these cadres, mostly of middle-class origin, were able to learn from the workers, as well as to give coordination and political consciousness to the spontaneous, localized, and scattered workers' struggles erupting at this time. Through these activities they were also able to recruit some workers into their ranks.

Early in 1930, under Ho's auspices, three different groups of cadres were organized into a single party, the Vietnam Communist Party.° Shortly thereafter, the party was able to escalate a hunger march by 6,000 peasants in Nghe Tinh (Ho's home province) into a

---

° The three original groups were the Indochinese Communist Party, organized by comrades in the North; the Communist Party of Annam, the central region; and the League of Indochinese Communists. We have not attempted to follow the various changes in name as the party was periodically reorganized, but have used the word "party" to refer to the vanguard organization which continued under Ho's leadership.

movement to divide up large estates and organize Soviets or People's Councils with self-defense units.

Then, between 1936 and 1939, in line with the Popular Front orientation of the Third International, the party carried out intense mass agitation for democratic liberties and a decent standard of living, and against fascism and war. These broad struggles gave the party contact with progressive sections of the middle class and the bourgeoisie, as well as the practical experience in combining legal and illegal struggle which is indispensable to every revolutionist.

The Nghe Tinh Soviets did not last long, but the party, with characteristic resourcefulness, extracted every possible political lesson from them. First, the party called them "Xa-Viets" rather than Soviets, using the Vietnamese word for village, *Xa*. By this means they were able to give the Nghe Tinh peasants an enlarged sense of the national and international significance of their actions. Equally important, from that point on, the party repeatedly used the example of the Nghe Tinh Soviets to educate the Vietnamese people in the meaning of working-class leadership.

During this same period the Vietnamese Nationalist Party (*Viet Nam Quoc Dan Dong*), with ties to the Chinese Nationalists (Kuomintang), staged a terrorist action at the Yen Bay garrison hoping to trigger a general uprising. Although both the Yen Bay mutiny and the Nghe Tinh Xa-Viets failed, the party seized the opportunity to point out the difference between them in class terms. The Yen Bay mutiny, it explained, was an example of the politics of the petty-bourgeoisie, who are reduced to adventurism and idealism because they lack the historical perspective which comes from Marxist-Leninist theory and the continuing contact with the working class which this theory encourages. The Nghe Tinh Xa-Viets, on the other hand, provided a model of working-class leadership because they organized the masses for improvement of their material conditions and for long-range political goals. The Nghe Tinh Xa-Viets were thus used by the party not only to give the peasants a broader national and international outlook but also to deepen the worker-peasant alliance and to make clear the need for the peasants to advance beyond their traditionally individualistic, undisciplined, and purely rebellious response to oppression. Much later, the self-defense units would be referred to repeatedly as embryonic examples of armed struggle.

Thus, in terms of actual struggles within the historical experience of its masses, the party carried out one of the major responsibilities of every vanguard organization, namely, to extend the concept of "class struggle" beyond the question of social origin or opposing material interests to the level of opposing forms of political activity.

The difference between Ho's implementation of the shifting orientation of the Third International during the 1930s and that of Western radical organizations is instructive. In Western radical circles during the thirties, millions of words were written and innumerable splits took place over whether or not to follow, first, the aggressively revolutionary Third Period orientation of the Third International and then the Popular Front orientation. What it shows is their own lack of any clear-cut revolutionary goals for their own countries. By contrast, Ho was able to make creative use of both the Third Period and the Popular Front period to achieve what the Russian Revolution had taught him was the prerequisite to successful revolutionary struggle in any country: the class distinction between the petty-bourgeois and the working-class approach to political activity; and seasoned cadres and a collective leadership sharing a common ideology.

By 1940 the party had reached a modest but perceptible level in relation to these goals. Perhaps the best indication of this was the collective leadership being forged which even then included Pham Van Dong, now Prime Minister of the Democratic Republic of Vietnam; Truong Chinh, secretary of the first Vietnamese Communist Party and an outstanding theoretician; and Vo Nguyen Giap, a former history teacher whose genius as a military strategist has since won the admiration of the world.

Hence the Vietnamese could now proceed to take advantage of the internal contradictions which were beginning to explode among the rival imperialists, indicating that a fresh cycle of war and revolution had begun. The French government, having capitulated ignominiously to Nazi Germany in Europe, would soon be reduced to calling in Japanese assistance in Indochina. At the same time the battle between the United States and Japan for the domination of Asia was on the verge of breaking into war in the Pacific. In the flux of the inevitable military victories and defeats among the contending powers, a vacuum, much like that in 1917 Russia, could be anticipated, and with it, a golden opportunity for a well-prepared revolutionary party to take power. Moreover, with the imperialist enemy weakened by its own internal contradictions and rivalries, even those mistakes which the party would inevitably make in undertaking this new phase of struggle might not be too costly.

So in December 1940 Ho Chi Minh returned to Vietnam for the first time in thirty years. In the following May, the Central Committee of the party, meeting at Ho's headquarters, a cave in Cao Bang Province not far from the Chinese border, set up the Vietnam Independence League (*Viet Nam Do Lap Dong Minh*) which has since become famous as the Viet Minh. In June, from a small Chinese town near the border, Ho broadcast an appeal to "Elders, prominent personalities, intellectuals, peasants, workers, traders, and soldiers" to unite in order to "overthrow the Japanese and French and their jackals." Shortly thereafter, he issued instructions to set up the first armed self-defense units in Cao Bang, the Viet Minh's first guerrilla base. Then, characteristically stepping back to ensure that the party was utilizing every possible resource for the next stage of struggle, he translated *The Art of War* by Sun Tzu, the Chinese military strategist who nearly twenty-five hundred years ago had emphasized the decisive importance to military victory of moral superiority, timeliness, understanding of objective conditions, leadership, ideology, and organization. Later Sun Tzu's ideas and their further development by Chinese Red Army commanders would be distilled into handbooks carried by every cadre.

Only then, in a continuing relationship of the party with its own masses* and in a determined struggle for power did the real theoretical and practical creativity of the Vietnamese revolution show itself. It had taken Ho Chi Minh twenty years of patient internal party-building to reach the point at which he could begin to create a specific revolutionary strategy for Vietnam. Having absorbed the lessons of the revolutionary experiences and developments of other countries, and having built a continuing leadership

---

* Ho's own contact with the masses was interrupted in 1941 by a nearly two-year sentence in a Chinese prison, during which time the party was not even sure whether he was dead or alive. But the leadership was already of sufficient depth so that his absence was not fatal, and the party's development may even have been accelerated by the opportunity given to others to assume responsibility.

which could collectively grapple with the new stage of struggle, the Vietnamese party was ready to exercise its own inventiveness and imagination to make the revolution at home.

The events of the next thirty years have been described many times. Under the leadership of the party, the Viet Minh proceeded to organize the political and armed struggles which culminated in the victory of the 1945 revolution and the founding of the Democratic Republic of Vietnam (DRV). In 1946 the French attempted to reconquer Vietnam, requiring the new government to wage the eight-year resistance which culminated in the famous victory at Dien Bien Phu. The Geneva Agreement having ended the war with the French on the basis of a temporary partitioning of the country, the DRV applied itself to the building of socialism in North Vietnam. But the United States, determined to maintain a base on the Asian mainland, set up its own puppet government in Saigon, and then launched a war against the Vietnamese people in an attempt to impose that government on them. As a result, the people of South Vietnam were forced to resume the national liberation struggle in 1960, under the leadership first of the National Liberation Front of South Vietnam (NLF) and then of the Provisional Revolutionary Government of South Vietnam (PRG). The strategy of people's war, first developed in the North under the leadership of Giap, was applied and expanded, and has now succeeded in forcing the United States to withdraw all its ground forces from South Vietnam.

The national liberation struggles of the Vietnamese fall into three main periods: 1. the struggles leading to the conquest of power and the foundation of the DRV in August 1945; 2. the struggles led by the DRV against the reoccupation by the French, beginning in 1946 and culminating in Dien Bien Phu and the Geneva Agreement of 1954; and 3. the struggles led by the NLF and PRG against the Saigon puppet government and United States forces from 1960 to the present. In each period the movement had developed on the basis of the achievements and mistakes of the previous period.

For us the details of those struggles are not as important as the fundamental concepts of revolutionary politics by which the Vietnamese cadres have guided themselves and the Vietnamese people over the last three decades, and which they have practiced so methodically that they have almost become second nature. This practice could not have taken place without the continuing and committed collective leadership which took so many years to create, and which has explained its every move to the Vietnamese people and to the world.° These methods were created and perfected in order to meet the exigencies of a tiny and technologically undeveloped nation struggling against powerful imperialist enemies. But they are now part of the fund of revolutionary knowledge upon which every revolutionist can draw.

In 1961 General Giap summed up "The Factors of Success" in *The Vietnamese People's War of Liberation Against the French Imperialists and American Interventionists, 1945–1954* (Hanoi: Foreign Languages Publishing House, 1961) as follows:

> The Vietnamese people's war of liberation was victorious because it was a just war waged for independence and the reunification of the country, in the legitimate interests of the nation and the people, and which by this fact succeeded in leading the whole people to participate enthusiastically in the resistance and to consent to make every sacrifice for its victory.
>
> The Vietnamese people's war of liberation won this great victory because we had a revolutionary armed force of the people, the heroic Viet Nam People's Army. Built in accordance with the political line of the Party, this army was animated by an unflinching combative spirit, and accustomed to a style of persevering political work. . . . It is an army led by the party of the working class.
>
> The Vietnamese people's war of liberation was victorious because we had a wide and firm National United Front, comprising all the revolutionary classes, all the nationalities living on Vietnamese soil, all the patriots. This Front was based on the alliance between workers and peasants, under the leadership of the party.
>
> The Vietnamese people's war of liberation ended in victory because of the existence of people's power established during the August Revolution and thereafter constantly consolidated. This power was the government of alliance between classes, the government of the revolutionary classes and above all of the workers and peasants. It was the dictatorship of people's democracy, the dictatorship of the workers

---

° See *People's War, People's Army* by Vo Nguyen Giap; *Forward Along the Path Charted by Karl Marx* by Truong Chinh; *The Vietnamese Revolution: Fundamental Problems, Essential Tasks* by Le Duan; *The Impotence of American Technique in Face of People's War* by Nguyen Khac Vien. The most detailed and concrete accounts by actual participants of the ways in which the party politicized the masses are found in Wilfred Burchett's many books and articles.

and peasants in fact under the leadership of the Party. It devoted its efforts to mobilizing and organizing the whole people for the Resistance; it brought the people material advantages not only in the free zones but also in the guerrilla bases behind the enemy's back.

The Vietnamese people's war of liberation attained this great victory for the reasons we have just enumerated, but above all because it was organized and led by the Party of the working class, the Indochinese Communist Party, now the Viet Nam Workers' Party. In the light of the principles of Marxist-Leninism, it was this party which proceeded to make an analysis of the social situation and of the balance of forces between the enemy and ourselves in order to determine the tasks of the people's national democratic revolution, to establish the plan for the armed struggle and decide on the guiding principle: long-term resistance and self-reliance. It was the party which found a correct solution to the problems arising out of the setting up and leadership of a people's army, people's power and a national united front. It also inspired in the people and the army a completely revolutionary spirit which instilled into the whole people the will to overcome all difficulties, to endure all privations, the spirit of a long resistance, of resistance to the end. . . .

If the Vietnamese people's war of liberation ended in a glorious victory, it is because we did not fight alone, but with the support of progressive peoples the world over, and more especially the peoples of the brother countries, with the Soviet Union at the head. The victory of the Vietnamese people cannot be divided from this support; it cannot be dissociated from the brilliant successes of the socialist countries and the movement for national liberation, neither can it be detached from the victories of the Soviet Red Army during the Second World War, nor from those of the Chinese people during the last few years. It cannot be isolated from the sympathy and support of progressive peoples throughout the world, among whom are the French people under the leadership of their Communist Party, and the peoples of Asia and Africa.

Note the six factors of success summed up by Giap: 1. a just cause; 2. a people's army; 3. a united front; 4. a government recognized by the people; 5. a Marxist-Leninist party; and 6. the support of people the world over. To one degree or another, and in one form or another, each of these ingredients must be present in any successful revolution, although the form each will take and its relative importance will vary from country to country and from situation to situation. At the heart of every revolution must be a cause the justness of which is recognizable by everyone, although everyone may not arrive at this recognition at the same time. International support would not play the same role in relation to a huge country like China as it does for Vietnam, although at the very minimum it requires a decent respect for the opinions of mankind. Similarly a people's army in an advanced urban society cannot possibly be patterned on one in an undeveloped rural one.

However, there can be no question as to the step-by-step functions which a revolutionary party must perform in any revolutionary period and which the revolutionary party in Vietnam has been carrying out since 1941. First, it must define the main contradiction facing the particular society, the main need and the main aspiration of the people, and hence the main task of the revolution. Then it must propagandize and organize the people to recognize this need and carry out this task. Finally, it must continually evaluate the objective situation, especially the contradictions which are always developing on the opposing side, so that it can seize the right opportunities to administer defeats to the enemy and/or to take power from him/her.

Giap makes clear that it was not until 1939–1941 that the party clearly conceived the task of national liberation, or the anti-imperialist task, to be the "most essential." Throughout the 1930s the party had been grappling concurrently with the two basic contradictions of Vietnam: between imperialism and the nation; and between the feudal landlords and the people, mainly the peasantry. However, once it recognized that a new cycle of war and revolution had begun, and with it the opportunity and responsibility to lead the revolutionary struggle to victory, it became necessary to choose the main contradiction upon which the revolutionary struggle would be made, relegating the other contradiction to the realm of reform. As with any choice, this entailed certain dangers, since a subordinated contradiction does not cease to exist, and can emerge to prominence at critical points. Thus, as Giap points out, by subordinating the agrarian economic reforms sought by the peasantry to the national liberation struggle, the party risked losing enthusiastic support of the peasantry. But having recognized this danger, the party was able to devise methods to cope with it. For example, in 1953, after the French forces had been strengthened by a heavy injection of military aid from the United States, the party disengaged its military forces from combat temporarily in order to carry out agrarian reforms that would increase peasant enthusiasm for the national liberation struggle. The speed with which the leadership disengaged and then re-engaged indicates how well they had internalized the fundamental dialectical law of all revolutionary struggle—that progress never takes place in a straight line.

The party had no illusion that just because it had defined the main need of the people as national liberation, the people themselves would immediately begin struggling for the aspirations attributed to them. Because your line is valid does not mean that the people will follow you. Hence the critical importance of the second main function of the party; first, to politicize the masses, and then, to organize them for struggle.

Through the process, the actual steps which are taken to politicize and organize the masses, the party leads the people to constitute themselves into a national force which is not only powerful enough to oust the foreign invaders but which embodies a new set of relations between different sections of the population on a national scale, i.e., a new nation.

Propaganda is the activity by which the party politicizes the masses. It is the party's way of building a political base in the hearts and minds of the masses whom it seeks to lead, the means by which the party infuses the people with a new concept of their humanity. In political terms this means giving them a vision of their political right and responsibility to control their own lives and the workings of their society. Only when a people have been imbued with this vision of themselves in a new political role can they exercise to the fullest their specifically human qualities of will and courage, of initiative and ingenuity, of intelligence and skill, of creativity and unity. Hence propaganda must precede their organization into physical bases or units of armed struggle. It is what the Vietnamese call the creation of the "mind behind the gun."

In the process of propagandizing and organizing the Vietnamese people to struggle for this new political identity, the Vietnamese arrived at the concept of revolutionary class struggle which distinguishes all the revolutionary struggles of our epoch. Revolutionary class struggle is not the same as the struggle for a special group interest, which is the way class struggle is conceived by the vulgar Marxist. It is the struggle of the most oppressed masses to transcend the political and social limitations which have been imposed upon them by a class society.

Although the Vietnamese were striving to develop all the masses, they did not believe that they could achieve this result all at once. To give the Vietnamese people a new concept of themselves, the party had to conceive and project the specific forms in which each of the different sections of the population could exercise their political capacities.

Hence political indoctrination was conceived as a three-pronged activity: 1. internal development of the party cadres to grasp the moral, theoretical, and practical responsibilities of revolutionary leadership (by this means those individuals who are already more committed are further developed so that they can sink themselves deeply into the mass, moving inwards, not upwards, to provide the core around which others can develop); 2. propagandizing the people to think differently about themselves; and 3. propaganda addressed to the enemy forces aimed chiefly at sharpening the growing internal contradiction between their professed function as a Vietnamese army and their actual functions as instruments and puppets of a foreign power.

Each level of political indoctrination was carefully worked out in terms of purposes and methods. For example, the propaganda aimed at creating a new self-concept in the people was organized so as to help the people to see their present, their past, and their future in a completely different light, to recognize their present condition as a social phenomenon rather than an individual misfortune, the result of imperialist exploitation rather than a natural disaster; to appreciate their own past of struggle against foreign invasion, the weaknesses of the enemy, and their own potential for self-government.

Propaganda to enemy forces, called persuasion, proceeded from the assumption of their basic humanity, i.e., that their hearts and minds were equally capable of conscience and patriotism, and that they were capable of repudiating the dehumanized activities which they were pursuing under the direction of imperialism. In NLF practice, this led to such extraordinary decisions in land distribution as the setting aside of equal parcels of land for all those serving in the armed forces, including those serving Saigon, and providing material aid to the bereaved families of soldiers on both sides.

Having infused the people with this new way of thinking, the party could then mobilize the initiative and intelligence of each group in the population to engage in programs of action.

Like all the great revolutions of this period, the Vietnamese revolution succeeded because the leadership was, on the one hand, absolutely clear at every stage about its long-range and short-range goals; and, on the other, unhesitatingly struggled to rally "the broadest revolutionary forces, securing allies, winning over all those who could be won over, neutralizing all those who could be neutralized if winning them over proved impossible—thus succeeding in utterly isolating the immediate concrete enemy and mustering all revolutionary social forces to smash him."

To rally the broadest social forces within any society, the party must be clear that no society is made up of faceless masses. In every society, no matter how atomized, fragmented, or alienated, the people themselves are not completely atomized or fragmented. Whether they are conscious of it or not, people already belong to various social networks just because they are human beings. Individuals live in the same village or neighborhood or have migrated to one area from the same place. They have had experiences in common, such as working in the same place or going to the same school. They have similar interests—in their children, in sports, or in music. The possibilities are obviously as infinite as the range of human interests and capacities. Often people have already organized themselves into structured groups on the basis of their common interests. If not, they can be encouraged to do so.

There is also a great variety in the depth of the relationships between individuals and between groups, ranging from the tight moral, ideological, and programmatic bonds which exist between comrades in a party, to momentary encounters between individuals or groups who happen to meet in the street or at a demonstration. Between these two extremes, a vanguard party which is very clear about its goals can create a long-term alliance for a whole strategic stage between groups and individuals in order to carry out a great variety of actions to accomplish a clear-cut political program.

From a careful examination of these possibilities, the party in Vietnam has created and perfected the organizational form of the United Front of which the Viet Minh, the National Liberation Front, and the Provisional Revolutionary Government of South Vietnam are the best-known examples. These United Fronts are long-term alliances of all kinds of social groups—women, youth, and workers; cultural, regional, and political—on a clear-cut political program.

They have included individuals from different popular strata as well as political parties and all kinds of mass social organizations. They have been built into a shadow government, or what has been described as "dual power structures" or "parallel hierarchies," which actually have more political authority and enjoy the loyalty of the people in a way that the Saigon government cannot, and which are therefore real governments.

These dual power structures were only possible because the party aimed consciously at both interdependence and independence in the relations between the party and the Front. The party has always maintained its independent organization and has never lost sight of or hidden its long-range goal or its maximum program for the socialist revolution. But by separating out shorter-range goals with which a greater proportion of the people could identify themselves, it has been able to rally the majority of the people behind its leadership. The party maintains close leadership over the United Front in the sense that it retains the responsibility for defining and keeping clear at all times the political program on the basis of which the Front has been formed. But it is equally concerned that the Front maintain independence from the party in carrying out this program, so that there is maximum opportunity for developing intiative and creativity on the part of the Front organization and its personnel.

The broader the social layers allied together in the Front, the more important it is that the party maintain close political leadership in order to ensure that the various strata within it continue to concentrate on the political program which originally brought them together and thus continue to act on the basis of what unites rather than what divides them.

In its programs for arming the people, the party has been equally methodical.

Arming the whole people did not mean that all the people could be equally armed to do the same thing at the same time. On the contrary, the evolving stages of armed struggle had to be laid out systematically, on the basis of the capacities of the different sectors of the population, the available arms, and the continuously broadening tasks.

Villages were conceived as Self-Defense Zones in which Self-Defense Units armed with elementary weapons defended the village against the tax collectors of the puppet government or enemy forces. Everyone in the village could function in some way in this armed struggle while at the same time continuing to participate in the productive work of the village. For example, at the beginning, the men used crossbows and guns, while the women and children laid mines and traps. As the struggle developed and the villagers began to break out of their traditional outlook with regard to the roles of men and women, the women, especially the younger ones, became as useful with guns as the men.

As the village Self-Defense Units began to see the need to go further afield to pin down or wipe out the enemy in nearby posts, they were organized into Mobile Guerrilla Forces with responsibility for defending a specific region. These Mobile Guerrillas played the role both of defense and offense. As long as a region was controlled by Mobile Guerrillas only at night, it was regarded as a Guerrilla Zone. It became a Guerrilla Base only when the guerrilla forces were strong enough to control it day and night.

Finally, as the strength of the guerrillas increased, it was possible to build a regular army for offensive operations.

At all levels of armed struggle, the principles of democratic centralism and criticism and self-criticism were practiced under the guidance of the unit's political officer. As Burchett describes it in *Vietnam Will Win* (New York: Guardian, 1968): "In discussions before an operation, commanders and men were on an absolutely equal footing; as long as any rank and file soldier raised any objection to an operational plan, discussion must continue until he was satisfied. During the operation discipline was total, the rank and file were expected to carry out allotted tasks and execute every command of their superiors without fail. But after the action was over, commanders and men were back on the same equal basis, in the critical summing up which followed each operation."

Obviously very skillful leadership was required to determine the point at which the number of units could be increased or at which the struggle could be advanced to a higher stage. The method used for expansion has been described as that of "growth and split." That is, when a particular unit had developed to sufficient strength, an individual or group of individuals was detached to form the nucleus of another unit. In such a process of development, there was obviously room for mistakes. Sometimes the leadership waited too long or was too conservative. Sometimes it moved too quickly or was rash. But every mistake was used as a basis for advance.

For example, in 1944, Giap, who headed the revolutionary committee in the Cao Bang region, came to Ho's cave with a proposal for an armed insurrection in North Vietnam. Ho rejected the younger man's plan on the ground that it was based on an appraisal only of the political development of people in his own region. "The phase of peaceful revolution is behind us," Ho is reported to have said, "but the time for general insurrection has not yet come." To bring that time closer, Ho proposed the formation of an Armed Propaganda Unit for National Liberation made up of the most resolute members of Giap's men. This unit would be responsible for guiding other units throughout Vietnam in their political and military development.

Out of Giap's premature proposal was born the structure for putting politics in command of the armed struggle, the concept which distinguishes the Vietnamese revolution and every revolution of this era. This example also underlines the importance of criticism and self-criticism to avoid stagnation and eventual retrogression. Had Giap responded subjectively to Ho's rejection of his proposal for immediate insurrection or had Ho not listened to Giap with an open mind, if a centralized leadership structure based on trust had not been created or if this leadership had not conceived of its own development in terms of the development of the Vietnamese masses, the Armed Propaganda Unit for National Liberation, i.e., a new and higher level of political activity, might never have been created. It is also unlikely that Giap would have become the master strategist that he has become.

Thus, out of many trials, tests and struggles, the Vietnamese revolution has developed to the point of achieving absolute superiority on the political and moral front, and the capacity to administer serious military defeats to the enemy. The basic concepts of people's war were first created by the party leadership in the North in the two earlier periods, between 1941 and 1945 and between 1946 and 1954. These concepts have now been practiced and developed in the South to such a point that Giap sees himself as a student of his Southern compatriots in the NLF.

In every phase of the struggle against French imperialism and U.S. imperialism, the Vietnamese have been guided by the strategic line that in the course of protracted warfare, their own strength would increase while that of the enemy could only decrease, due to the fundamental contradiction inherent in U.S. technological overdevelopment and political underdevelopment. Never forgetting this fundamental contradiction, and confident that it would continue to manifest itself in a variety of forms, each causing the enemy to lose even more of its initial superiority, they have been able to make the passage of time one of their most powerful allies. More than any generation which has preceded us in the three thousand generations of *Homo sapiens*, ours has had the opportunity to learn from concrete experience the importance of looking at time in this way and not just as lifeless moments ticking away on a clock. We have seen how, as the strength of the NLF has grown over the past decade, all the internal contradictions in the U.S. position have multiplied. The mobility of the resistance forces increased continually, because they could depend upon the population for information as well as supplies. Meanwhile, the United States and Saigon forces, depending upon advanced weaponry and therefore upon longer defense lines, became increasingly immobilized. Afraid to venture out among the people, their forces holed up in bases like Khe Sanh, which became easy targets for mortar attacks. Unwilling to face the guerrilla forces in hand-to-hand, i.e., mind-to-mind, combat upon the ground, they were reduced to increasingly savage and generalized air strikes. The more unpopular the Saigon regime became, the more dependent it was on the United States. The more dependent it was on the United States, the more unpopular it became. As the antagonisms between the puppet Saigon and U.S. troops increased, so did desertions in the ARVN and demoralization in the U.S. forces. As the chances for victory became more remote and the costs and casualties mounted, so did questions at home in the United States as to the purpose of the war.

The people's war of the Vietnamese has now clearly initiated a new cycle of revolution in the world. Everywhere, even in the United States, people are beginning to see the war in Vietnam in a new light, as

> not only a struggle between an oppressed people and an oppressor nation but also between two kinds of life, two outlooks, two roads for the future of Mankind. It is a struggle between seeing men and women

as subjects and seeing them as objects, between seeing men and women as social beings capable of fighting, working, acting together to transform themselves and transform each other, and seeing them as isolated individuals, bundles of appetites, neuroses and fantasies, as so many bodies to be manipulated and programmed.

The Americans fight a mechanical war but the Vietnamese fight a people's war. For the Vietnamese the human element always comes first. There is nothing they can do without the people. The people are their support, the people are their warriors, and the people are their political belief. The Vietnamese are organized, that is, they have a sense of themselves as a people. The Vietnamese are also politically conscious —they understand why and for what they are fighting. The American army is just the opposite. Each man in it is a trained individual, each for himself. The American forces possess a great deal of technical know-how but they have absolutely no sense of political know-why. They fight with machines according to machine principles. There is nothing they can do with the people in Southeast Asia—except exterminate them by converting them into body counts or pacify them by removing them into refugee camps. People have to become numbers and objects first before the American forces know how to deal with them.

On the other hand, not only people but Nature itself is a friend to the Vietnamese, an enemy to the Americans. The jungles cover the Vietnamese liberation forces, so the jungles have to be defoliated. The crops feed the resistance, so the crops have to be destroyed. Under the earth the people build tunnels, so the earth has to be bulldozed away. The guerrillas march at night, so the night has to be conquered with laser sensors. Only the monsoon rains are so far invulnerable to the Pentagon think-tank. To the Vietnamese fighting the people's war, the whole land is alive; the trees are alive, the stones are alive, the waters are alive, and the people are alive. To the American forces everything is dead, including the people. The frustrated comment of an American officer: "The only way we can win this goddamn war is to pave the whole country into a giant parking lot" sums up the philosophy of America.°

This is the philosophy which kept the United States trapped in Vietnam. This is the way in which the great majority of the American people still think they can solve all problems from the most minor to the most mammoth. This is the way of thinking and acting from

---

° From *Asian-Americans and the War* (Detroit: Asian Political Alliance, 1971).

which this country must now struggle to extricate itself and which it must replace with another way of thinking, the indispensable basis for another way of acting, if we are to cope with our mounting problems and our increasingly antagonistic relations with one another, and if we are to rejoin and enrich the mainstream of advancing humanity.

6

DIALECTICS AND REVOLUTION

Down through the many thousands of years of our continuing evolution as human beings, men and women have thought in many different ways about themselves and about the world in which they lived. Until a few hundred years ago, most people had no concept of change as development, principally because there was really very little progress in their lives from which to derive such a concept. Year after year, decade after decade, generation after generation, they did the same things in the same way. They hunted the same game or tilled the same soil, ate the same food, were born, gave birth, and died in the same way as their ancestors had done. During their lifetimes they were subject to the same kind of arbitrary rule by tribal chiefs, feudal lords, or kings. Under these unchanging circumstances, their concept of change could only be based on their perception of such phenomena as constant repetition of the seasons, the agricultural cycle of sowing, planting, and harvesting, or the human cycle of birth, growth, reproduction, and death. So their concept of change was a cyclical concept: the more things change, the more they return to the beginning and start all over again.

At a certain point in our evolution our ancestors developed the concept of gods, seeking to create some entities more powerful and more exalted than their human rulers, entities to whom they could look for ethical and moral standards. They themselves were not yet ready to accept the responsibility for creating and enforcing moral and ethical standards. Since their rulers came and went, and most of them were hardly representative of the standards which every society needs to govern the relations between people, man/woman created gods to embody and validate these values.

These gods were mythical creatures. But having invested these gods with such authority, man/woman began to look to them to fix all kinds of earthly problems, to deliver them from pain and suffering, from toil and misery, or to reward them in heaven for their hardships on earth. This kind of thinking is idealism, i.e., it is the kind of wishful or subjective thinking by which people create an ideal in the form of a person or a state of being and then begin to believe in its independent reality and rely on it to "fix" things up for them.

Idealistic thinking became very deeply entrenched in the thinking of the great masses of the people because they did not believe that they could change anything in reality. Only the chief, the lord, or the king had the power to bring about changes in reality, and these changes rarely benefited anybody except the chief, the lord, or the king. Therefore the masses' only hope of change for the better was in a mythical realm. In this way, until a few hundred years ago, the great masses of people accepted their lot, their place, as subjects.

About twenty-five hundred years ago philosophy began in both the East and the West when a few men began to wonder about the contradiction between what actually existed, the real, and what should exist, the ideal. But these philosophers did not see any real possibility of changing reality for the better. They had no idea that the great masses of the people might be organized and mobilized into a social force for progress. This very advanced idea or concept did not emerge until after the French Revolution, two hundred years ago. Therefore, the only progress that philosophers, particularly in the West, could envisage was ideal progress, i.e., progress towards the ideal in the minds of individual philosophers.

It is important to realize that men and women thought this way for many thousands and thousands of years if we are to appreciate the great leap forward, the revolution in human thinking two hundred years ago, and the even greater leap forward in thinking which we have to make today.

Some indication of the long historical process by which man/womankind has developed can be obtained by watching the development of the individual from infancy through childhood and youth to adulthood and advanced years, since the historical development of the species is to some degree recapitulated in the development of the individual. However, we also know that simply advancing in age does not mean a development in social thinking. Many who reach chronological maturity still do not ask themselves the kind of fundamental questions or are not prepared for the kind of critical thinking and struggles which are essential to the development of the social thought process. Most people spend their whole lifetime just being utilitarian or materialist, preoccupied only with questions of physical survival and comforts. They do only what they have to do in their own self-interest and/or what they are told to do. They accept whatever occurs in society as beyond their control, as being fixed by others.

There are others who begin to wonder. But most of these are not ready to go to the organized effort necessary to put their visions into practice. Therefore, if any good comes out of what they think or envisage, it is purely accidental. In this sense most people have a philosophy or a set of assumptions and convictions by which they live, but few become philosophers. A philosopher, believing that ideas do matter, organizes his/her assumptions and convictions into a body of ideas. Still, most philosophers only contemplate these ideas. They do not progress to the next stage, the stage of politics. That is, they do not try to find a way by which they can propagate their convictions to people and especially to the masses of the people and attempt to organize these people to struggle to make these convictions real. This is what revolutionists do, because revolutionists are profoundly convinced that the society in which they live must be changed, and that the ideas which they have developed are advanced ideas, i.e., ideas for advancing society. They are profoundly convinced that until the great masses of the people at the bottom of a society acquire the motivation and the determination to change their society, there can be at best some improvements or reforms in a society, and more likely only an exchange of positions by those at the top. For a fundamental reorganization of any society to take place, the eyes and hearts of those at the bottom must be opened to a new, more advanced way of human beings living together. Only then will they be able to exercise their previously unused initiative and creativity to bring about those many changes in oppressive relations which are visible only to those who see them from below. That is why revolutionists devote so much effort first, to exploring and creating advanced ideas, and then, to finding the ways by which these advanced ideas can be grasped by the masses of the people and thus transformed into a material force to change themselves and society. It is in this very important sense that revolutionists are neither idealists, i.e., concerned only with ideas or ideals, nor materialists, i.e., concerned only with matters of economic survival. On the contrary, their lives are devoted to the struggle to establish a new unity between advanced ideas and the great masses of the people, a unity which is neither idealism nor materialism, but the truth uniting both.

We are at the stage today where we are seeking to discover the next step in the evolution of man/womankind. Therefore, what matters to us is that, regardless of the differences which have separated human beings from one another down through the ages (differences of sex, of caste and class, of tribe or nation, of race or religion), men and women in the course of our three thousand generations of evolution have become more profoundly and uniquely human insofar as they have sought more profound, more enlarged concepts of what it means to be human. Because what makes men and women distinctively human is not how well or how badly they behave, how meek or aggressive their temperaments, how moderate or militant their actions, or how skillful or clumsy their practices. What distinguishes man/woman as human and differentiates us from all other living things is our ability to reflect upon our past and present experiences and to project visions and programs for human struggle to create a new future. It is in this sense that those individuals who have assumed the responsibility for creating and projecting to the great masses of people an enlarged vision of their humanity play such an important role in the advancement of humankind.

Less than two hundred years ago the poor of Paris, rising out of the gutters, sewers, and cellars, created by their actions the basis for the new idea that oppressed people can change their lives. In the French Revolution the masses, by their actions, created the concept of citizenship for poor people where previously the world had only known the relationship of ruler and subject. If today we can talk about, wonder about, define a social revolution as a profoundly new and profoundly original transformation in man/woman's concept of self, in their conditions of life, and in their relations with other classes, races, nations, and cultures, it is because the epoch of social revolution was initiated by the poor people of Paris in the French Revolution.

The French Revolution brought onto the political stage great masses of ordinary people, ready to clash with their oppressors in order to transform reality in the name of reason and of the advanced ideas of Liberty, Equality, and Fraternity which the intellectuals had been talking about. Through their actions the French masses overthrew the feudal aristocracy, which had been acting as a fetter or brake on the development of the productive forces, and made it possible for the Industrial Revolution, already under way in England, to get under way in France.

The French Revolution opened the minds of the Western world to the possibilities within existing reality for sudden and rapid developments toward an ideal. It thus weakened the concept of reality as static and unchanging, and began to replace it with a concept of reality as evolving and dynamic. The French Revolution also made apparent the existence of opposing classes and interests both within society and within a revolutionary movement that at the beginning or on its surface had appeared as a unity. It thus weakened the idea of reality as basically homogeneous and harmonious and suggested a new idea of reality as inherently contradictory, or as containing duality within unity.

In the wake of the French Revolution, the Industrial Revolution began a rapid transformation of the physical environment of people from one dependent on natural forces (weather, seasons, soil) to one that was man-made (cities, factories, machines). Theoretically a man-made environment should have increased human freedom, but the money economy and increasingly oppressive relations within the factory subjected growing numbers of people to new and terrible bondage. Thus, what had been created in the name of human freedom was in turn becoming a fetter on human freedom. The resolution of one set of contradictions had led to the creation of others.

The French Revolution began in 1789 and kept Europe in turmoil throughout most of the nineteenth century. The early years of the century were years of evaluation much like our present period, during which thinking people were striving to make some sense of the world-shaking events through which they were living and which they were aware had destroyed the old values and the old society.

It was not difficult to see that what was happening had both a positive and a negative side. On the one hand, the French Revolution had obviously meant progress in human dignity and identity in the sense that it had made Liberty, Equality, and Fraternity a part of the normal outlook of millions. It had led to a much broader and deeper participation of the population in the shaping of their destiny, and, after the rebellion of the Parisian masses in 1792 and 1793, it had even led to government acceptance of greater responsibility for economic justice. On the other hand, the Reign of Terror under the Jacobins and the Napoleonic dictatorship, both of which had been supported by the masses, aroused widespread fear as to what would happen if the masses really had their way.

The same negative and positive features characterized the Industrial Revolution. On the one hand, by destroying superstition and promoting scientific thinking, the Industrial Revolution promised miracles not only in production but in more reasonable relations between people. On the other hand, it also brought about the concentration of former peasants in city slums, where men, women, and children were forced to sell their labor power as a commodity simply in order to live. As a result, the traditional skills of the craftsman were destroyed, as were all relations between people not based on money.

Confronted with this situation, most people didn't know what to think. Some said that so many bad things had come out of the Industrial and French Revolutions that society ought to go back to the past. So there were constant attempts at restoration of the old regime, attempts to push the clock back. Others, and particularly the new capitalist class, were very satisfied with the new situation and made glowing promises of the abundant future it offered for everybody.

The French and the Industrial revolutions had made clear that man/woman's consciousness does not only reflect the world; it also creates, determines the world. But the negative consequences of the French and Industrial revolutions also suggested that man/woman's struggle to create a new human world was bound to be a protracted one, involving the successive overcoming of ever deepening contradictions. Thus, together, the French and the Industrial revolutions created the need and the basis for a new way of thinking.

It was within this historical situation that Hegel, a German philosopher who as a student in Germany had hailed the beginning of the French Revolution in 1789, began to formulate the philosophy of dialectical thinking. It cannot be too strongly emphasized that Hegel's philosophy arose out of a historical situation, a historical need on the part of thinking people for a systematic way to reflect about what was happening in relation to the past and the future. Because we, too, are living in a period of great historical transition and confusion, it should not be too difficult for us to understand the importance of the three basic principles of dialectical thinking as formulated by Hegel.

In the first place, Hegel said, social reality, and indeed all reality, is constantly developing, constantly evolving from a lower to a higher form.

Second, the basic reason or cause for this continuing evolution is internal, not external. It stems from the drive within everything to achieve its highest potential, a drive which creates a continuing contradiction within things and the internal necessity to negate what they are in order to arrive at what they can be.

Third, it is through conflict and contradiction that progress to a new positive takes place. This is what is known as negation of the negation.

This dialectical concept of change as development was a sharp break away from the old concept of change as cyclical, i.e., the idea that things just continue to go around until they return to where they started, or in its more modern formulation, "it has always been this way and it will always be this way." The concept of change from internal causes also differs sharply from the widespread concept of change as dependent upon external causes which most social scientists have borrowed from the physical sciences. The external cause concept is a mechanical way of thinking which attributes change only to others or to outside forces. Applied to human beings, it acts as a barrier to revolutionary thinking because it leads the oppressed to depend on others or on changes in external conditions to make changes in and for them. The dialectical thinker, on the other hand, recognizes that external causes contribute to change but they are not the primary cause. Temperature conditions help the egg develop into a chicken, but temperature could not possibly bring about the development of a chicken from a stone. Foxes don't act like chickens nor do foxes come from chickens.

Using the dialectical concept of internal causes, we can see how the drive within anything to achieve its own potential creates a conflict with its present state of reality which has become a fetter upon its continuing evolution. In order to resolve this contradiction, a struggle must take place. Out of the resolution comes a new unity. But this new unity in turn is only temporary, since within it a new duality or a new contradiction between the actual and the potential is emerging, creating the basis for further struggle towards a still higher form of existence. This concept, usually called the unity of opposites, also makes clear why progress or development never takes place in a straight line or just by quantitative increase or decrease. In other words, progressive development is never just evolutionary; it requires great and sudden leaps, drastic changes in direction. But neither does it take place, as Hegel puts it, "like a shot out of a pistol." Maturation through the overcoming of one contradiction after another, or what Hegel calls "the labor, patience and suffering of the negative" is continually necessary. There is no "final struggle," no ultimate unity, no "promised land" in which we just sit back and reap the benefits of past struggles.

The concept of negation of the negation makes clear that in every struggle to change an existing reality, we must keep clearly in mind the new positive or the new unity which we are trying to create. Negating the present reality is never just to create chaos or uncertainty; it is always to create a new positive. Negation is not just for the sake of negation; it should always have definite goals.

The dialectical method of thinking is in essence critical and revolutionary. Using this method of thinking, an individual will refuse to admit the authority or permanence of an existing state of reality. He/she will be confident that within any particular reality there are internal contradictions which are the basis for negating this reality. He/she will constantly seek to find and hold fast the new positive or the new and higher unity which can emerge out of the resolution of these contradictions. The creation of this advanced way of thinking was therefore an indispensable step on the road to revolutionary thinking and practice.

Revolutionists seek to change reality, to make it better. Therefore, revolutionists not only need the revolutionary philosophy of dialectics. They need a revolutionary ideology, i.e., a body of ideas based on analyzing the main contradiction of the particular society which they are trying to change, projecting a vision of a higher form of reality in which this contradiction would be resolved, and relating this resolution to a social force or forces responsible for and capable of achieving it. It is only after you have arrived at a correct ideology that it makes sense to develop your revolutionary politics, i.e., the programs necessary to mobilize and organize the revolutionary social forces. If your ideology is wrong, i.e., misdirected or limited, then all the most brilliant programs for militant activity by the masses will be of no avail. Every revolutionist must be absolutely clear about this sequence—from revolutionary *philosophy*, to revolutionary *ideology*, to revolutionary *politics*.

Karl Marx, born in 1818, was the first person in history to develop a revolutionary ideology. While his fellow students were using the ideas of Hegel for intellectual gymnastics (Marx ridiculed them as "The Holy Family"), Marx set himself the task of changing the Europe in which he was living, a Europe torn by struggles between the aristocracy seeking to restore the feudal past and the capitalists seeking to build their own power through exploitation of the new freedoms created by the French Revolution. Looking beyond the obvious struggle between the restorationists and the capitalists, Marx saw the new antagonisms which were developing within the process of production between the capitalists and the workers. This was the main contradiction of bourgeois society, Marx said, and out of it would inevitably grow an increasingly powerful social force to build a new socialist society, the social force of the working class, organized and disciplined by the process of production itself.

Together with Friedrich Engels, who was to become his lifelong collaborator, Marx created the foundations of an ideology for European revolution in the *Communist Manifesto*, published in 1848, a year of ferment in Western Europe much like the 1960s in the United States. Since few people paid any attention to the bold new ideas which the youthful Marx was advancing, he devoted the major part of his remaining years to theoretical work in the form of systematic analyses of the contradictions in capitalist production and historical interpretations of the class struggles and civil wars of his time. Hence he did not make the transition to revolutionary politics, which involves continuing contact with the revolutionary social forces defined in your ideology.

As we have seen, the first man to practice and in fact to create the practice of revolutionary politics was Lenin. While a young man in his twenties, Lenin had come to the conclusion, based on his studies of Marx and Engels, that the chief task of the Russian people was to get rid of the autocratic regime controlled by the landlords and the capitalists; and that the Russian working class was the chief social force to lead the great masses of the Russian people in this task. He then devoted the remainder of his life to creating the disciplined organization, called the vanguard party, which could lead the working class to power.

A vanguard party is the instrument by means of which the militancy and the rebellion of the revolutionary social forces can be transformed from purely reflexive, trial-and-error reactions into purposeful, planned, and programmatic struggles for power. The vanguard party thus increases not only the political awareness or consciousness of the revolutionary social forces but also their self-consciousness, i.e., their capacity to reflect upon and learn from past experiences and practices and out of these reflections to develop programs and plans for the future.

Lenin's concept of the vanguard party was not created overnight or easily "like a shot out of a pistol." Just as Marx had arrived at his revolutionary ideology out of his political determination to shape the course of nineteenth-century Europe, Lenin arrived at his concept of the vanguard party out of his political determination to make the revolution in Russia. This led him into ideological struggle with other socialists who also claimed to be Marxists but who insisted that Marxism meant that socialism in Russia could be achieved through the spontaneous rebellion of the workers (the Economists) or through the gradual development of the contradictions within Russian capitalism (the Mensheviks). In line with their evolutionary concept of socialist development, the Mensheviks argued against a disciplined vanguard party and for a mass party; thereby, in Lenin's words, leaving "the door wide open for every kind of opportunist and stretching the boundaries of the party till they become quite blurred."

In October 1917 the Russian workers and peasants, under the leadership of the Bolshevik Party, seized power. To many revolutionists, from one end of the world to the other, the ideology and the organization which had achieved the Russian Revolution appeared to be the final solution to the contradiction between ideas and reality.

Meanwhile, however, Lenin himself, at the head of the Bolshevik Party and of the Workers' Government, was discovering the new dualities within the new unity which had been established by the revolution.

Lenin recognized, and struggled tirelessly to make his colleagues and the Russian people understand, that only the first task of negating or destroying feudalism and capitalism had been achieved by the October Revolution. There still remained the much more difficult and protracted task of creating the new positive of a new social system. Such a social system would be superior to capitalism only if it involved the great masses of the people in continuing, creative, cooperative, self-critical, and self-disciplined practical and productive activity, only if the people themselves were transformed so that they would naturally and unhesitatingly assume responsibility for decision-making and control over the economic and political development of the country.

In his efforts to lead the Russian people in this practical activity of creating a new positive, Lenin, until his death in 1924, had to carry on a fierce struggle against two sets of opponents. On the one hand, there were those who idealized or romanticized the masses (Anarchists), denying the need for leadership and calling for the dictatorship of the masses against the dictatorship of the party. Lenin accused these people of revolutionary rhetoric and of infantile leftism because of their refusal to take into consideration the individualism which the masses had inherited from the past.

On the other hand, there were those who were concerned only with rapid economic and industrial development, insisting that this material development would automatically bring in its wake the political development of the masses. Lenin accused these people of putting economics in command of politics and warned that their policies would lead to state capitalism, to the domination of experts and technicians, and to the eventual isolation of the government and the party from the people.

Thus, out of the Russian Revolution, a new set of contradictions had been born. This new set of contradictions centered chiefly around:

1. the relation of leaders to masses (Is leadership necessary?);

2. the relation of economic development to political development (Does the improvement in material conditions necessarily bring about the political development of the masses or does it sometimes bring about the opposite?); and

3. the contradiction between the "abruptness" of revolution (to use Lenin's word) and the protracted period required for the cultural revolutionizing of the masses.

For the last fifty years Mao and the Chinese Communist Party, in their determination to make a revolution in China, have also been creating new answers to these questions which are critical to every revolution.

The Chinese Communists have only been able to create these answers because they have constantly borne in mind and constantly deepened through practical struggles the dialectical conception of reality as inherently and increasingly contradictory (one always divides into two) and the revolutionists' goal of making the most advanced ideas a practical part of the lives of the masses so that they can transcend the limitations which have been imposed upon them by class society. The great historical contribution of Mao is that he has demystified the fundamental laws of dialectics to the point where they can be consciously applied by hundreds of millions of peasants and workers to the most elementary as well as the most complex questions of production and politics.

The Chinese Communists anticipate and utilize contradictions as a powerful catalyst to further development. Thus, instead of rejecting the concept of leadership altogether because of the obvious potential within it for bureaucratic domination, the Chinese Communists welcome the tensions implicit within the relations between leaders and masses, or between central committees and local committees, as a means of arriving at more correct, more vital, and richer ideas on both sides. Only through a true dialogue between those who are more developed, or who have more overall responsibility, and those who are less developed, or who have more particular responsibilities, can reciprocal education, and therefore change and development, take place. This tension suffuses the famous passage defining the role of leadership. Leadership must "take the ideas of the masses (scattered and unsystematic ideas) and concentrate them (through study turn them into concentrated and systematic ideas), then go to the masses and propagate and explain these ideas until the masses embrace them as their own, hold fast to them and translate them into action, and test the correctness of these ideas in such action. Then once again concentrate ideas from the masses and once again go to the masses so that the ideas are persevered in and carried through. And so on, over and over again in an endless spiral, with the ideas becoming more correct, more vital, and richer each time. Such is the Marxist theory of knowledge."

The same appreciation of the reality of contradiction underlies the concept of criticism and self-criticism. Criticism and self-criticism is the way in which individuals who are united by common goals can consciously utilize their differences and their limitations, i.e., the negative, in order to accelerate their positive advance. The popular formulation for this process is "changing a bad thing into a good thing." Hence the Chinese Communists emphasize, first, the need to prevent mistakes (through the most thorough discussion and preparation of all involved); second, the need to recognize, admit, and correct (rather than cover up) mistakes; third, the need to pin down exact responsibility for mistakes. This is not for the purpose of placing blame on an individual but to enable the individual and others to learn the appropriate lessons from the mistake and thus avoid repetition. Failure to pin down responsibility (liberalism) for fear of offending the individual or on the basis that "it's not their fault" actually retards individual development because it leads people to make fewer demands on themselves to develop. Often the reason for a mistake is not just technical but social, e.g., stemming from an attitude of individualism or élitism, or of arrogance or complacency, or from disregard of other's opinions, or from fear of making mistakes. Self-criticism, as distinguished from criticism, stems from the individual acknowledging that there is a continuing contradiction within him/herself between a social or socialist outlook and an individualist or bourgeois outlook, and therefore the continuing need to remold his/her outlook.

From the Yenan days to the present, the Chinese have been

conscious of the trap of vulgar materialism, or economism, which gives priority to the development of productive forces and material incentives. To avoid this trap they have insisted that the essential aim of revolution is the most rapid possible development of the human potential within the masses for political consciousness and social responsibility. Mao launched the struggle against the vulgar materialist tendency within the party as early as 1937. To have built the party on the basis of vulgar materialism would have meant certain failure, since semi-colonial China was too undeveloped economically to have produced a proletariat. In 1966, when liberated China was undergoing rapid economic development, the economist tendency again emerged in Liu Shao-ch'i, one of Mao's closest comrades. That tendency posed such a threat to the Chinese Revolution that Mao risked the turbulence of a revolutionary struggle within the party and in the whole society in order to crush it. It is obvious therefore that the economist or vulgar materialist concept of human development as dependent upon economic development, is a tendency with deep roots in the Marxist movement and in all industrializing or industrialized societies. Lenin fought against it, Mao continues to fight against it, the present conflict between China and the Soviet Union is based on this duality within Marxist theory. In one form or another, every vanguard party must carry on a continuing theoretical and practical struggle against the vulgar materialist tendency in the pre-revolutionary as well as the post-revolutionary period.

The Chinese Cultural Revolution shows revolutionists everywhere that dialectical materialism, as opposed to vulgar materialism and idealism, means the continuing struggle to make the most advanced ideas the property of the masses so that they can turn them into a material force to change society and the world.

With this enriched understanding of dialectical materialism, it becomes possible to give a more meaningful answer to the third question which we have been bequeathed by the Russian Revolution. Beginning with the Chinese revolution, all the great revolutions of our time have reversed the process by which Lenin and the Bolsheviks came to power in Russia. They have consciously and deliberately postponed the confrontation with the regime and the seizure of state power until after there has been a protracted struggle to unite and transform the masses economically, politically, and socially. Acutely aware of the bureaucratic degeneration and depoliticization of Soviet Russia, they have concentrated on a protracted struggle to develop self-reliance and responsibility in the masses as well as the basic social and political structures necessary for the formation of a new government and a new society. Confident that time will only deepen and widen the contradictions on the side of the enemy, and taking seriously the post-revolutionary reflections of Lenin, they have concluded that if the masses have not begun to develop a sense of social responsibility before the seizure of power, the new revolutionary government will, sooner rather than later, find itself confronting disappointed and hostile masses who expect miracles from the new government, and are much less patient with it than they ever were with the gods.

The practice of these advanced ideas in the Chinese, the Guinea-Bissau, and the Vietnamese revolutions has disclosed political consciousness and social responsibility to be a necessary ingredient of human dignity and human identity.

It must never be forgotten that the Chinese, the Vietnamese, and the people of Guinea-Bissau could never have achieved this advance in revolutionary politics had it not been for the leap made by Lenin in the Russian Revolution, and the new contradictions which this leap created. Analogously, Lenin's revolutionary politics, and the Russian Revolution, developed from the revolutionary ideology which Marx and Engels created. Finally, Marx and Engels could never have created their revolutionary ideology had it not been for the dialectical philosophy which Hegel formulated, and which, in turn, came out of the French and Industrial revolutions.

For revolutionists, it is much more important to appreciate the successive struggles which have made possible this historical development from dialectical philosophy to revolutionary ideology to revolutionary politics than it is to know in detail the scenario of every revolution, much less to get involved in second-guessing what should have been done or should not have been done in each revolution. It is obvious also that the ideas and the initial leadership in most revolutions have come from intellectuals of petty-bourgeois origin. Whether or not they remain petty-bourgeois intellectuals depends on the depth of their conviction and their readiness to devote their lives to a protracted struggle to make their advanced ideas the property of the masses. Marx and Engels, his collaborator; Lenin; Mao; Castro; Nkrumah; Ho—none of these was a poor peasant or worker.

Toussaint L'Ouverture was what we would today call a "house nigger." Cabral was an engineer. Each grappled with the contradictions of his particular society at a particular time in order to change that society. Each had to transcend the limitations in the thinking of his predecessors and contemporaries and boldly create a new set of advanced ideas before that society could make a great leap forward into the future.

The most dangerous enemy of the revolutionary theoretician is not the external enemy but the potential within all theory, and especially the boldest theories, to become dogma. The more a revolutionary thinker is isolated from systematic dialogue and practical interaction with revolutionary social forces, the greater this danger.

In the one hundred and twenty-five years since the *Communist Manifesto*, we have witnessed the emergence of many new contradictions: contradictions between rival imperialisms in two world wars, between the socialist camp and the capitalist camp in the wake of the Russian Revolution, between the imperialist powers and the colonialized peoples, within the socialist camp between Russia and China, as well as within individuals between the bourgeois and the socialist outlook. The revolutionist utilizes all these contradictions and anticipates that there will be even more in the future.

Marx did not call for a separate Communist Party to lead the workers. The Communists, he said explicitly in the *Manifesto*, do not form a separate party opposed to other working-class parties. "They do not set up any sectarian principles of their own, by which to shape and mould the proletarian movement."

More than a generation later, Lenin, also an intellectual, created the new idea of a party to lead the workers. It is important to realize the very advanced stage of reflection and responsibility on the part of human beings which the vanguard party represents. Most people use the term "vanguard" today to apply to the most militant, the most rebellious, the most oppressed, the most ready for confrontations with the enemy, regardless of whether that person has a body of ideas or is responsible to a body of people who have themselves accepted continuing responsibility. Lenin created the vanguard party precisely to combat that kind of reactive politics. He realized that merely to react to this or that issue is to say, in essence, that the people in power ought to change the way things are, whereas the aim of a vanguard party is to replace those in power with a social force which will change the way things are to the way they ought to be.

With Lenin the party is no longer the representative of the needs and interests of the working class, as it was for Marx. With Lenin the party has become a transmission belt taking from the masses their issues and grievances, organizing these into programs, and then taking these programs back to the masses to raise them to a higher level of struggle and of consciousness as to what must be done and what must not be done.

Lenin was the first to appreciate the importance of what few so-called Marxists in the advanced countries have gotten around to recognizing, i.e., that the laws of dialectics which govern the development of the revolutionary social forces also govern the development of the capitalist counter-revolutionary forces. If the revolutionary social forces antagonized by capitalism do not develop the revolutionary power to overthrow capitalism, capitalism will continue to develop dialectically to a new stage or new stages, and thereby acquire the means to incorporate sections of the revolutionary social forces within itself.

That is what has happened with imperialism, which is a new stage of capitalism. Other economists, prior to Lenin, had recognized how the relatively primitive industrial capitalism of Marx's day had been transformed into large-scale monopoly and finance capitalism in the advanced countries, and how these countries were dividing Africa, Asia, and Latin America among themselves, maintaining the peoples of these continents in a state of systematic underdevelopment so that they could continue to serve as sources of raw materials, as markets, and as spheres of influence. Other economists had described this new stage of development of capitalism as imperialism. Lenin's specific contribution was to recognize the new duality within this new stage of capitalism. This new stage of capitalism had not only made it possible for the capitalists to corrupt a substantial section of the working class inside the advanced countries; it had also created a new revolutionary social force inside the systematically undeveloped countries which would be striving for national liberation.

Lenin saw that imperialism, which he called a new stage of capitalism, had set into motion a process both for the continued advance of capitalism and for the regression of the workers inside the imperialist countries, because it set these workers into an antagonistic relationship with the masses of the colonial countries still trying to set themselves free from feudalism while fighting the new enemy of imperialism. How important the dialectical way of thinking was to Lenin's analysis of imperialism can be seen from his spirited comments on Hegel's writings, which he studied, for the first time, in 1915.

What has been taking place in China for the last few decades is the result of Mao's reflections not only on the contradictions of Chinese society but also on the problems that the Russian Revolution raised and failed to resolve.

Just as we can say that the Chinese revolution is the granddaddy of revolutions today in the Third World, we can also say that the United States is the granddaddy of advanced capitalism, the most highly developed capitalism, with the most highly advanced technology that the world has ever known. We must pioneer in creating a model of socialist revolution for the advanced capitalist countries.

This fact alone presents us with the dilemma that there is not, there cannot be any historical model for a revolution in this country. There has never been a revolution in an advanced country from which we can learn. We recommend that our readers compare the *Communist Manifesto* with the *Manifesto for a Black Revolutionary Party*, which we published in 1969. This will help them appreciate what has happened in one hundred and twenty years. The working class of the United States, whose development we have traced in *The American Revolution*, is not the one Marx knew in nineteenth-century England. A revolutionary ideology for the United States must be based on the development of the revolutionary forces in this country. All we can take from Marx is his method of dialectical analysis.

The 1926 General Strike in England showed that the workers in an advanced country can close down the country by striking all the plants, but it takes more to make a revolution than the power of the workers to paralyze production. A revolution requires a revolutionary political apparatus which will enable the great majority of the people to defeat the power of the state and reorganize all its institutions. France in 1968 came closer than any advanced country has come to the transfer of power in the last hundred years. Yet with power lying in the streets, there was no revolutionary organization in France that wanted power or that was prepared for power, because there was no revolutionary organization with any vision of what it would do with that power.

To conclude, let us state categorically some of the things that the United States revolution in the twentieth century is *not* going to be for.

1. The revolution to be made in the United States is *not* going to be for Liberty, Equality, and Fraternity. That was the goal of the French Revolution, in order to get rid of feudalism.

2. The revolution to be made in the United States cannot be for socialism as defined by Marx. Capitalism has already developed productive forces to the point where material needs can be satisfied. This is one of the great contradictions facing a Marxist movement which has put economics rather than politics in command of its thinking.

3. The revolution to be made in the United States is *not* for civil rights. Civil rights are what any society gives to every individual in that society if it treasures its legitimacy or its right to exist. The kind of rights that will exist in a new society will be qualitatively different from the rights in this society. The revolution to be made in the United States is *not* to increase the freedom of individual choice. Rather it is to increase the collective consciousness of how to choose, how to grasp both ends in order to pull forward the middle.

4. The revolution to be made in the United States is *not* for majority rule. Our society is the final proof that majority rule is not the most advanced form of human rule. Counting noses cannot be the fundamental way for determining political direction or for making political choices and political judgments.

5. The revolution to be made in the United States is *not* just to give to the poor the same rights and privileges that the rich have had. It is *not* to spread the wealth, *not* to give the poor an equal right to be as materialistic and as opportunistic as the rich. It is *not* just to end poverty or to bring peace so that those in power can concentrate on the reforms that will pacify the masses. The question to be answered by a revolution in an advanced country like the United States is whether man/woman's wants are going to be allowed to dominate and define man/woman's needs as human beings.

6. The revolution to be made in the United States is *not* just to have population control. The Chinese have three times the population of the United States in approximately the same area, and they

are much healthier because they make socially conscious choices between what people want and what people need.

7. The revolution to be made in the United States is *not* for "Peace, Bread, and Land" as it was in Russia in 1917. It is for total political power to make decisions as to what should be done and what should not be done with land.

Only when we understand what the revolution to be made in the United States will *not* be for, can we begin to reflect on what it will be for. For if we approach an American revolution with the lack of clarity with which the Civil War was fought, then we might wind up with power—although that is doubtful—and then repeat the tragic errors of the post-Civil-War period. At that time, in order to fit the economic aspirations of some of the people, the black masses were forced back into a state of servitude worse than that of slavery itself, by the 1877 Compromise. Every successive generation has suffered the social consequences of this failure to develop a clear idea of the awesome responsibilities of power. Our generation has the opportunity to make a fresh start.

The revolution to be made in the United States will be the first revolution in history to require the masses to make material sacrifices rather than to acquire more material things. We must give up many of the things which this country has enjoyed at the expense of damning over one-third of the world into a state of underdevelopment, ignorance, disease, and early death. Until the revolutionary forces come to power here, this country will not be safe for the world and revolutionary warfare on an international scale against the United States will remain the wave of the present—unless all of humanity goes up in one big puff.

It is obviously going to take a tremendous transformation to prepare the people of the United States for these new social goals. But potential revolutionaries can only become true revolutionaries if they take the side of those who believe that humanity can be transformed. Those who have already given up on America, those who have condemned it as hopelessly racist and fascist, will never make an American revolution. If this book, and particularly this chapter, accomplishes its purpose, it will help readers to appreciate that this country is only two hundred years old, and, by comparison with most of the countries of the world, in its infancy. The people of this country have lived together continuously a much shorter time than any of the peoples whose revolutions we have studied. The ancestors of most of us were not among those who founded this country only two hundred years ago and established the political, economic, and social patterns by which it has developed to its present state. The American people have never really engaged in the revolutionary struggles by which any great nation is created. That great humanizing experience still lies before them.

Only with this sense of historical perspective, historical duration, and historical proportion can we undertake the task before us of revolutionizing this country. Objectively the task is colossal.

The United States is the citadel of world capitalism. Capitalism in the United States has gone a long way beyond the primitive capitalism, the manufacturing capitalism, and the industrial capitalism of Marx's day, to embrace imperialism and colonialism, neocolonialism, multinational capitalism, and the military-industrial complex with its client states all over the world.

Capitalism has developed to the point where money-lending itself is an industry. The banking industry makes more profit, exploiting all of us through its savings and lending mechanisms, than old private capitalists exploiting the workers in production. Banks have become as common as filling stations.

U.S. capitalism has brought together an unholy alliance of the old bourgeoisie, the new managers of industry, the ex-generals and the existing generals, scientists and technicians from Germany and the United States multi-university, war workers, mercenaries from all classes, and particularly the "lumpen"—double agents and agents-provocateurs, media manipulators, cost accountants, and petty careerists from one end of the world to the other. All these are supported and subsidized by the American taxpayer. So that when we talk about the bourgeoisie today, we have to be very scientific. Are we so naive as to think we are talking only about America's sixty families—or are we ready to include millions of people, of divergent social types and origins, whom we are all supporting and subsidizing by our taxes without any kind of representation except that which is achieved through a national or local lottery, called voting, every two or three years?

Many people recognize that technological man/woman has outstripped ethical or politically conscious and socially responsible man/woman. This too is the result of dialectical development.

Technological man/woman developed because human beings had to discover how to keep warm, how to make fire, how to grow food, how to build dams, how to dig wells. Therefore human beings were compelled to manifest their humanity in their technological capacity, to discover the power within them to invent tools and techniques which would extend their material powers. We have concentrated our powers on making things to the point that we have intensified our greed for more things, and lost the understanding of why this productivity was originally pursued. The result is that the mind of man/woman is now totally out of balance, totally out of proportion.

That is what production for the sake of production has done to modern man/woman. That is the basic contradiction confronting everyone who has lived and developed inside the United States. That is the contradiction which neither the U.S. government nor any social force in the United States up to now has been willing to face, because the underlying philosophy of this country, from top to bottom, remains the philosophy that economic development can and will resolve all political and social problems.

7
REDISCOVERING
THE AMERICAN PAST

Every revolution is a struggle to resolve the particular contradictions which have evolved out of a particular past. Every country's past is particular, but America's past is so particular that it almost seems to have evolved on another planet. Except for the native Americans, whom Europeans named Indians, everyone in this country is a descendant of someone who came here from another continent and another culture less than four hundred years ago—in most cases, much less. The economic, social, and political institutions of this country have been shaped by the struggles of very real and very different people, mostly of humble origin and all seeking to make a new and prosperous life for themselves here, on this earth, as quickly as possible, regardless of the cost to other peoples, especially to those of different ethnic backgrounds, and to future generations. They have thus made it inevitable that at some future time the American people would be compelled to face with sober senses the real, i.e., historical, conditions of their lives and their relations with their kind.

As the Indians were meeting in the eleventh century, somewhere near Ticonderoga, to reconcile the territorial claims of different tribes, they had no idea that technical advances in navigation and aspirations for freedom by ordinary people on another continent would lead to their becoming one day the first people in history to be placed in a concentration camp called a reservation. Nor did the members of a religious sect, seeking, in the early seventeenth century, a place where they could exercise what they conceived as their God-given right to interpret the Bible in accordance with their own consciences, have any idea that they would set into motion a chain of events which would lead, a hundred and fifty years later, to the creation of a new nation founded on concepts of freedom and equality more advanced than any hitherto dreamed of, but a nation that would eventually exterminate and enslave people on a racial basis as they had never before been exterminated or enslaved in human history.

Thus, one group, seeking to escape the contradictions on one continent, began to create new contradictions for itself and for another set of people on another continent, contradictions which have remained to this day and have become more complex and challenging with the years.

It is only by reflecting on the political, social, and economic climate of Europe in the sixteenth and seventeenth centuries that we can understand why so many thousands were ready to embark on a journey to the new continent, a journey as daring and as historic as Mao's Long March more than three centuries later. Most of them had no idea what life would be like in the new land, what were the customs of the people already living there, how they would grow food or what kind of food the soil would grow. The voyage itself was long and dangerous. If you were lucky, you made it from Plymouth, England to Plymouth, New England, in ten weeks, as the Pilgrims did. But it might well take twice that long. A ship had to be stout enough and carry a crew skillful enough to cope with the tropical hurricanes which led to watery graves for many. Enough water and provisions had to be carried for both passengers and crew on the long voyage. The tools and implements needed to grow food, hunt game, and build dwellings had to be brought along. And finally, it was crucial to begin the journey with a sufficient number of dedicated and capable persons so that, after the inevitable attrition from illness and death en route, there would be enough people left to establish and maintain a minimum settlement. Because the last consideration was so important, it was customary for ships to set out together in a fleet.

Yet despite the known and unknown perils, many individuals contemplated the Long Voyage because a new spirit had begun to stir in the ordinary man and woman, the artisans and the clerks, the housewives and the vagabonds, of Western Europe. It was an era of what we today call "rising expectations." Instead of dreaming about happiness in heaven, as the masses of Europe had done for centuries under the tutelage of the Roman Catholic Church, they had begun to think about achieving it here on earth.

As the word spread of a new and bountiful land across the ocean that was not already owned by kings and queens and feudal lords, those imbued with these rising expectations began to wonder how they could get to it. Some joined groups sponsored by kings and queens anxious for the gold and silver and furs of the New World. Others acquired merchant sponsors who were on the lookout for groups reliable enough to back. Many were simply adventurers and scoundrels, running away from their obligations. Others saw themselves as agents or servants of the Crown. Some only planned to grab as much gold and silver as they could and then make a fast getaway back to their homeland to enjoy their new wealth. A very few thought of America as a place where they could settle, raise their families, and build a new society. But adventurer or settler, most of those who came to this country, then and since, have been humble and unhappy folk because, as Tocqueville° put it, "the happy and powerful do not go into exile."

Among those who came to settle and raise their families were the Pilgrims who made the Long Voyage on the *Mayflower* in the fall of 1619, and whom subsequent generations of Americans have rightly honored. This is not because the Pilgrims endured more hardships or had more physical courage than the others who had come or were still to come. It was because they had a body of ideas, the radical ideology of Puritanism, which they were trying to implement by creating a new society in a new land. Many other settlements were established—in Virginia by the British, in New York by the Dutch—but these were only company- or Crown-sponsored. Their

---

° Tocqueville's two-volume *Democracy in America* remains the most penetrating analysis of the contradictions of American society ever written.

members were bound together only by ethnic or family (biological) ties or material (self) interests.

The radical ideology of the Puritans was formulated in terms of religion because, as we have seen, the aspirations of the masses have been, until recently, expressed in relation to God. In feudal Europe the Roman Catholic Church had arrogated to itself the right to interpret the will of God to everyone, from peasant to monarch, and had become the continent's most powerful institution, both politically and economically. Therefore it was only natural that the first generalized revolt by the European masses against feudal rule had taken a religious form in the Reformation, which repudiated the right of the clergy to interpret God's word to the masses.

The Pilgrims were, to begin with, Puritans. The Puritans were English men and women of enterprising spirit who came from the lower middle class of printers and postmasters, clerks and apothecaries, tailors and saddlers. Usually able to read and write, and with some members who had attended the university, they were in revolt against the Church of England because it seemed to them as hierarchical and as restrictive of the independent thinking and activities of the ordinary man and woman as the Roman Catholic Church from which Henry the Eighth had split. Separating one by one from the Church of England, they organized their own congregations and elected their own pastors to help them practice in their daily lives the ideas they derived from their studies of the Bible. Not only did they insist that no priests or representatives of the Establishment had the right to interpret the Bible for them. They were convinced that if they worked hard and lived very strict moral lives in accordance with the Bible, God would see to it that they prospered. Through their joint worship, they constantly reinforced one another in the conviction of their human dignity and righteousness, as contrasted with the sinful and luxurious living of those who persecuted them for their efforts to build the Kingdom of God here on earth. For their subversive ideas, which the Puritans were very aggressive in propagandizing, they were harassed and persecuted. Many were put into prison, and not a few leaders were executed.

One congregation, which later became our Pilgrims, fled to Holland, where they found religious tolerance. But among people speaking another language and with their own prosperous and tidy culture, there was no opportunity for the Puritans to make converts or to implement their hopes for a "New Jerusalem." So after many disappointments, they arranged with a joint stock company for a ship and provisions, as well as additional recruits and a crew, so that they could establish a settlement in the New World and send back the furs and gold and the other resources of America which would justify the money invested in them.

The Puritans were men and women with strong convictions about the ideal relations between people. But they were soon to find that there is a big difference between ideals and reality. They had embarked on the *Mayflower* in order to establish a new and united community of true believers. But the new recruits to their contingent were "strangers" who did not share the ideas or the past experiences of the Puritans.° The "strangers" had no interest in ideology whatsoever; they had only undertaken the journey for the economic opportunities which the New World promised.

As the ship approached the shores of New England, it dawned on these economic opportunists that the King of England no longer had any authority over them and that they were in a position to extract a price for their skills and labor. So they suggested that, once ashore, they go off on their own.

Thus threatened, the Puritans drew up the Mayflower Compact, which pledged all the signers to "combine ourselves together into a civil body politick, for our better ordering and preservation." Through the Mayflower Compact, the Puritans gained assurance that the economic opportunists would stick with the ideologists, while the economic opportunists gained a voice in the decision-making. The Compact is a historic document because it represents the fruit of the first bargaining by working people for political rights in exchange for their contributions in labor. It is a forerunner of the present labor contract, and an example of the kind of concessions which those with official power can make to those without power when they are linked by material considerations. The Puritans were able to come up with

---

° For an engrossing account of the contradictions and developing relations between the two groups, see *Saints and Strangers* by George F. Willison (New York, 1945), which is based on the manuscripts of William Bradford, a member of the original congregation and a leader in its inner councils until his death in 1657. Bradford's manuscript, which he called his "scribled writings," was begun in 1630 and completed in 1650. It was first discovered, by accident, in 1855, two hundred years after his death.

this new concept of compact because over many years they had been practicing the idea of a body politic among those who shared their ideology. Now, driven by practical necessities, they were ready to enter into the same relations with those with whom they only shared material interest.

On shore, economic exigencies became more important each year. As the struggle to survive in the new land grew more desperate, as it became increasingly necessary to trade with the Indians in order to get the furs with which to pay their debts to the sponsoring Londoners, as many members of the original company succumbed to hardships and were replaced by new shiploads, those with fewer convictions and more self-interest in economic opportunity began to dominate the leadership. Thus, step by step, in order that the settlers might endure and prosper in the new country, economics began to take command over religion and principled politics.

The growing priority of economic self-interest was most critically manifested in the settlers' relations with the Indians. On board the *Mayflower* the Pilgrims created the advanced idea of the Mayflower Compact to meet the challenge from the "strangers" because the two groups had shared a common cultural background in Europe and a common material interest in establishing a settlement in the New World. But this unity was not present in their relations with the Indians. The desire of all those coming over on the *Mayflower* to escape their state of subjection in Europe and to prosper in the new land was very real. The Puritan search for a land where they could practice their convictions was also very real. However, they had come to a country where there were some very real people who were living in accordance with a completely different set of beliefs, with an entirely different culture. When the Indians met to decide which tribe would have hunting and fighting rights over different sections of North America, their decisions were based on the various cultures of the different tribes. There were some who hunted small game in the East, those who hunted large game in the West, those who fished in the myriad lakes and rivers, others who planted corn. On a continent where there was plenty of land and very few people, and where kings and church and aristocracy had not seized huge domains for themselves, no concept of private land ownership had been developed. Nor had the Indians created structured armies and clerical institutions to protect private ownership and aristocratic privileges.

When the Indians told the settlers that nobody owned the land, they meant that everybody owned it. But it was easy for the settlers to misunderstand the Indians, not only because it was in their economic interest to do so, but because their historical experience had been limited to Europe, where practically every piece of land was somebody's private property. Their bodies had left Europe but they had brought their European past with them in their heads.

From their earliest search for a "New Jerusalem," the Puritans had been imbued with a vision of a new society of the common man and woman. As they established themselves in New England, they began to translate their vision into reality. They were ready to work hard and to make sacrifices for their convictions. They were courageous and daring in their determination to hew out an existence in their new surroundings. But since the Indians had not gone through the historic experiences which they had endured in Europe, and since their own concept of the nature of man/woman was limited to European man/woman, it was easy for them not to include the Indians in their concept of humankind. Their ideas had been advanced enough to take them across the ocean, but not universal enough to include people from another cultural background. Up to then, the only patterns that had been established for relations between peoples of widely different cultures had been either that of the more advanced dominating over the less advanced and forcing them to assimilate the culture of the advanced; or those with a less advanced culture conquering those of a more advanced culture and then gradually assimilating the achievements of the more advanced culture—as in the case of the conquest of Rome by the barbarians from Northern Europe or of China by the Mongols.

The Indians had neither the will nor the power to conquer the Pilgrims. The Pilgrims made no attempt either to incorporate the values of the Indian culture into their own or to assimilate the Indians into their culture. Nor did they set an outer limit beyond which no Pilgrim could settle, so that on the other side of that limit the Indians could continue their own way of life or develop at their own pace and by their own efforts toward a technically more advanced civilization under their own leadership. Instead economic expediency was allowed to govern. The Pilgrims first took from the Indians such skills in hunting, fishing, and the growing of corn as served their interests, and then entered into an increasingly unequal trade relation with the Indians. They traded trinkets and alcohol and resold corn to the Indians in exchange for beaver and fox furs with which they bought supplies and paid the debt they owed their sponsors back in England. To meet ever increasing demands from Europe, they stepped up their profit in the exchange with the Indians. For less corn they demanded more fur and more land, leaving less land and less game for the Indians and therefore greater Indian need to buy corn and cloth from the settlers. Each year more and more settlers poured in from the tyranny of Europe, and more and more land was taken from the Indians. That which was not taken outright became worthless to the Indians because the wild animals on which they depended for food and skins fled before the tide of advancing settlements. As the antagonisms between desperate Indians and avaricious colonists became more bitter, some of the most avaricious even began selling guns to the Indians, guns which they knew would be used against other colonists. Thus, in the course of their determination to advance their own humanity, which was progressive in relation to their persecution in England, the settlers became increasingly backward in relation to another section of humanity and even among themselves. The same domination and restrictions from which they had fled in Europe, they imposed on the Indians.

Today many Americans think that the rapid development of this country is the result of the Pilgrims having been a "chosen people," a people blessed by Providence because they were brave enough to turn their backs on Europe, leaving behind its persecution and tyranny, risking the dangers of the ocean voyage to come to the new continent where there were such unlimited opportunities. Such an explanation introduces an element of predestination and inevitability into the decisions made by the Pilgrims. More important, it evades the contradiction within which the settlers were trapped in their relations with the Indians because their concept of man/woman was, not surprisingly, limited by their historical experiences. We must rid ourselves once and for all of this concept of "chosen people," not to berate the Pilgrims for their historical limitations but in order not to get trapped ourselves in the limitations of this concept. Once you begin to use divine providence or a supernatural power to justify self-interest, you impose limits on your own human capacity and responsibility to reflect on and develop an enlarged concept of humanity in relation to those different from yourself and thus in relation to your own humanity.

How much the American mind has crippled itself by using divine Providence to sanction the country's rapid economic development can be seen by the assertion of Benjamin Franklin a century later regarding the Indians. "If it be the design of Providence," Franklin said, "to extirpate these savages in order to make room for the cultivators of the earth, it seems not improbable that rum may be the appointed means. It has already annihilated all the tribes who formerly inhabited the seacoasts." This from the man who served with Thomas Jefferson on the committee to draft the Declaration of Independence!

Thus the philosophical basis was laid to bring in and enslave a whole people from another continent to achieve the rapid agricultural development which is a prerequisite to rapid industrial development. This philosophy led, in the Mexican War, to the seizure of millions of acres of land from "greasers" and the destruction of the culture of the indigenous people of the Southwest; in the Spanish-American War, to the subjugation of the Cubans and the Filipinos; and, finally, in our day, to the genocidal war against "gooks" in Indochina. All in the name of "Manifest Destiny."

In 1763 the war between the British and the French for the domination of the American continent ended in victory for the British. The war is known as the French and Indian War, since the Indians fought with the French on the basis that the latter, being less interested in settling, constituted less of a threat to their way of life than the British. The British came out of the war with a powerful empire, but also with a huge post-war debt and the increased costs of policing their empire. To pay these costs, the British Parliament decided to impose heavy taxes on the colonies, since, after all, it could be claimed that the war had been fought in their interests as much as in the interests of those remaining at home.

In resisting the British effort to tax them, the colonists were undoubtedly motivated by economic self-interest. But as the struggle over the tax issue intensified, these heirs to the Puritan tradition of ideological controversy and propaganda began to develop political ideas of a scope previously unheard of. At first, the argument took the form chiefly of legal reasons why the British Parliament had no right to tax the colonists who were not represented in Parliament. But before very long the intellectual leaders of the rebellion, reflecting on the historical experience of the colonies over the previous hundred and fifty years, began to realize how far they had advanced beyond those who were still trying to govern them, in their concepts and realization of the nature and potential of man/woman.°

When most Americans think of the American Revolution, what comes to mind is the 1770 Boston Massacre in which Crispus Attucks lost his life, the dumping of tea in Boston Harbor, the ride of Paul Revere, or the shot fired at Lexington and Concord and heard round the world. They see the American Revolution as a series of spontaneous and rebellious actions, which in turn led to other militant actions and finally to a war for freedom from colonialism. Such a scenario of the American Revolution is very similar to that which most radicals have of the revolutions in Russia, China, Cuba, Africa, Vietnam.

Actually, the protracted process of creating a vigorous, independent, self-confident, self-reliant people capable of making decisions for themselves had been taking place for over a hundred and fifty years, beginning with the Mayflower Compact and continuing through township meetings and the creation of representative institutions. It was to take more than ten years of ideological struggle and propaganda, from the passage of the Sugar Act by the British Parliament in 1764 to the outbreak of hostilities at Lexington and Concord in 1775, before a political base had been laid in the hearts and minds of the American people deep enough to wage military struggle against the most powerful military force of their day.

Writing letters, publishing pamphlets, holding meetings, men and women from every strata of the population, in the North and South Atlantic colonies, began a vigorous ideological struggle around their right and duty to resist taxation by the British and what this meant in terms of their own past, their present and future relations with the motherland, and their own future in America. Young radical Northern intellectuals like Sam Adams and Mercy Otis Warren, and John Adams and Abigail, his wife; Southern aristocratic intellectuals

---

° *A Dissertation on Feudal and Canon Law,* written by the youthful John Adams in 1765, reveals the philosophical and historical scope of these reflections.

like Thomas Jefferson; Pennsylvania conservatives like James Wilson; or farmers like John Dickinson; the British-born Tom Paine; all struggled for ten years to convince each other and to win the people to their views. Not until the ideological struggles to discover the right road for the Chinese revolution inside the Chinese Communist Party during the Yenan years, would democracy again be practiced on such a broad scale.

The intellectual leaders of the American Revolution did not only speak and write. Between 1763 and 1775 they organized Committees of Correspondence in every colony, and in nearly every town, county, and city, to maintain contact with one another and to organize a common resistance. Then, as the framework of the colonial administration began to disintegrate in the sharpening conflict between the American colonists and Great Britain, these Committees of Correspondence were turned into Committees of Inspection and Committees of Safety, which exercised executive power in their jurisdictions, becoming, in effect, what we would today call a "dual power structure."

As with any other people who have shared the same general historical experience, there were many differences or tendencies within the unified conviction that they should not pay the tax to the British. These reflected actual differences within the population. Some colonists were content with the prevailing relations with England ("don't rock the boat"). Often they were motivated by their desire for profits in trade with England and the incipient Triangular Trade—Africa (slaves), West Indies (sugar), New England (rum)—with which it was linked. Many were afraid of losing their positions as administrators for the Colonial Office. Some had accumulated warehouses of tea, and relished the idea of British tea being tossed overboard so that they could sell their own stock. Many were afraid of being isolated from Europe, which was in their eyes the only civilized continent in the world, and the home of relatives and friends.

As the ideological struggle became more heated, those who had intended only to reform the relations between empire and colony became aware that debate and protest and reform had already unleashed the hopes of the masses to the degree that there was no longer any room for compromise between the expanded concept which the people now had of themselves and the concept of them as subjects which the British government held.

As the confrontation drew near, many of those who had put forward ideas to rid the colony of the British began to retreat. Like liberals, they wanted to be on both sides. Some vacillated for the entire period of the struggle. Some even moved as far inland as possible to evade the issue. Some fled to Canada and are now part of that country's history.

Essentially the American colonists were able to make and win the revolution for independence against Britain because they had experienced a degree of freedom from feudalism that no other people had known. They had experienced both the opportunity and the necessity not only to struggle for survival, but to make decisions for themselves. They had learned that freedom is not just an abstract concept but a way of life involving both opportunity and responsibilities. They began to appreciate that on this continent they had been creating in reality what such European philosophers as Locke and Hume and Rousseau had only been discussing from an ideal viewpoint. They began to see themselves as creating a new way of life, a new way to achieve happiness, which made them the vanguard of man/womankind, the social force of a new humanity.

It was within this milieu of intense theoretical and practical activity that Thomas Jefferson, then only thirty-three years old, was able to write the Declaration of Independence in 1776, evoking a new vision of humanity. To this day people all over the world are still moved to struggle by the words:

> We hold these truths to be self-evident, that all men are created equal, that they are endowed by their Creator with certain unalienable Rights, that among these are Life, Liberty and the pursuit of Happiness.—That to secure these rights, Governments are instituted among Men, deriving their just powers from the consent of the governed,—That whenever any Form of Government becomes destructive of these ends, it is the Right of the People to alter or to abolish it, and to institute new Government, laying its foundation on such principles and organizing its powers in such form, as to them shall seem most likely to effect their Safety and Happiness.

A few years later, inspired by this Declaration, the French Revolution would explode in Europe and a similar movement in Santo Domingo.

Many years later, at the beginning of the nineteenth century, John Adams would write: "The revolution was effected before the war commenced. The revolution was in the minds and hearts of the people." As a result of the revolutionary propaganda, especially of the Adamses, the Paines, and the Jeffersons, the colonists had discovered that there was a noble purpose in their struggle against the British Crown, namely, to establish the dignity of the common person. Armed with this new political concept of their human identity, the colonists were able to defeat the more experienced British forces. The American forces won the war for independence with small contingents of local forces, mostly fighting on their own terrain and with the support of the people. What they lacked in technology and military experience, they made up for in ingenuity and energy, and most of all by the conviction that their cause was just.

When the war ended in 1783, the contradictions and differences which had been submerged in the struggle against the common enemy came to the surface. In his original draft of the Declaration of Independence, Jefferson had accused the King of England of many crimes. These included bringing "on the inhabitants of our frontiers the merciless Indian savages, whose known rule of warfare is an undistinguished destruction of all ages, sexes and conditions of existence" *and* the waging of "cruel war against human nature itself, violating its most sacred rights of life and liberty in the persons of a distant people who never offended him, captivating and carrying them into slavery in another hemisphere, or to incur miserable death in their transportation thither."

In the final draft of the Declaration of Independence, which was adopted by the Congress on July 4, 1776, after heated debate and threats of withdrawal by the slave-trading and slaveowner representatives, the passage concerning the Indians remained but that on the slaves was completely deleted. Jefferson agonized over the deletion, but, in the interests of unity, he capitulated.

The fifty-five delegates who came together in 1787 to frame a Constitution for the new nation were almost all men of distinction—patriots, scholars, merchants, and landowners. The most distinguished among them—whether from the North like John Adams, Benjamin Franklin, and Alexander Hamilton, or from the South, like

George Washington, Thomas Jefferson, and James Madison—had all expressed their abhorrence of the institution of slavery in the strongest terms. But none of them believed in the equality of blacks and none of them was ready for a principled political struggle over the question of slavery.

The immediate question which had brought the delegates together was the urgent need to create a central government strong enough to defend the nation against foreign encroachments, to negotiate trade treaties with foreign powers, to keep the thirteen states from clashing with one another, and to establish the sound currency necessary for trade and economic development. But the delegates also represented different states, based on different and potentially conflicting social and economic relations, and fearful of domination by a government in which other interests were represented.

In order to increase their representation in the central government, the slaveowning states demanded that slaves be counted in the census as whole numbers, while the Northern states, where slavery was virtually non-existent, did not want slaves counted at all. They compromised on the provision to count the slave as three-fifths of a man. Neither Northern nor Southern delegates were talking about slaves voting. They were only concerned with the interests of their respective states.

Thus the United States became the only nation in history whose best and brightest minds first led a revolution from colonialism in the name of life, liberty, and the pursuit of happiness for all men, and then built a contradiction into their society by explicitly denying human dignity to a quarter of the population they aspired to govern.

The Constitutional Convention had exposed and polarized real contradictions in the country. But in the interests of unity, the Founding Fathers covered up the contradictions. They evaded their political responsibility to carry out ideological struggle and create a principled political leadership for the country. They thereby laid the groundwork for the Civil War.

At the time it appeared that the cover-up compromise would work. Many blacks had fought in the War of Independence (some on the British side). There was also a general sentiment, particularly in the Northern and border states, that slavery would gradually disappear. In fact, during and after the revolution, many slaves had actually become free men and women—some by simply running away, others through legislative action, court decision, or individual manumission in the Northern states.

However, almost before the ink was dry on the compromise document, free blacks began to sharpen the contradictions by agitating for the freedom of those still enslaved. In the afterglow of victory in a just cause, many whites sympathized and supported the black freedom movement. Then, in 1793, only six years after the Constitution was adopted, Eli Whitney invented the cotton gin, which made it possible to utilize many more slaves in the production of cotton than had hitherto been required on the tobacco plantations. Cotton was a most precious commodity for the textile mills which would provide jobs for workers and profits for capitalists in New England. Cotton was also shipped to England, assuring a more favorable trade balance for the infant nation, as well as the capital it needed for new factories. So once again the economic thrust took over, white support for the black freedom movement subsided, and the country was flooded by racist propaganda, using the Bible, pseudo-science, greed, and fear to justify the enslavement of blacks.

But slaves continued to rebel and to run away. Freed blacks, like David Walker in Boston, issued appeals to their brothers and sisters to rise up and throw off the yoke of slavery. Periodically, spectacular rebellions—among them those of Denmark Vesey in 1820 and Nat Turner in 1831—struck terror into the hearts of the slavemasters and aroused hope and anger in the blacks.

In the 1830s a number of radical intellectuals in the North began the Abolitionist Movement, a comprehensive attack upon slavery and all the political, economic, and social institutions which had made it possible and continued to enforce it. The Abolitionists, men and women like William Lloyd Garrison, Wendell Phillips, Theodore Parker, Angelina and Sarah Grimké, John Brown, were part of a cultural renaissance which developed in the coastal cities of New England, and which found expression not only in the anti-slavery movement, but in the creative writings of men like Emerson, Thoreau, and Melville. These New England intellectuals were very different from the Southern intellectuals of an earlier period like Thomas Jefferson, whose opportunities to reflect and create new ideas had been made possible by slave labor and who worried about, but were still able to live with, the contradiction between their lofty ideas and the ownership of slaves.

In the first place, these men and women were very conscious of their continuity with the distinctively American intellectual tradition which had begun with the Puritans and assumed such an advanced political form in the ideological struggles, propaganda, and organization leading to the American Revolution. Without such a historical consciousness of a continuing tradition, real creativity is impossible. But they were also very conscious of going beyond this tradition. Their horizons had been immeasurably broadened by the whaling industry and the China trade, which took young people like Herman Melville, as well as ordinary seamen and merchants, to the far corners of the earth. Enriching their historical tradition with these new experiences, they had developed an enlarged concept of humanity, which included, and even idealized, South Sea islanders, Indians, and African blacks, because they had not yet been caught up in the nexus of commercialism. Their concept of equality was not individualistic but universalistic. As Melville put it, in *Moby Dick,* a "just Spirit of Equality" had spread "one royal mantle of humanity over all my kind."

In response to the black rebellions and black agitation and propaganda, these New England intellectuals now began a ferocious attack on the culture of the marketplace, which justified the degradation of some human beings in order to further the economic well-being of others. Americans, they said, had thrown off the yoke of theocracy, aristocracy, and monarchy, only to set in its place the yoke of money. The Constitution, they said, was a bastard document, a compromise between the high ideals of the Declaration of Independence and the selfish economic interests of slave traders and slave owners. They challenged other Americans to base their decisions on putting human beings first rather than the Almighty Dollar. They were ready to put their lives on the line, to hide runaway slaves, to wrest them from sheriffs trying to return them to the South, to defend their meetings against attack, and, even as in the case of John Brown, to organize a massacre of white settlers in the Kansas-Nebraska armed conflict, and, five years later, an insurrection at Harper's Ferry.

There were many differences among the Abolitionists over strategy and tactics. They debated and split over whether it might be best just to let the South go, rather than allow its poison to spread into the rest of the nation; or whether there was any point in using the electoral process. But none of them had any use for the proposal to ship the slaves back to Africa in order to rid the country of the "Negro question," the new compromise (favored by Lincoln) which was gaining popularity and leading to the formation of Colonization Societies. Instead they were absolutely convinced that Americans, for the sake of their own humanity and development, must struggle to resolve this contradiction which they had created for themselves. They were very much aware of the fact that blacks had lived in this country for as long as any whites—and longer than most.

The Abolitionists concentrated on the slavery question, but they were also active and vocal on other issues: women's rights, peace, debtors' reform, abolition of capital punishment, prison reform. No issue which involved oppressed humanity was alien to them. However, they had very little idea of the power that would be necessary to realize their advanced ideas or of the systematic mass struggles which blacks would have to carry on if they were going to be able not only to free but to develop themselves to become a powerful part of a developing nation. Hence their propaganda and agitation tended to appear abstract and idealistic, despite the militancy of their actions. Objectively, they were too remote geographically and socially from the blacks who were their chief social force. They therefore were unable to develop what we now call the "from the masses, to the masses" relationship out of which could have developed the revolutionary politics and programs for land reform around which the black masses might have organized themselves. There were black Abolitionists who had come out of the masses, men and women like Frederick Douglass, Sojourner Truth, Harriet Tubman, Samuel Ward, Henry Highland Garnet, Charles Remond. But these were individuals, distinguished for their courage, their eloquence, their organizational ability, rather than a political body developing its ideas and programs through a collective and continuing process of theory and practice.

It is not just hindsight which leads us to raise the land issue. The struggle over who would settle the land from which the Indians were being driven had been a burning issue ever since the Louisiana Purchase and the first decade of the nineteenth century. At first the slaveowning interests of the South fought to have new states admitted as slave states in order to increase their power in Congress. But as the soil in the slave states was threatened with exhaustion by the wasteful methods of cultivating cotton, they began to regard their own westward expansion as a matter of economic life and death. On the other hand, the growing industrial capitalist class in the Northeast saw the West chiefly as the breadbasket indispensable to the feeding of workers in the cities, while many of these same workers were insisting that the West remain free soil so that they could eventually pull up stakes and go homesteading and farming. For both the Northern worker and industrialist, economic ties to the West were becoming more important than their economic ties to the South.

Compromise after compromise had been attempted by Congress and the politicians on the continuing conflict between North and South over western lands. The first was the Missouri Compromise of 1820, which provided for Maine to be admitted as a free state, Missouri as a slave state, with slavery prohibited elsewhere in the Louisiana Purchase north of 36°30'. That compromise failed, and Congress tried the Compromise of 1850 and the Kansas-Nebraska Act of 1854. Both of these provided for "squatter sovereignty," i.e., Congress evaded the responsibility for deciding whether new states should be free or slave, and left the decision to whomever got there first. The 1850 and 1854 Compromises were open invitations to armed struggles between the contending forces. These struggles led directly to the Civil War.

Thus the issue which led the majority of the American people into the Civil War was not the abolition of slavery as a fundamental contradiction in the American concept of man/woman, which could have been resolved only by mass struggles to realize an enlarged concept of humanity. Rather it was the question of how the western lands would be used for production, i.e., whose economic interests, those of the cotton-growing South or the industrial Northeast, would prevail.

In failing to give principled political leadership at the Constitutional Convention, the Founding Fathers had given the go-ahead signal for politics to become the handmaiden of economics. Every individual and every interest group was given official sanction for the pursuit of individual or sectional advancement through economic development under the benevolent auspices of a fatherly government. This meant, for many city workers, settlement and expansion toward the West, exterminating and driving the Indians before them, while for new immigrants, fleeing the poverty and tyranny of Europe, it meant jobs in the mushrooming factories. Although many people believe that the immigrants rushed from their ships to the frontier, the historical fact is that most of them stayed in or near their friends in the Eastern cities. Usually those who had lived in the new nation for some time moved West, while the new immigrants replaced them in industry, becoming the first labor force rooted to the mines, the mills, the tanneries, and the foundries.

In this ideology economic development was both goal and method, end and means. Every political decision made by government and people was governed by how much it would further or retard the rapid economic development of the country.

This left to the Abolitionists, and their few supporters in the North, and the blacks in the South, the social and political responsibility for putting principled politics in command of economics. The Abolitionists and the blacks were governed by social thought because they believed that what was good for the most oppressed was good for the country as a whole. But they were geographically separated from each other and neither had reached the stage of consciously struggling for power in order to put their politics in command of the entire country. On the other hand, Southern whites, Northern industrialists, the old workers leaving the city to become farmers, and the new immigrants swarming off the ships to become workers, were all expressing bourgeois values. That is, they believed that what was good for their own special, material interests was best for the country.

Ironically, and not surprisingly, forces with conflicting interests—Northern industrialists, workers become farmers, Abolitionists and blacks—would all line up on the same side in the Civil War. It was an unholy alliance, and could not last.

In order to lend a semblance of legitimacy to their cause, the Southerners used the legal or Constitutional issue of States' Rights. The colonists had originally fought a war for independence on the principled basis of human rights, and on this basis, it was conceivable that, until the adoption of the Constitution, any individual could have appealed to a national government over and above the states.

But when the slaveowners won States' Rights at the 1787 Convention, they effectively blocked off any legal or constitutional way for dissidents in the South to transcend the control of the Southern states.

Lincoln did not try to discover or propagate a deeper philosophical basis or human vision for carrying out the struggle against the slaveholding states. Instead he reacted to the secessionist challenge within the framework which they had created, making "Save the Union" the only objective of the Northern cause. In the bloodiest internal struggle that any nation has ever undergone, the question of unity rather than principled politics was the central issue. For whom, by whom the nation was to be saved was obviously a matter of conflicting interpretations on the part of the different forces on the Northern side. Yet Lincoln's goal, like that of the Founding Fathers, was unity at whatever cost. He made no effort to appeal to an enlarged sense of human identity among those on both sides, to urge them to recognize the role which whites had played in bringing blacks to this country by force and hence their responsibility for developing a new society in which everyone could play an equal role. Not until it looked as if the North might lose the military struggle did he even issue the Emancipation Proclamation in 1863, which freed only the slaves in Southern territory. The result of this narrow and opportunistic approach to a long and bitter struggle was that the more hardships the Northern workers endured in the war, the more they tended to blame the blacks. This was especially true of the Irish immigrants who had poured into the country in the decade preceding the 1849 Irish famine. In the New York Draft Riots of 1863 they were foremost among those who burned and raped blacks with more ferocity than any Southern lynch mob.

Lincoln was assassinated in April 1865, just as the war had come to an end. There was no one around like George Washington, who had commanded the respect of the entire country after the War of Independence because he had been a masterful and successful general, determined to rid the country of foreign domination. The contradictions among the victors had advanced beyond the point where they could be covered up by an individual figure symbolizing unity. Vice-President Andrew Johnson, who took over the Presidency, tried to carry out Lincoln's program for binding up the wounds of the nation, i.e., reconciling the interests of the victors with those of the defeated. But what was needed after such a costly conflict was not reconciliation but a revolutionary policy, backed by force, which would have enabled the blacks to take over the land of their defeated masters, and thus set the nation on a new road. So Johnson ended up trapped by the various factions in the administration and in Congress, each of which had different views on how to end the chaos.

Some wanted to punish the Southern planters by denying them the vote and taking over their property; others wanted to treat them like prodigal sons. Meanwhile, Confederate veterans were roving the country in the South and West, raiding, looting, killing blacks and Indians. The newly emancipated blacks in the South were like stateless people without land to till, homes to live in, or food to eat. But all the capitalists were interested in was expanding production; all the workers wanted were jobs and land; and all the newly arrived immigrants wanted were jobs.

In this brief period of chaos, with the South under military control by federal troops, black people in the South for the first time in this country came to exercise some aspect of political decision-making. In the process, several were elected to Congress. But far more important was their contribution to education. The freed blacks owned nothing, had nothing. The only chance they could see for developing themselves was through education. And if they were to get some education, it would have to take a social form because only rich whites could afford private schools. So they established public schools which not only enhanced their own opportunities but those of the many poor whites who could not afford private schools. A few of them were able to establish plantations, and fewer still opened up small stores. They forced the opening up of public places, like restaurants and hotels, and rode in the same cars on trains with whites. For a brief period the socially conscious black forces, aware of their destitute existence, put forward such humanitarian ideas that even poor whites who had small landholdings as well as those who had formerly acted as slavedrivers for the master plantation owners, were in sympathy with their cause.

At this point the blacks were still the largest ethnic group within the working class. Although westward expansion was still going on, the bulk of production of agricultural goods and industrial commodities was still east of the Mississippi River, in the Northeast and Southeast.

But the efforts of the blacks to develop new social institutions depended at this stage upon military support from a federal government which was under pressure from profit-hungry industrialists, land-hungry workers, and job-hungry immigrants, to get back to business as usual, i.e., to the pursuit of private happiness through economic expansion. The result was that in 1877, still another compromise was reached between the North and South. In exchange for "home rule" (i.e., States' Rights under another name) or the withdrawal of federal troops, the South agreed to support Rutherford Hayes, the Northern businessman's candidate, for President in a disputed election. Thus once again the best and brightest minds of this country capitulated to blackmail. After fighting a bloody civil war allegedly to free the slaves, then declaring them legally free, the North allowed them to be put back into a state of servitude equal to or worse than that of slavery. In exchange for the opportunity to develop the West and North as they saw fit, the Northern industrialists gave back to the Southern slaveholders the right to exploit the blacks as they saw fit. Once again, the nation had put economic development, economic expansion and the material self-interests of the individual ahead of all human considerations. Economics was put in command over politics, degrading politics to a tool of economics—to "dirty politics." Once again, it was confirmed to those already in the country and to the millions of immigrants still to come, that the pursuit of economic development and economic expansion was the ideology of this nation whatever the cost in terms of human development.

Following the 1877 Compromise a flurry of restrictive laws, Jim Crow laws, were passed in Southern towns, counties, and states, all designed to keep blacks in their place—their place being what any white person, even a small white child, said was their place. Thus the United States became two nations, a nation with two sets of laws, one for blacks and one for whites, with more laws than all the rest of the world combined. State laws duplicate and conflict with national ones, local laws conflict with and duplicate state and national laws. Passing a law has become the passing-the-buck method for attacking all social problems, because the nation, beginning with the Constitutional Convention, had put behind it any concept of the transformation of people through ideological and political struggle over principles and practice. Thus "that's the law" has become the excuse to evade contradictions, just as economics has become the excuse to evade social and political issues. Courts, lawyers, prisons, guards, and probation officers proliferate to service the proliferating prisoners produced by the proliferating laws.

For a brief period in the 1880s and 1890s, black and white farmers in the South attempted to come together in what has been called the Populist Movement. But the Populist Movement was no less a self-interest movement just because it united two self-interested groups. Poor blacks and poor whites, mainly farmers, combined their forces to fight for their economic interest in credit, cheap money and lower shipping rates against Northeastern railroad and banking interests. The movement developed primarily in the border states and did not include the white workers in the North nor the new immigrants who were taking over so many of the jobs in the expanding heavy industry. In the North these white workers were already beating up blacks who attempted to get jobs in the mills and mines. Motivated only by self-interest, they regarded their jobs as private property to be protected against other workers from other ethnic groups, much as the farmer regards his/her piece of land.

Although the Populist Movement had as one of its objectives to bring poor whites and poor blacks together, the narrow concept of economic self-interest on which it was based made it easy for the landowners and aristocrats of the South to combine with the Northern industrialists to whip up racist prejudice and split the movement. Recognizing the economic threat in any united action by blacks and whites, the landowners and industrialists stirred up white fears that if the blacks became equal economically to the whites, blacks would easily take away white women from white men and mongrelize their race. Inflaming the poor whites against the blacks on the basis of their color was not difficult in a country where the extermination of Indians and the enslavement of blacks had been for so long justified on the basis of their racial inferiority.

The effect of this racist propaganda was to increase lynching to a level which it had never reached even under slavery. With blacks thus terrorized and kept forcibly on the cotton plantations as sharecroppers, the country was free to drive forward towards economic expansion. Henceforth, all but a small minority would be blind to any human or social responsibilities which might interfere with economic self-interest. From top to bottom, depoliticization would become the rule, reversing the process towards politicization which had begun with the Puritans and had reached such a high level in the period preceding the American Revolution.

Henceforth the separation between the best and brightest minds and the mass social forces, which had not existed in the American Revolution but which had prevented the Abolitionist Movement from developing into a revolutionary movement, would become polarized into a division crippling to both sides. In the pursuit of their own careers, American intellectuals would put their talents at the service of the Establishment, while those who refused to do so would be condemned to lives of isolation and frustration. At the other pole the masses would become even more exclusively preoccupied with material interests, using the excuse of "dirty politics," i.e., politics under the command of economics, to justify their own evasion of social and political responsibility. Politics would become increasingly degraded to the struggle to get "a piece of the action" or a piece of the power for your own individual, ethnic or sectional interest—and eventually to the attempt to get total control of a swelling state apparatus for yourself and your machine of dehumanized supporters. Only occasionally, as in the first decade of the twentieth century, and again in the 1930s and the 1960s, would the opportunity arise to bridge the gap between the intellectuals and the masses. But each time, because there had not been the necessary philosophic, ideological and political preparation, the opportunity would be wasted.

At the turn of the century, Theodore Roosevelt took this depoliticization of the American people and their obsession with the pursuit of economic interests to the international level. Realizing that the United States was beginning to approach the economic strength of Britain, and that the two were now the world's most powerful nations, he became convinced that it was America's "Manifest Destiny" to rule the world. With Theodore Roosevelt, the government took upon itself the role of encouraging rapid economic development of the productive forces at home and the imperialist role of this country abroad. Production for the sake of more production and for expanding mass consumption at home, and

economic and military expansion for the sake of American production and world power abroad, were consciously accepted as the
responsibility of the central government.

The effect of this new concept of the role of government has been
the accelerating growth over the last seventy years of big government and executive power completely alien to the concept of feeble
central government, inhibited by regional loyalties, provided for in
the Constitution. Constantly intervening at home, to meet the
recurring economic crises of recession and inflation, and abroad, to
meet the competition of rival powers and crush the socialist and
nationalist aspirations of other peoples, the United States is now
ruled by a Warfare-Welfare State, a state which aims both to satisfy
the expanding economic appetites of an increasingly self-interested
population and to achieve domination over other powers and other
peoples. Instead of the powerless central government conceived by
the Founding Fathers, we are now confronted with a powerful
monster dedicated only to the increase of its own power.

Once again, the people of this country are faced with the kind of
arbitrary power which John and Abigail Adams, Thomas Jefferson,
and Tom Paine faced in the 1760s, and which they could effectively
resist only after the most sober historical reflection on their previous
development, passionate ideological struggle, and revolutionary
propaganda and organization, in the course of which they arrived at
a new vision of human identity for "all men." In *our* hindsight we
have the advantage of almost twice as many, much more concentrated years of rapid economic development and social crisis. We can
draw not only on our own historical experiences but those of the
whole world. And, most important, the oppressed peoples in this
country and the world whose attitudes and aspirations could only
have been inferred two hundred years ago, have over the intervening
period, and particularly since World War II, stood up and made
known to everybody the infinite variety of their grievances, their
aspirations, and their contradictions.

8
A UNIQUE STAGE IN HUMAN DEVELOPMENT

What time is it on the clock of the world? Is it just 8:30 p.m. on the evening of July 4, 1973? What is time? Is it just the measurement of the distance traveled by the hands of a gigantic clock? How do we estimate time in terms of the evolution and development of humanity?

In the preceding chapters, we have tried to restore for our readers a sense of time by dealing with the dialectical development of man/womankind through the evolutionary and revolutionary process. We have also tried to impart a new appreciation of the critical role which revolutions play in the evolutionary process of humanity.

We have said that when we come to the United States, we are at a different time, a different stage in the development of man/woman, a time and a stage at which human beings have never been before. Hence we are confronted with different choices, different decisions, different directions, different opportunities, from those presented to man/womankind in the past.

We are confronted with a unique development in the phenomenon of human development.

Whenever you are dealing with living organisms, and especially with human beings, the most important thing is to see them in terms of their *development*, which can only be evaluated over a period of time. People develop slowly, as they struggle to resolve internal contradictions, making choices, seeking to avoid misery and achieve happiness.

It isn't easy these days to think about people in terms of development through struggle. We are all profoundly influenced by the mass media. Television news reporters, trying to catch the attention of the public for their advertisers, all live in their minds from moment to moment and try to make us live the same way. They think in the way that philosophers call "empirical." Whereas, with human beings and societies, nothing is more important than to think *dialectically*.

We are all changing all the time, and our development never takes place in a straight line. Every one of us advances in a certain direction; then we find ourselves confronted with unanticipated contradictions or obstacles. Some of us charge ahead anyway—trying to bulldoze away the obstacles. Others stop to reflect. Some of us drift backwards. But whether we drift backwards, charge ahead, or stop to reflect, eventually we must confront reality again in its new form. Then we have the opportunity to make another choice as to which way to go, and to begin anew the process of struggle which is the only way that anything or anyone advances.

The most important fact in today's world is change. Some changes take place *within* us and some *to* each of us. Some changes we *want* in ourselves or in others or in the world and are (sometimes) ready to struggle to achieve; some changes we *resist* in ourselves or in others or in the world, and are (usually) more ready to struggle against. America and Americans have always been characterized by extreme mobility and by tremendous growth, i.e., by physical and quantitative change. But today's changes go beyond the quantitative or physical.

Various images have been used by various writers to try to bring home to us what has been called the "change revolution" or the revolutionary speed-up in the rate of change itself which characterizes modern scientific and technological developments. For example, in the best-selling *Future Shock* (New York: Knopf, 1970) (whose conclusions reinforcing a throwaway mentality towards people and things we repudiate) Alvin Toffler suggests that we divide the last fifty thousand years of *Homo sapiens* into lifetime units of approximately sixty-two years each. On that basis, there have been approximately eight hundred lifetimes since human beings first began to make and use tools and to create in terms of artistic sensibilities.

Most of the material goods and technical equipment we are using today have been developed only within the last or the eight hundredth lifetime of *Homo sapiens*.

Or to take another image, this time from *Teaching as a Subversive Activity*, by Neil Postman and Charles Weingartner (New York: Delacorte Press, 1969). These authors suggest that we imagine a clock face with sixty minutes on it. Let the clock face of sixty minutes represent three thousand years, the period that human beings have had access to writing systems. On that basis, each minute would represent fifty years. Using this unit of measurement, the printing press came into use only nine minutes ago; television into general use only in the last twenty seconds; the computer only in the last five seconds; and communications satellites only in the last couple of seconds.

On this same clock face, we can say that:

1. only in the last four or five minutes, beginning with the American and French Revolutions, have we witnessed *revolutionary struggles*;

2. only about two minutes ago, with Karl Marx and Friedrich Engels in nineteenth-century Europe, did we begin to develop *scientific revolutionary thinking*, i.e., a scientific method for combining the creativity of the revolutionary intellectual with the creativity of the revolutionary masses;

3. only about thirty seconds ago, at the end of World War II, did we enter the *epoch of global revolution*, with the simultaneous struggles by millions of people on all continents to shape and to better their own lives;

4. only about fifteen seconds ago, with the Montgomery Bus Boycott, triggered by a black working woman, Rosa Parks, and led by Martin Luther King, Jr., did *nationwide revolutionary struggles*, shaking up all sectors of the population, begin in the U.S.A.

All of us now living within this eight hundredth lifetime of *Homo sapiens*, and particularly those of us living in the United States, now have the responsibility and opportunity to decide whether the hands on the clock of social progress are going to stop or continue.

Whether there will be additional lifetimes depends on *all* the world revolutionary struggles which are now going on in China, in Vietnam, in Africa, in Latin America, and in the United States. All the struggles in the world today affect Americans more immediately and directly than they ever have in the past. They have shaken up this country, posed new fundamental issues to this country, given new hope to some and appeared as a terrible threat to others.

However, the struggles most important to us are those taking place in *this* country, because they are the only ones we can really shape. They are the only ones whose direction can be in *our* hands. Therefore it is necessary that we examine them carefully, to understand what must be the essential thrust of a new American revolution.

In other words, we must not begin by imposing a theory upon the struggles developing in this country over the last decade and a half. Rather, we must derive our theoretical understanding from our examination of reality.

A great many people have said—although all do not mean the same thing by it—that in the United States technological man/woman has outstripped ethical man/woman. If we trace scientifically the development of man/woman in the United States, we must conclude that our political development has not kept up with our economic or technological development. Hence the increasingly agonizing contradiction between our advanced technology and our backward politics, between our material abundance and our spiritual emptiness.

Historically this contradiction has been developing throughout the two centuries of this country's existence. From the very beginning, this nation, and every citizen within it, has been confronted with never-ending choices between economic interests and social justice. Periodically this contradiction has been written into law and deepened by a particular decision, as when the Founding Fathers decided to delete from the original draft of the Declaration of Independence the section condemning slavery and the slave trade.

There is no question that the founding of this country involved a revolutionary advance in the concept of human dignity. The concepts projected in the Declaration of Independence and in the Constitution involved a profound rejection of ideas, which had theretofore prevailed, as to the appropriate relations of the common man and woman to government, to propertied persons, to the church, to the police, and to the courts, and asserted the rights of the common man and woman to Life, Liberty, and the Pursuit of Happiness. But precisely because the American Revolution aspired to so much, it exposed its own contradictions, in its actions and in its documents. How could it reconcile the conviction which it had stated so eloquently, ". . . that all men are created equal, that they are endowed by their Creator with certain unalienable Rights" with the fact that the revolution did not free the blacks from slavery? Only by actually writing into the Constitution itself that the slave was only three-fifths of a man!

Then came the Civil War, which many people, including some whites and most blacks, interpreted as a war to end slavery. But the majority of Northerners who actually fought the war were fighting for their economic interests: for free land in the West, or to accelerate economic and industrial development in the Northeast. Once the war was over, it was only a matter of time before the great majority of whites were ready to accept the 1877 Compromise, which permitted the South to maintain blacks in a state of economic and legal servitude even more restrictive than chattel slavery. That was a crime much more serious than the one perpetrated in the American Revolution, because after allegedly fighting a civil war to free the slaves, at the cost of hundreds of thousands of lives, and after millions of words professing the noble political purposes of the war, the nation permitted blacks to be systematically degraded again. At the time of the Revolution the citizens of the new republic might have been entitled to plead ignorance. But not after the Civil War.

It is when we look at China today that we can appreciate the lower stage in the evolution of man/womankind that the Civil War and the Compromise of 1877 represent. In China today the people are ready to hold back economic development to allow all the people to develop to the same level. But a hundred years ago the United States was ready to consign a certain segment of the population to servitude so that another segment, distinguished from the first only by its lack of color, could enjoy social mobility. The segment condemned to underdevelopment had up to that time constituted the chief labor force of the society, which was then agricultural. The blacks were, in fact, this country's first working class. Thus, by condemning a section of the working class to servitude, the Compromise of 1877 destroyed the possibility of "Black and White, Unite and Fight" which Marx had expected to emerge from the Civil War.

A few years later came the first effort to unite blacks and poor whites on a class or economic basis, in the Populist movement. Since by this time the poor whites had already begun to see the counter-revolutionary political advantages, i.e., the life-and-death power over blacks, that they could derive from uniting with propertied whites on a race basis, the Populist movement failed. Economics had been put in command of politics after the Civil War. Thus it was only a matter of time before white racism would destroy any possibility of revolutionary politics on a class basis.

The emigration of white workers from South and Central Europe in the late nineteenth and early twentieth centuries appeared to skirt this contradiction. In fact, it was only making it more difficult to resolve. As each shipload of immigrants landed, everyone pursued the American Dream by attempting to climb up the social ladder, ignoring the fact that opportunities were open to them because they were closed to blacks. From this first step, it was simple to move to the next step, of whites refusing blacks the right to work alongside them, on the grounds that blacks would lower wages. Opportunity had become opportunism.

In *The American Revolution*, we pointed out how the United States has compromised itself on the question of the rights of blacks until political evasion has become a part of the American way of life. The country fought the American Revolution inspired by the belief that all men are created equal, but it did not free the blacks from slavery. Next it fought the Civil War to save the Union which was breaking up because blacks had not been freed by the Revolution, but then it stuck the Union together again by resegregating the blacks. In World War I this country allowed blacks to fight in order to save democracy and to work in the plants in order to build the materials that were needed to defeat the Kaiser—but only because the war had made it impossible to bring in more immigrant labor from Europe. In World War II Roosevelt issued Executive Order 8802 allowing blacks to work in defense plants—but only to keep the nation from being torn asunder by a threatened march of blacks on Washington. On the eve of the Korean War, Truman integrated the armed services—in order to save the country from Communism. Now the Kerner Commission has denounced racism in order to stem rebellion, but proposes upgrading of whites to higher jobs so that blacks can remain in the scavenger role of taking over second-hand jobs, second-hand homes, second-hand schools, and second-hand neighborhoods.

A nation which has compromised so often, which has taken the road of opportunism again and again, no longer has the same options as it had two hundred years ago. Its people are no longer the same people as they were at the time of the American Revolution. Too much water has flowed under the bridge. With each compromise they have been more deeply incorporated into the *system* of compromise. With each evasion of political and social responsibility, their political backwardness and their irresponsibility have been intensified. So that not only their political institutions but they themselves are now embarked on a road accelerating and worsening their political irresponsibility, their powerlessness, their unreadiness to reverse the direction in which they are moving.

As we enter upon the 1970s, practically every American citizen, black and white, recognizes that the traditional view of the United States as a "melting pot" is no longer valid. Many will insist, quite correctly, that it has always been a myth. It is only one of the many myths, both superficial and fundamental, that the black movement has succeeded in exploding one after another during the last twenty years.

Today there are two Americas—one black, one white. For some Americans, black and white, the key question is whether, or how, these two Americas can live together in harmony. For others, the question has come to be whether, or how, they can peacefully co-exist as two entities, geographically and/or politically separate.

There is no simple solution. It is this naked fact—that no simple solution exists—which torments United States citizens, be they black or white. The people of this country have for so long believed that, if things were just left to the politicians while they pursued their own individual wants and desires, somehow, some day, some leader would come up with the necessary answers. Now that the working out of solutions depends increasingly upon the people themselves, there is widespread confusion and demoralization.

After World War II the black movement began as a struggle for integration in order that black people might reap the benefits of the system. But as the movement has deepened and widened, the system into which blacks once sought integration has begun to crumble, while those with whom it once sought equality are themselves faced with a crisis unprecedented in United States history.

At the time of the Birmingham explosion in 1963, few people realized that the coming North of the movement would also explode the myth of integration as a simple solution and force the movement to re-examine the American economic, social, and political system.

Looking back at the state of the movement in 1963, we can see that nearly everybody approached the problem as if the struggle for rights up North would follow the pattern of the struggle down South. It is only after Northern blacks began to examine the issues and grievances on which to focus their struggles, that they began to realize that *every* institution, North and South, has been structured for the express purpose of keeping blacks at the bottom. The role assigned to blacks in this society since colonial days has been that of scavengers, taking the leavings in every sphere, whether it be jobs, homes, schools, churches, or neighborhoods that whites have run down and now consider beneath them.

Since 1963, the Northern movement has been confronted with the dilemma of how to organize a struggle for rights when, according to law, Northern blacks already have those rights, and when the grievances which most directly affect the great masses of Northern blacks involve the very structure of all American institutions. The Southern movement now faces the same dilemma.

In the last ten years the black movement in the North has tried many different solutions, from mass demonstrations to mass rebellions, from voting black to buying black. Through its many activities it has produced a social force of millions of blacks, formerly apolitical and apathetic but now anxious to act. At the same time the movement had rid itself of a number of illusions, discovering that the solution did not lie simply in integration, or spontaneous eruption, or militant rhetoric, or the unity of sheer numbers. It is now clear that the problems of black people cannot be solved by the most charismatic or most militant spokespeople for black grievances, or by economic aid from city, state, or federal governments, or by programs for hiring the hard-core unemployed.

Faced with these realities, the black movement is now painfully evaluating its past actions and seeking a program for the future, precisely at the time when those actions have brought into the political arena a white counter-revolutionary force which feels its way of life threatened by the black movement and seeks to wipe out this movement before it acquires more power.

Unlike the black revolutionary forces, the white counter-forces do not have to search for an ideology before they can plot their actions. Their ideology is that of the existing society: economic development regardless of the cost to human beings, everyone advancing at the expense of everyone else, and all whites advancing on the backs of blacks and other colored peoples. Even though they are themselves exploited and dehumanized by the system, even though they are powerless to affect major decisions about what to produce or when to go to war, they still believe that the American system is the best of all possible systems because it has allowed them to climb up the social and economic ladder on the backs of blacks and other people of color. It is, for them, a system of privileges, which they are determined to maintain by all means necessary. The attacks on student anti-war demonstrators by "hardhats" hint at the lengths to which white workers are ready to go to defend the American way of life. These attacks also reveal how dangerous is the illusion, spread by white radicals, that black and white workers in this country can unite and fight for revolutionary social change on the basis of common economic self-interest.

One hundred years ago, after the Civil War had ended slavery, Karl Marx thought that race would no longer be a barrier to the unity of black and white workers in the United States. "Labor cannot emancipate itself in the white skin where in the black skin it is branded," he wrote in *Capital*, in 1867. Even the most cursory glance at the context in which this passage appears makes it obvious that Marx wrote this, not as a slogan urging the unity of black and white workers but as a description of a situation which he assumed had been ended by the Civil War. Today, we know what Marx *could not have known in 1867*—we know that racism became even more deeply entrenched in American life with the expansion of capitalism after the Civil War because it provided a means for white workers to advance on the backs of others. Hence it would be naïve to expect white workers to liberate blacks from racism. Blacks must liberate themselves, but they can do so only by liberating American society as a whole from the system which has achieved such rapid economic development at the expense of peoples and races.

Before we analyze why this is the only road open to blacks and the nation as a whole, we must examine why it is that so many well-meaning American Marxists could have been so mistaken in their use of the above-stated quotation from Marx. We must do this because, as we have seen, every successful revolution in our epoch has been based on utilizing the methods of Marxist-Leninism, and at the same time pursuing a relentless struggle against those who insist on dogmatically following the scenarios from other revolutions and who get their ideas from books rather than from the contradictions arising from the specific historical development of the particular country.

Marx, in the middle of the nineteenth century, concluded, from his studies of the revolutions of 1830 and 1848, that the capitalists and the liberal intellectuals would never be able to destroy the remnants of feudalism which continued to exist in Western Europe; that the capitalists, threatened by the growing strength of the working class, would compromise with the landed aristocracy; and that the petty-bourgeoisie would shrink back in horror from a life-and-death clash with the bourgeoisie. Therefore the tasks of completing the bourgeois revolution, as well as of making the proletarian revolution, would fall upon the working class, the only class organized and resolute enough for such an awesome undertaking. This is the theme of all of Marx's historical writings.

In the 1930s, the United States Communist Party borrowed this scenario, which Marx had arrived at in nineteenth-century Europe, introducing some minor variations in the cast of characters and the scenery in order to give it an American flavor. Stripped of rhetoric, their interpretation of the American past and the American future ran something like this:[*]

The American Revolution was progressive because it freed both

---

[*] Jack Hardy: *The First American Revolution* (New York: International Publishers, 1937).

the bourgeoisie and the common man. The bourgeoisie was freed from vested interests in Britain in order to develop the productive forces which would eventually make it possible for the common man to control his own destiny. The common man was freed to enjoy Life, Liberty, and the Pursuit of Happiness. However, the bourgeoisie has become competitive and monopolistic, and now fetters the productive forces needed to create sufficient abundance for a classless society. Fortunately, however, capitalism has produced a social force, the working class, which can carry on the historic task of developing the productive forces and creating the objective conditions for Liberty, Equality, and Fraternity for the common man, thereby completing what the capitalists could not complete. The only barrier to working-class success in this historic task is the disunity between black and white workers, which is partly the result of feudal remnants in the South and partly the result of a conspiracy by the big bourgeoisie in order to divide and rule. Therefore black people should fight for their rights and white workers should support them, in the interests of completing the bourgeois-democratic revolution, so that we can advance to the next stage of the socialist struggle against capitalism. This scenario usually concludes with a sententious quotation of the passage from Marx beginning: "Labor cannot emancipate itself . . ."

This is the picture that most radicals still have of the revolution in the United States—although some groups may introduce variations into the scenario. For example, the black proletariat or the black lumpenproletariat may take the leading role in place of the white workers. We must recognize this in order to understand the unhealthy and essentially neocolonialist relations which have developed between white radical organizations and black individuals or groups over the years.

Until a few years ago acceptance of this scenario for the American revolution was not only relatively harmless, but even progressive. It provided the inspiration and the courage for innumerable middle-class whites to challenge the racism of their neighbors and of workers, to expose the national chauvinism and the general refusal to admit any defects in this "best of all possible worlds," to defy official and unofficial persecution by the FBI, the McCarthys, and the average American white community of any unorthodox ideas, and to face up to the real terrors of fascist rule in the American South. For the average middle-class white American, who has provided the hard-core of American Marxist organizations, a set of radical convictions, and association with others of like mind, were necessary to gain the inner strength to perform socially responsible but essentially liberal acts which the average American considers un-American. Hence it would be a serious error to underestimate the valuable role which these ideas and these individuals have played in puncturing the curtain of mental tyranny and conformity that the silent majority in this country has traditionally maintained.

However, since the black movement in the mid-1950s began setting into motion genuine revolutionary and counter-revolutionary social forces, therewith opening up the present revolutionary period, these ideas, so completely at variance with the actual and specific historical development of this country, have led and can only lead to a disastrous misreading of the dangers and opportunities now at hand. At this point, following or staging this scenario is both a farce and a tragedy because of the democratic illusions which it fosters and the aura of legitimacy which it gives to the white radicals' tendency to sponsor blacks who are victims of U.S. racism, to make political capital of their martyrdom, and then to export them back to the black community as its leaders.

Today the life and death of the entire human race depends on the revolutionist in the United States recognizing that there are no models for a revolution in the United States. It is not enough simply to emphasize the general rule that *every* revolution is unique. We must understand and appreciate the very specific historical process by which capitalism has developed in this country.

As we have seen in the last chapter, the United States has been from its very inception a society without feudal remnants and without any need to make a bourgeois-democratic revolution, except against the British Crown. Unlike Europe and Asia, where the aristocracy and the Church owned most of the land, this country has been from its beginning sparsely populated, with land freely available, and hence, until the 1930s, with a continuing shortage of labor. Once the native American was slated for extermination because she/he refused to provide the labor needed for agriculture and to accumulate the capital necessary for capitalist production, United States capitalism has had to import labor, either by force or by hope. The Southern plantocracy and black slave labor in this country were not a feudal remnant but the means by which U.S. capitalism achieved its primitive accumulation of capital—first from trade in slaves, and then from the cotton which the slaves produced and which was sold to the textile industry in England to obtain the capital needed for U.S. manufacturing. (Few people are able to appreciate the fact that the United States was also once an undeveloped country in need of foreign capital.) Black slave labor also freed whites to become: (a) the labor force in industry without which capital accumulation could not have taken place; and (b) the farmers needed to produce the food for the urban labor force. From the beginnings of capitalism in this country in the eighteenth century, racism, or the stigmatization of blacks as an inferior people to be confined by force to an inferior place in the social structure, was a necessity for a rapid rate of capitalist development. In the nineteenth century, following the Civil War, racism again was necessary as a means for U.S. capitalism to keep blacks on the plantations down South and thus to provide the incentive, the hope, for the tired, the poor, the wretched refuse of Europe to come to work in the mushrooming mines, mills, and factories.

In the twentieth century, as technology was constantly being revolutionized from the surplus value derived from exploitation of labor within the process of production, making many factories and machines obsolete, racism again proved indispensable to capitalism. It made possible the relegation of blacks and other people of color to jobs in the outmoded plants, thus maintaining the capacity of these plants to produce profit and continue their contribution to the total social capital available for investment in new technology. In this way racism has enabled U.S. capitalism to maintain an internal colony from whose super-exploitation the United States has been able to develop into the economically most advanced country in the world. In this way also racism has been of benefit not only to the capitalist class. It has from the very beginning benefited white workers, providing them with a platform on which to rise, steadily upgrading their jobs, their working and their social conditions, while blacks have been the scavengers, taking the jobs, homes, schools, and neighborhoods that the whites no longer wanted.

This is the specific way in which capitalism and racism have developed inseparably in the United States, each acting as both cause and effect in creating a unique society in which there has been no limit on the pursuit of production for the sake of production and in providing opportunities, unparalleled in any country or in the history of the world, for the common man, i.e., the great majority of whites, to enjoy life, liberty, and the pursuit of happiness, i.e., to join the rat race, in complete disregard of all human values except those of material need.

It is necessary to stress the inseparability of racism and capitalism in the specific historical development of this country, not in order to blame the capitalists and workers, but in order to rid ourselves of the widely held belief that racism has been an imperfection or wart on the face of capitalism in the United States.

Racism has been an integral part of the historical development of U.S. capitalism, enabling it to achieve the material abundance which has made it possible for Americans to pursue happiness and enjoy material comforts far beyond anyone's expectations or even imagination two hundred years ago. And whoever pretends that this is not so or that racism is some kind of "feudal remnant" which has stood in the way of U.S. capitalism developing productive forces without limit or of the common man's pursuit of material happiness, rather than the means by which these two goals have been achieved under U.S. capitalism, is propagating lies about the past and the present.°

Today, because of the inseparable development of capitalism and racism, the main contradiction in the United States is the contradiction between its advanced technology and its political backwardness. We are a people who have been psychologically and morally damaged by the unlimited opportunities to pursue material happiness provided by the cancerous growth of the productive forces. As a result, the pursuit of happiness for most Americans means the rejection of the pain of responsibility and learning which is inseparable from human growth. Liberty has turned into license. Equality has become the homogenization of everybody at the lowest common denominator of the faceless anybody. Fraternity has become mass-man cheering and groaning at the various modern spectacles—sports, lotteries, and television give-aways.

The social anarchy in the United States today is not the result of the economic anarchy of competition on the market, or of the

---

° See "Uprooting Racism and Racists in the United States" in *Racism and the Class Struggle.*

anarchy of economic crises used by the capitalists periodically to destroy the previously created productive forces in order to make way for capital accumulation on a higher level (as in the Depression of the 1930s); or of the anarchy which comes from the absence of a planned economy. The social anarchy in the United States today is the result of the lack of any human values or *qualitative* standards imposed by human beings on the *quantitative* cancerous growth of production for the sake of production or the expansive virulence of quantitative expansion which by its very nature cannot limit its own growth. Such a humanly destructive situation cannot be corrected by replacing one form of economic man/woman, the wealthy, with another form of economic man/woman, the poor black or white, and/or black and white.

It requires the intervention and the creation of other kinds of human beings, human beings who define their identity and conceive their human dignity in terms of social responsibility rather than in terms of material and/or ethnic interests.

From its beginnings in this country nearly two hundred years ago, immediately after the Constitutional Convention, and again at the very beginning of the current movement some twenty years ago, the black struggle derived its force chiefly from the determination of blacks to enlarge the concept of human identity and human dignity beyond the biological or ethnic limitations which have been placed upon the people of this nation through a long series of corrupting compromises. However, unlike previous struggles, the current movement has been a self-developing movement, i.e., each year the movement gained momentum as ever widening forces joined the struggle. The result was that at a certain point great masses of people began rebelling outside the confines of the movement, because they felt that the progress which had been made was inadequate to that which could and should be made. Out of these rebellions the Black Power movement erupted in the mid-1960s.

When the Black Power movement exploded, blacks had the opportunity to add a new revolutionary political dimension to what had been up to that time chiefly a moral and philosophic concept. That is, for the first time, blacks could have proposed Black Power as the taking of state power by blacks in order to revolutionize the entire country on the basis of their enriched concept of man/woman. Instead the black movement has allowed itself to become bogged down in a kind of black nationalism which is as biologically narrow and as economically opportunistic as the white nationalism which has corrupted this country for so long.

Black nationalism was and can be progressive insofar as it creates in black people the historical consciousness of the uniqueness of their oppression and of the role which they have played in the historical development of this country. From the vantage point of such a historical consciousness, black nationalism can provide black people with an understanding of the historical reasons why they should struggle for a new society in a country where their progenitors have lived for as long as any other ethnic group—except for the native Americans—and longer than most. Having endured the oppression of slavemasters, having built the infrastructure in agriculture which was a necessary foundation for the rapid rise of industrial capitalism, and, finally, moving into industry, blacks have a greater right than any other segment of this society to confront and challenge every segment of this society, every ethnic group within this society, to discover a new and higher form to express their humanity at this stage of technological development and of world revolution.

This is an awesome challenge which blacks have tried to evade. They are hesitant to face up to it because it is so challenging. They have the fears which always haunt the revolutionary social forces; they are not convinced that they can win, and they lack confidence in their ability to create a better society.

These fears are not unique to blacks. All revolutionary social forces have fears as they come face to face with the revolutionary responsibility of changing the whole society. Because the task is so great, it is much easier to evade the tremendous challenge and responsibility for the disciplined and scientific thinking and disciplined political organization which are necessary to lead revolutionary struggle.

Many of those who have been frustrated by the failure of the civil rights movement and the succeeding rebellions have begun to put forward all kinds cf fantastic ideas as to what blacks should now do. In a revolutionary period, if you do not try to resolve your contradictions by going forward, the chances are that you will go backward.

Some say blacks should separate and return to Africa. Some say they should separate but should remain here and try to build a new black capitalist economy from scratch inside the most advanced and powerful capitalist economy in the world! Some say blacks should join the Pan-African movement in Africa and build a military base in Africa from which we will eventually be able to attack the United States.

Instead of probing the historical past of blacks in this country for the rich political lessons that it has to offer, blacks have become African scholars, both in the universities and the streets, going back thousands of years to prove that Africans also had kings and queens (as if black kings and queens didn't have subjects just like white kings and queens). Using the African past as a justification, some are even doing the same thing to women that blacks used to find so ridiculous in the Southern whites—keeping them pregnant and making them walk a few steps behind on the street.

Many think in purely ethnic and biological terms, dreaming of going back to Africa. Others scheme to get a piece of this country for themselves—three states or five states. For many Black Power has begun to mean the pure symbolism of long hair (the longer the better) or doing the same kind of dances that blacks have always done in this country, but in African garb. For a whole lot of people, Black Power has come to mean just "doing my own thing" regardless of the consequences to anybody else.

Many blacks who were in the movement have dropped out completely, trying to "make it" for themselves as doctors or lawyers or businessmen or directors of various pacification projects. Others say blacks should just struggle for survival from day to day, doing whatever has to be done for survival. And finally, others have just given up struggling for anything at all, and have turned to astrology or drugs or religion in the old-time belief that some metaphysical force out there in the twilight zone will rescue them from their dilemma.

The chief weakness of the black movement in the United States at this stage arises from the fact that most black militants view nationalism as an end in and of itself. They cannot face the fact that nationalism is not a revolutionary ideology; it does not provide a revolutionary solution to the contradictions of society. It is only a means to an end, a stage in the development of revolutionary struggle—just as rebellion or insurrection are stages in the development of revolutionary struggle.

In developing a revolutionary ideology for the United States, it is necessary to be very scientific about the *difference* between the role that black people have played in the development of this country and the role that colonial people play in the development of the imperialist country which exploits them. In relation to U.S. capitalism, blacks have played a role which is both *like* and *unlike* that of colonial peoples. They have been superexploited like all colonial peoples, but they have also played an integral part in the internal development of this country *from its very beginning*. This country has no history separate and apart from the history of black people inside it. By the same token the history of black Americans cannot be separated from their history in the development of this country. The cultural traditions which black Americans have already created, in the sphere of music (work songs, spirituals, blues and jazz) and in the sphere of politics (the continuing and protracted struggle for nearly two hundred years, to move beyond mass religious and community organizations to mass political organization, beyond rebellion to revolution, and beyond nationalism to socialism) are a vast resource upon which all Americans can draw.

Therefore, nationalism in this country cannot possibly have the same meaning as nationalism in countries like Kenya or Ethiopia or Ghana. Those countries have been trying to rid themselves of an oppressor who has invaded them from outside. Therefore they can fight *first* for independence, for self-rule, to get the imperialists to leave; and *then* for liberation, to rid their economies of control by neocolonialism.

In the United States there are no colonial settlers or colonial administrators to expel. Americans, be they descendants of settlers or immigrants, indentured servants or slaves, have all been an integral part of the development of this country. *Whether they came by choice or in chains*, whether their ancestors are in Africa or in Asia or in Europe or in Latin America, their culture, their history, is now a part of this country's history and not with their ancestors on other continents.

Because they are reluctant to face the revolutionary responsibilities which flow from this historical truth, many black Americans continue to call themselves Pan-Africanists, thus encouraging greater confusion and disarray in the black movement. Many Pan-Africanists in the old days lacked deep roots either in this country or in any country. Most of them were West Indian intellectuals, often very gifted individuals, who left their homelands because the little islands on which they were born offered little hope for individual advancement. Today's Pan-Africanists have been heavily influenced by Marcus Garvey, the Jamaican who formed the Back-to-Africa movement after World War I, at a historic juncture when it appeared that the European powers had been so thoroughly weakened by the war and by the Russian Revolution that black Americans could re-take Africa from them. For *that* period, it was an extraordinarily bold conception.

But Pan-Africanism in the United States today is mainly a confession of revolutionary frustration and failure by people who were first in the civil rights movement, *then* were lifted to revolutionary enthusiasm by the rebellions and the Black Power movement, and who are *now* evading their responsibility to lead a revolution in the United States. This would require them to grapple with the real contradictions *of this entire society*, because a revolutionist aims to change the political, social, and economic relations of everybody in the particular society.

The present flourishing of separatist tendencies inside the black movement shows that blacks share the characteristic American reluctance to assume the awesome responsibilities of revolutionary political struggle and leadership. As we wrote in *The American Revolution*:

> Americans find excuses where there are no excuses, evade issues before the issues arise, shun situations and conversations which could lead to conflict, leave politics and political decisions to the politicians. They will not regain their membership in the human race until they recognize that their greatest need is no longer to make material goods but to make politics.

Meanwhile, because blacks cannot possibly solve their own contradictions separate from a solution of the fundamental contradiction in the United States between advanced technology and political backwardness, and because black revolutionary political leadership is pivotal to the progressive movement of other social forces in this country, the nation as a whole moves closer and closer to chaos.

Frustrated by its inability to crush the people of Indochina by technological and military might, bewildered and bedeviled by the challenges of great numbers of young people to a system which justifies such wholesale destruction of people and nations in a remote area of the world, appealing to the most selfish material interests of each section of the country against every other, unable to cope with the foreign trade deficit and inflation at home, reacting to all contradictions with spectacular measures which are supposed to control the contradictions but which only encourage them to fester, the executive branch of the government uses its vast powers chiefly to increase its own power and to barricade itself against all who challenge this power or who seek a way to build a new society and a new world based upon the respect of nations and of human beings for each other and for themselves.

Meanwhile, the cities decay, health facilities soar in cost and decline in availability, crime rules the streets; one-third of the nation remains ill-fed and ill-housed; rivers, lakes, and streams are turned into sewers, streets are littered with the residue of purposeless consumption; public transportation scarcely exists except in the skies, where competing planes by the thousands spew out their gases to fill the atmosphere with cancer-producing pollutants.

A crisis of such critical importance in the evolution of the human species and in its relation to the planet on which it depends for its continuing evolution, cannot be resolved by reform measures, such as a change in administration or the expenditure of more millions by those in authority, or the election of blacks to carry out the same policies by which whites have brought this country to its present state of chaos. The solution entails a social revolution which will reverse the whole course of dehumanization by which the United States has achieved its present state of technological and material eminence, giving priority instead to the development of the American people as a politically conscious, socially responsible, independently creative, and unashamedly self-critical people. The crisis, like every historical crisis, not only represents a danger to all man/womankind. It is also an opportunity to advance man/womankind another step in its evolution.

The challenge to blacks to struggle for revolutionary power cannot be evaded indefinitely. Until blacks are ready to face the fact that "Black Power" which is not revolutionary power is sheer rhetoric, that revolutionary power means the power to govern, and that the power to govern in the United States means the responsibility to govern all the people, regardless of race or national origin or creed; until blacks are ready to lead both blacks and whites in the struggle for revolutionary power, they will be unable to use the opportunities which exist at this historic juncture when the United States power structure faces defeat and discredit abroad and chaos at home.

But what about the White Left? By White Left we do not mean the old radicals who have spent the last fifty years either defending the Russian Revolution and/or hoping for the completion of the *first* American Revolution to bring *more* Liberty, *more* Equality, *more* avid pursuit of *more* Happiness; who have fragmented into a variety of sects, each seizing on one particular aspect or interpretation of the Russian Revolution or of Lenin's or Trotsky's writings as the reason for its separate existence; none of whom has ever seriously conceived of itself as carrying on a serious struggle for revolutionary power in the United States, but who all continue to hope that some day, some way, the American workers will be miraculously driven by the economic breakdown of capitalism to take over production and establish Workers' Power; and who until that day, preoccupy themselves with issues of democratic rights or ad hoc campaigns of various kinds.

The White Left that we are concerned about is the white youth who, beginning with the civil rights movement, gave of their energy, their time, their talent, their money, and often even their lives in the struggle for civil rights for blacks. These whites, like blacks, began by believing in integration; in other words, that the dilemma of U.S. society could be resolved without tampering with the economic, social, and political system that had created and maintains the separation of the races and without disrupting those who had benefited by this separation, especially the white workers. As long as they were welcome in the civil rights movement, the conviction, the dedication and the courage of these white youth could not be questioned. It was only when blacks themselves began to question the perspective of integration that these whites had to begin to ask themselves more fundamental questions.

Were they rebels with a cause of their own? Or were they only rebels for someone else's cause? Cast off during the Black Power phase of the black movement, these white youth then drifted to the peace movement which until that time had been kept alive by the old pacifists. In the anti-Vietnam war movement, these youth found a cause of their own—for not only were they themselves threatened by the draft but they could see the continuing drift of the United States toward being the counter-revolution to the Third World revolutions. Infused and imbued with a cause, the New Left initiated sit-ins, particularly in the educational institutions of the country, mobilizing liberals and youth for mass marches on Washington and on the old political parties, as in Chicago. Thus, chiefly through the efforts of white youth against the Vietnam war, the political machinery of this country is now in chaos.

However, the White Left has had no perspective of who would take the power in this country and who would reorganize our society or how it would be reorganized. Although many denounce the system and talk of revolution, no one has ever seriously asked how a revolutionary struggle would take place in *this* country, which social forces could be mobilized, who would lead them, and who would benefit, directly and indirectly. In this respect the white movement is less well developed than the black, which has at least begun to recognize which social forces would benefit by revolutionary change and which ones would be upset by revolutionary change, even though it has not clarified the goal of revolutionary change nor assumed responsibility for organizing the necessary forces. The White Left moves even more pragmatically and empirically and reactively from issue to issue than the blacks: from war, repression, ecology, to voter participation, educational reform, anti-consumerism—dropping out, drugging in, collectivizing, communing.

The New Left has two fundamental weaknesses, one objective and largely outside its own control, and the other subjective. Objectively, it has no mass base in any community with which it can interact systematically in the course of concrete struggles and thereby develop the revolutionary organization and the revolutionary programs necessary to transform itself and the masses. Hence its tendency to live vicariously through the revolutions of other peoples. Even more serious, however, is its unreadiness to make an objective criticism of its pragmatism and empiricism, its opportunism and adventurism, its individualism, its competitiveness and the tendency towards ultra-democracy, all of which have such deep roots in the American past and the American present. Through the labor, patience and suffering of such an objective self-criticism, the New

Left could take the first step toward thinking dialectically. Without such a consciously developed method of thought, the New Left can only continue to react to wrongs, trying to put things right by sheer rhetoric and rebellion, and becoming demoralized when these methods fail, as indeed they must. The New Left has been trying to make amends for the wrongs done to blacks throughout American history, thereby abdicating its own responsibility to make political judgments and political decisions. It has acted from guilt, the worst possible foundation for revolutionary politics, constantly trying to prove its repudiation of the American past (and of American parents) by generosity and by militant, but essentially futile, efforts to destroy the system at one blow. It has made no serious effort to use what is progressive in the American past to get rid of what is backward. Instead it has concentrated on strategy and tactics rather than on ideology, trying to develop the latter from the former when it should be the other way around. Hence, instead of advancing politically, young whites have regressed, some going the way of bourgeois politics as in the McGovern campaign and ending up as Jesus freaks or guru admirers.

It takes courage as well as vision to project an entirely new way for people to live, instead of just reacting to others, getting more violent when others get violent, or making more money because the opportunity is available to make more money, or buying a Mark IV because someone else has gotten a Cadillac.

In an advanced country a fundamental distinction has to be made between *wants* and *needs,* and people must be brought to understand the necessity to choose between them. For example, people in this climate *need* shoes to protect their feet from the elements, but a lot of people *want* alligator shoes. One may *need* a car for transportation, but one *wants* a Cadillac or Rolls Royce for social reasons. The same is true of clothes, homes, furniture, or television. Many people even demand fancy telephones. People move to certain neighborhoods because they want a better house or better schooling for their children, when what is needed is the improvement of their old neighborhood. The failure to distinguish and choose between needs and wants, in every sphere, from the trivial to the important, has created a nation of consumer addicts who, because they *want* the new look in everything have acquired a throwaway mentality, and have lost the sense of human values which any society *needs.*

Is it possible to project advanced ideas, ideas of a more human way to live, to the rebellious but politically backward masses of an advanced country? That problem in itself demands recognition of the fact that it is possible to be economically advanced and politically backward, whereas Marxists have generally assumed that the masses of a technologically advanced country are also politically and culturally advanced. In fact, the masses in the United States have been content to remain on the fringes of the political arena, so involved in pursuing their own individual economic interests that they have gladly left politics and the solution of fundamental problems to the politicians. Even those who feel most oppressed in this country still respond only as victims, and have not seen themselves as the potential creators of a new man/woman.

In an undeveloped country the vast majority of the people have a model or a vision of what they want to achieve. Essentially they strive for the material development of the advanced countries, while at the same time (because they are aware that these countries have developed economically by damning them into a state of underdevelopment), they seek new, more humane methods by which to effect their own material development. Hence the almost universal acceptance of socialism by the new nations. Mao and Castro have been particularly aware of the dilemma involved in allowing technology to command politics; hence their emphasis on political development as the means to technical development. Nevertheless, revolution in all the undeveloped countries has had a clear and concrete goal. The oppressors had to be destroyed because they have kept the oppressed in a state of backwardness and the productive forces in a state of stagnation. The advantages enjoyed by the oppressor have been clearly visible to the oppressed.

Today, in this technologically advanced but politically backward society, we must introduce into the thinking of the oppressed the idea of what they need to achieve, because without real goals, it is difficult for people to strive. Most rebels, black or white, react to an idea purely in terms of the social position of the person advancing the idea. Usually they will not even consider an idea unless it comes from someone in the most oppressed strata of society. They never stop to consider that any ideas of serious value will have to be highly advanced ideas—they cannot be ideas of the past, because, like it or not, the United States is a highly advanced country, and one in which the contradictions are not material or economic, but within the realm of human choice. Where else in the world have people been paid *not* to grow food? Where else in the world is the class of petty-bourgeois employees and technicians so much larger than the industrial working class and the farmers?

How to project an advanced idea in tune with our unique stage of human development is a serious revolutionary problem, more serious even than that which Marx faced in projecting his ideas to the European radicals of his time. Malcolm X used to chide the masses, because he began with the idea that the masses were not perfect, and that they *had* to be transformed. He had the courage to attack the Establishment while chiding the masses for their backwardness, their superstitions, their myths and fears. Malcolm realized that the masses would have to repudiate much of what they had accepted as normal and natural, and transform themselves into new people with new values, and with a new vision of new tasks to be performed, if black people were ever to be free. In fact, Malcolm repudiated his own past as not consistent with a new life and new values.

But in the years since Malcolm's death, when we should have been developing a new revolutionary vision, we have wasted our time in so much rhetoric that black and white radicals today make a virtue of irresponsibility and a virtue of vice—so long as it is the vice of an oppressed person. Today anything can be called revolutionary, regardless of how inhumane it is, so long as an oppressed militant is involved. The result is that, despite the spreading militancy and rebellion, we are moving further away from, rather than closer to, the revolutionary goal of building a new society.

Our challenge today is how to project a notion of the next stage in the evolution of man/womankind. We have to be concerned about the development of man/womankind, not in the undialectical way that sociologists and anthropologists are concerned with human development, but by projecting another, a new notion of man/woman, one that will replace current notions of what it means to be human. To do this is not a technical problem. It is not a matter of taxing the rich to spread the wealth among the poor, thereby depriving the poor of the human right and responsibility to make the choices and decisions which represent the next stage in the evolution of man/womankind, or making them passive recipients rather than active participants in defining and creating the new man and new woman.

A potential revolutionist can't just start with the specific problems, such as what to do with eighteen-year-olds or what to do with the university or what to do with the environment. One must see the whole, grasping the essential nature of man/woman. We may have to destroy many things in order to make it possible for these new human beings to establish themselves, but we will not be doing this just because we don't like things as they are. We will be tearing things up because we have in mind doing something entirely different with the world. For example, we will have to discover how to give up or to deny ourselves a lot of things before we can become related to nature again. We can't stop pollution if we are not ready to give up fancy wrappers, throwaway bottles, pesticides, enzyme detergents, and new cars every few years. The city will have to be reorganized, industry will have to be reorganized, the schools will have to be reorganized.

All these problems pose for the potential revolutionist some very serious choices. Are you just going to please the masses or are you going to give leadership to the masses? Up to now revolution has been seen or thought of as a way to give everybody *more* of everything rather than *less* of many things. The development of the United States has posed many unanswerable questions; for example, if blacks had become integrated or assimilated into the American way of life as were the immigrants after the Civil War, would they not have been equally responsible for and/or equally hostile to the development of revolutionary struggles in Latin America, Asia, and Africa?

People in this country have an extremely limited view of what man/woman should strive for. Most people think in terms of objects or property or skills, and they are unable to think of what humanity might become. The movement in the United States has exaggerated, glorified, and romanticized events that have taken place. It has made no distinction between rebellion and revolution, and has failed to understand the difference between what must take place in a pre-revolutionary period and what can take place in a post-revolutionary period.

We must be scientific and precise about what a commotion such as that which took place in Detroit in 1967 really represented. We can't call rebellion revolution just to make ourselves feel better. What we call something today, particularly with the mass media waiting to make political stars, in itself becomes an action. We have to know the difference between a rebellion, a riot, a revolt, and a revolution. If we don't, we will be calling everything revolutionary, from how we comb our hair to what color panties we wear on Monday morning.

Are the young revolutionary or just rebellious? Rebellion springs from specific social conditions, but does not go beyond rejection. Hence it can degenerate into cults, sects, and separatists. Revolution must contain a powerful element of political responsibility. Anyone who speaks of "revolution for the hell of it" or "revolution for the sake of revolution" is not revolutionary. We have for too long accepted the old categories of revolutionist vs. reformist—as if every rebel were a revolutionist, while those who are for fundamental social change but not for tearing everything up mindlessly are "just reformists."

We have to reject categorically the idea that the Jerry Rubins are revolutionists, regardless of the good work they may once have done in the movement. A revolutionist has a continuing responsibility—the word is not an honorary title bestowed for past valor. The theatrical view of revolution belongs on the stage, not in politics. For those who think that this judgment is too harsh, remember the judgment that Lenin had to make about his brother, a terrorist—a judgment that most of us are not yet ready to make of Che's activities in Bolivia because we love him so much for what he accomplished in Cuba.

Potential revolutionaries remain just that, potential revolutionaries, so long as they can't bring themselves to make political judgments of Che's attempt to import into Bolivia what had succeeded in Cuba, without making a systematic effort to evaluate and understand the specific social conditions in Bolivia. We do not condemn Che because he failed—there is never a guarantee of success. But we do judge Che's politics because they were wrong. We can't deny, nor do we want to, what Che did in Cuba. For that we embrace him. But our responsibility as revolutionists starts by making responsible judgments.

Similarly, every serious revolutionist has to make political judgments about the Black Panther Party, which professed to be a revolutionary vanguard party and claimed to be a defender of the people. In fact, the politics of the Black Panther Party has been so much shaped by reactions to the enemy that its members were constantly asking the people to defend the party. Anyone who makes a serious study of the Black Panther ten-point program will see that this program is just an ultra-democratic demand for civil rights. It contains no vision of what the party in power will do with technology, with industry, with housing, with the environment, with education, with scientific research, with international relations—in a word, with any of the main ingredients of a modern society.

If every time someone hollers on the corner, or gets into a fight with the cop on the beat or the boss on the job or the teacher at school, you call it revolutionary, you end up by demoralizing your own forces. It is impossible to organize if everybody believes that revolution is everybody doing their own thing. If that is really true, then someday, somehow, somewhere, somebody will rise up and that will be the revolution. As long as you believe that, you will be constantly turning to where the action is, which is just about the state the movement is in today. In essence, the New Left's behavior toward black militants is not too different from that of the Old Left—which used to get excited whenever the workers went on strike because of the conviction that a strike meant that revolution was just around the corner, and because of the theory that the revolution was essentially a spontaneous outburst of workers.

If an eruption can go in any direction, then it is not revolutionary, even though it may contribute to increasing social chaos. Only actions and movements that are along the path of advancing humanity are revolutionary. Everyone who rejects the society doesn't thereby become revolutionary. Some of these rejecters turn to banditry, thuggery, and some just plain cop-out. For example, what was the objective of the mass assembly of five hundred thousand people at Woodstock? Were they advancing humanity or was it just mass self-indulgence? Many young rebels have gone to countries that have achieved revolution and come back to America insisting that all we need to do is what those nations are doing—never realizing that what people are now doing in those revolutionary countries is only possible because they have already gone through a long struggle for power and can now, therefore, carry out post-revolutionary reconstruction. For example, Cubans carry guns in revolutionary Cuba because the power of the victorious revolution makes it possible for them to do so. But Cuban revolutionaries did not go around in Batista's Havana openly flaunting guns to be used in overthrowing Batista. They knew very well why Batista's forces carried guns—to protect the system. If romantic rebels (or provocateurs) carried guns in Havana or talked about going out to the bush to join Castro, Fidel didn't run into Havana to defend their democratic right not to be hanged by Batista. Revolution is not a game of chicken. There is a fundamental difference between the duty of a revolutionary to carry weapons for the purpose of defending the community, and merely flaunting weapons in the face of the overwhelming armaments of a repressive state.

There are millions of Americans who are seeking answers to questions about what is to be done in the present very critical period, and who are not necessarily wedded to the current system. This has always been true of any society in a revolutionary period, and if it were not true in the United States today, we would have to re-examine our evaluation of the country as being in a revolutionary period. The point is that when you have a serious idea of where you are going, the number of people that you can hope to recruit either as cadre members or as supporters is very much greater than most potential revolutionaries believe. Marx was not as aware of this as were Lenin and Mao, because it is the kind of thing you become concerned about when you are seriously struggling for power and must begin to assess forces in a concrete, realistic way.

Revolutionary social change in man/woman must begin with those who propose to do the transforming. We are faced not with the task of applying the ideas of Marx or Mao to the United States but with that of developing a new concept of human identity as the basis for the revolution in America, a concept which must extend the dialectical development of humanity itself.

9

CHANGING CONCEPTS FOR CHANGING REALITIES

During the past seventy-five years we have been experiencing a technological revolution without precedent in human history. As this revolution gained momentum, and with each spectacular advance, the idea that humankind can find solutions for its problems through material things and through technical developments has taken deeper root.

But now we find that despite these technological miracles, American men and women in every walk of life are deeply troubled. They feel that they have lost their sense of direction, their sense of purpose, their sense of identity, their sense of history.

The very purpose of life is now in question, because life has, in fact, become purposeless for great numbers of people.

Our problems flow from solutions which were created in response to problems in the past, solutions which served to resolve those problems. In resolving or negating the problems, however, those solutions created new contradictions, many of which now serve as strong dehumanizing factors in our society.

That is why philosophy is so necessary. It is the essence of philosophy to provide a concept of the relationship between ideas and reality (past, present, and future) and the critical bearing which each has on the other. Philosophy begins when individuals question reality. Philosophy is the continuing struggle to find more adequate questions regarding the nature of man/woman and reality. It is an advance beyond religion, which is the search for certainty and for absolute answers.

Usually the search for a new philosophy begins with the break-up of old values and old standards, and a growing suspicion that the old ruling class is not fit to govern or has lost what the Chinese and Vietnamese call "the Mandate of Heaven."

Such a situation exists in the United States today.

In this country it is estimated that one out of every five persons is mentally ill; in fact, the number of mentally ill people exceeds the number of people with all other forms of illness combined. There are seven million known alcoholics. Countless millions are addicted to drugs, from tranquilizers to heroin. The number of persons simply unable to cope with life here has reached epidemic proportions. All the efforts of psychiatrists cannot help us to solve this problem, because the goal of psychiatry is to help the individual adjust to the society, which is precisely what millions of Americans cannot do.

At the other pole, those who have adjusted successfully to the society have done so only because they have accepted the dominant philosophy of our society, that one should strive to get as much for oneself as one can, regardless of anyone else, and that one's life should be organized around that purpose. Go to school so that you can get a better job and earn more. Cater to those in the upper echelons because they may be able to help you get a better job. Go on strike so that you can make more money—no matter what you are producing or what this means to the community.

According to this philosophy, government exists only to secure everybody the opportunity to live this way, and the best government is that which provides the most effective umbrella for this kind of life. For that government the majority of the people will come out every four years and, through the ritual known as voting, make clear that they are ready to obey the President as if he were a god for the next four years. The rest of the time that god is left to do what he will with our affairs.

By this process, the American people evade responsibility for decision-making, and invest the government and its many agents with the power they want to meet the recurring crises of a world in rapid technological and social change. As a result, corruption in government is as common as crime in the streets. The difference is that no one votes for the criminal in the streets, but the people still vote for the government.

Today in the United States the Vietnam war has come home to Americans in ways that they never suspected. Instead of maintaining full employment for Americans, which is how most workers viewed the criminal war in Indochina, it has brought on a runaway inflation whose end no one can foresee. Blacks, Chicanos, Puerto Ricans, Asian-Americans, Indians, Appalachian whites, young people—all are in a state of rebellion, inspired or accelerated by their realization that the citadel of world capitalism can be breached by a tiny nation lacking in the technological might which was heretofore considered necessary for military victory. Millions of middle-class and working-class whites feel threatened and bewildered by these rebellions and this inflation and wonder where it will all end. They continue to live in accordance with their philosophy that the pursuit of economic benefits will solve all their problems and the problems of this society. But they are not so sure that this is still true. They sense in their relations with their children that the entire family structure, which provided a kind of social rationale for chasing the buck, is disintegrating. Even their many credit cards do not help them to keep up with the inflated economy. And the war in Indochina has upset their preconceptions more than they are ready to admit, even to themselves.

In the midst of this crisis has come the Watergate scandal, destroying the myth that the President knows best, and revealing instead that what he knows has in fact been acquired by his technocratic hirelings using the same kind of electronic gadgets that have already failed to win the war in Vietnam. These hirelings have not even won their power through the political rituals by which the American people have up to now legitimized their representatives. Instead they see themselves as a football team running and blocking their way downfield against all opponents, for the glory and power of their chief, or as a spy ring as unrestricted in its activities against other Americans as the CIA has been against the citizens of other countries in actual or potential conflict with the United States. Instead of being a benevolent god, the government begins to look like a monster, capable of manipulating and shredding the American people with the same callousness it has manifested in manipulating ideas, shredding papers, and raining napalm down on the people of Indochina.

Having dehumanized themselves by exploiting the natural resources of the whole world and destroying whole peoples in the pursuit of their own material comforts, the American people are now confronted with reality in the form of shrinking world markets and the shrinking dollar for American tourists and occupation forces abroad, the energy crisis, and the growing suspicion that this country must soon begin to live on its own resources. Having treated so many other people like "gooks," the American people are increasingly treating each other this way. Americans treat each other like enemies, using and abusing each other as if each person had the inherent right to do anything, no matter what, which serves his/her desires and ambitions.

These problems cannot be solved by technology, any more than the war in Indochina could be won by technology. In fact, the application of technology to human relations only introduces more distance into these relations and encourages people to treat each other like things. Human relations can only be changed by human beings who have brought about a fundamental change in the view they have of themselves and of other human beings.

Up to now, satisfied with the pace at which private capitalism was producing the abundance to gratify their pursuit of material happiness, and with a government which acted "for the people" by intervening periodically, with economic projects and wars, to keep the economy from slowing down too much, the American people have gone their merry and not-so-merry way, often complaining about the bosses, the government and the system, but always acting as if the system was somewhere outside themselves. This was a convenient fiction to help them evade the fact that the system is a very concrete thing, functioning through shared values, structures, and institutions of which everyone in the United States is a part and which everyone keeps in operation.

So deeply ingrained in every American are the ideas of private industry, free enterprise, private ownership, and the right of every individual to exploit other individuals, that even when these ideas produce chaos people continue to believe in them. At one time, these ideas, these values did work. They produced an abundance of goods which made possible the access, by people of humble origin and of diverse ethnic groups, to social mobility and material comforts far beyond those of people elsewhere in the world.

But, although most people don't like to admit it, no matter how hard they work to make the final payment on a house, big appliances, or car, so high are the taxes, the insurance, and the various licensing fees that their continuing payments may well be more than the initial cost. So shoddy are the goods you buy in the race to consume that the increase of mass consumption is clearly for the sake of continuing mass production, and no one is quite sure just what the purpose of continuing mass production is.

At a time when the American people cry out for leadership, the national government is being exposed as a sink of corruption. Local governments exhibit daily their impotence to deal with the most elementary community problems.

With foreign policy crises coming one after another, U.S. diplomats must be ready on a moment's notice to put out brush fires that threaten to turn into forest fires.

In the marketplace a cold war is brewing across the length and breadth of the continent. Hundreds of thousands of housewives have begun to protest against the threat to their private standard of living from soaring prices. The same people who refused to join any protests against the genocidal racist war in Indochina—a war which has helped to create our current inflation—are now resentful that, since the cease-fire, things have gotten worse instead of better.

Those whom the government has tried to pacify with the "War on Poverty" are bitter at the administration's plans to shift funds from pacification projects to rebuilding the military forces defeated in Vietnam.

Black people, who in the 1950s and early 1960s injected new life into American society by their fight for human rights, have degenerated to such a point that they have failed to identify themselves with the Vietnamese in their fight against the mass killings, rapes, and environmental destruction of Indochina by American troops. In fact, some blacks took part in the massacres, while others stood by and watched. Some now welcome the returning soldiers, just as the whites do. Separated or integrated, the dehumanized attitudes of most black and white people have become indistinguishable.

The moral deterioration of Americans in their daily social relations is apparent everywhere. Burglary, muggings, armed robbery, murder, rape, dope-taking, and dope-peddling are now as American as apple pie. *The spirit that led to the Mylai massacre pervades the nation.*

Many people sense the breakdown of the American Dream. Some respond with a strident patriotism; others with growing militancy on behalf of their own special interests—thus creating more social conflict and fragmentation.

This situation, coming to a head in the 1970s, did not begin yesterday. It is the culmination of a long history during which the American people have allowed economic development and technical know-how to shape the course of their political organizations and social relations.

For the purpose of economic development, black slavery was instituted and maintained by force and ideology. To foster economic expansion, Indians were virtually exterminated, and their survivors herded into concentration camps. To buttress economic development and raise the standard of living, Cuba and the Philippines were subjugated by U.S. imperialism through military invasion in the Spanish-American War.

A half-century later, the atom bomb was dropped without warning on Japan in order to proclaim to the world that the American Century had begun, and that the United States now had the military power to shape the world as it saw fit. In pursuit of this aim America embarked on the Korean war and then the war in Vietnam.

These brutal, arrogant acts were supported by the majority of the American people because they believed that the sky was the limit. Now that the people of Vietnam have exploded this myth, it has become not only necessary but possible for Americans to take a good look at themselves, to ask *why* we are where we are, *where* we are headed, and *whether* that is where we really want to go.

During the last two hundred years we have been traveling ahead with gathering momentum to make economic development the governing principle in every decision. Now it is necessary for our very existence that we change directions, that we embark on a new road. The old direction, the old road, created by one philosophy, one set of values, has become destructive not only of others but of ourselves as well. The old concepts have taken us on a road where material things have become not just the means but the very end of human aspirations. We have replaced man/womankind as the end and goal of living with the things which we originally created to serve us as means. We now value human beings for their economic possessions and their economic status rather than for their humanity.

It was a great advance in human evolution when the Puritans, four hundred years ago, began to struggle to better the material conditions of the ordinary man and woman and seek happiness on earth instead of in heaven. The philosophy behind this struggle was the new and rich value which the Puritans put on ordinary men and women, placing on them the responsibility for determining their own course rather than leaving it to priests and bishops, and for living simple and austere lives in contrast to the corrupt and venal lives of those priests and bishops.

As modern Americans, taking pride only in material things, we now have more than 200,000,000 citizens alienated from their own humanity and from each other, each pursuing his/her own material ambitions, related to one another only in terms of envy and competition, and the hatreds and antagonisms which inevitably flow from these. As more goods become more available, the stakes get higher, and the external pressures mount. Meanwhile we have been trying to export the same values, the same hatreds and antagonisms, to people elsewhere in the world, through multinational corporations, puppet governments, the Marshall Plan, NATO, SEATO, Alliance for Progress, Point IV programs, SALT—all in order to block the struggle and search of other peoples for a more human way to live. Military operations, elaborate espionage systems, one plan after another, come off government planning boards in an attempt to impose a dehumanized way of life upon the world, until today the President and his hirelings, Senators and Congressmen, all use the same kind of military and technological jargon to discuss human beings and human relations—e.g., "inoperative," "capability," "input," "feasibility"—as were once used only in describing machines and weapons.

One of the first steps toward creating an enlarged concept of our humanity is to develop an enlarged concept of our relation as human beings to politics. The Declaration of Independence and the original Constitution put forward broad and lofty assertions about the nature and the aspirations of human beings. But the Constitution was created nearly two hundred years ago in a very different era. It set forth the standards and the structure necessary for ongoing relations. But it was written at a time when popular loyalties were mainly to states and regions, when the country was primarily agricultural, when industry had not been developed. Moreover, this country at the time had consciously and deliberately disengaged from foreign affairs, from which the country felt protected by two great oceans.

Since then the United States has fought four major wars—the Civil War, the Spanish-American War, World War I, and World War II—as well as countless unofficial wars. Since World War II the United States has replaced Britain as the Western imperialist power responsible for policing the rest of the world, instead of being the associate in world power which Theodore Roosevelt had envisaged.

Through the years the U.S. government has moved from a feeble apparatus dependent upon the states and regions for its power, to an apparatus of enormous power in its own right, by virtue of its size and the far-reaching national and international decisions it has been expected to make. In a world as complex as ours, it is difficult to keep domestic issues separate from issues of national security, but it might be possible if one struggled scrupulously to do so. If, on the other hand, a President and/or his staff becomes obsessed with his own indispensability and historic mission as an international politician, it becomes easy, under the cloak of national defense, to confuse national and international affairs and to justify any domestic action deemed necessary to maintain, enlarge, and perpetuate that President's power. In relinquishing their political responsibilities and leaving all decisions to the government, the American people have created the conditions which have made possible the monstrous self-serving espionage apparatus employed by Richard Nixon. Instead of seeing their citizenship as a responsibility, the American people saw it only as a right, leaving it to others, and to the city, state, and national government to deal with every important issue, reducing themselves to children who react with "I like" or "I don't like," "I support" or "I don't support," restricting their relation with the government to the minimal one of voters (or taxpayers) who can be calculated on a computer.

By what concept of politics have the American people guided themselves that they could accept such a childlike, such a diminished human role for themselves all these years? What *is* politics? What is the appropriate relation between ethics and politics? What is a nation? What is freedom? What is equality? What is truth? And what is the purpose of a constitution? The answers to these questions cannot be found in any dictionary. They have to be created.

What is politics? What did former Chief Justice Warren mean when he said, at the Fifth International World Peace through Law Conference in Yugoslavia, "We have grown up in the comfortable sense that politics is the art of the possible. Few of us have faced the fact that science has transformed politics into the art of the indispensable."

What we need is an entirely new notion of politics. It would appear that politics includes much more today than it has ever included before. For example, if you decide that you don't want nuclear power plants, that is politics.

Most people think of politics as a "thing." What we must understand first is that politics is a process, the process by which the political and social decisions involving the organization of society are made.

First, let us review what politics has been; then find out what it has to be. We do not have to be governed by what politics has been. Rather we should explore what politics should be in order to accomplish what it must accomplish.

If we are going to talk about a new revolution, we have to talk about a new man/woman. The concept of a new man/woman requires not only new concepts of the relations between people, but new concepts of the relations between government and people. These new relations must spring from new attitudes in the people themselves. New institutions cannot be created without new concepts; only human beings can create new concepts.

In the eighteenth and nineteenth centuries, Western political economists drew a sharp distinction between economics (civil society) and politics (the superstructure) and claimed that the latter should be subordinated to the former. Thus the Physiocrats and Adam Smith fought for "freedom of trade" and "laissez-faire" for the bourgeoisie against the intervention of the state, as the best way to achieve the harmonious development of society. Marx's nineteenth-century vision of the "withering away of the state" and of

Communism as a new form of civil society in which each receives "according to his needs" and gives "according to his abilities," was in the antipolitical tradition of the eighteenth century.

On the other hand, when we think about politics today, we have to think in terms of the mutual responsibilities of government and people, and not just in terms of the relations between individuals within the civil society.

Most radicals still have a concept of politics that flows from the Marxist antipolitical tradition. If a militant worker says nothing about politics, that is considered profoundly political because his/her actions presumably express the instinctive drive of the working class to reorganize society on socialist foundations. For most radicals, revolutionary politics is little more than being "on the right side," the side of the oppressed masses: Yet often (although it takes courage to say so), you can learn more about the modern crisis of Western Civilization from people who have been thinking seriously about the dilemma of modern man/woman, but who are not on the "right side" in terms of class, social origin, or political policy.

Not until Lenin did a Western revolutionary attack economism and seek instead to put "politics in command." Lenin recognized that the workers were concerned chiefly with their economic needs and that a political party was required to raise them to political consciousness. After the Russian Revolution, he developed the concept of "politics in command," warning that if the Bolsheviks allowed economics to command, the workers' state would turn into state capitalism. After Lenin's death, the Bolshevik Party, under Stalin, gave priority to the development of the productive forces, i.e., they put economics in command, and Soviet Russia degenerated into the state capitalist bureaucracy so well exemplified by Brezhnev, who has more in common with Nixon than he has with any revolutionary socialist or communist.

When we come to the Chinese Communist Revolution, politics clearly takes command, both because the Chinese were able to learn from the Russian experience, and because the Chinese tradition stemming from Confucius stresses the political responsibilities of the scholar.

In our technologically advanced societies, where so many social decisions need to be made about what should and should not be produced and in what quantities, we are going to find it very hard to distinguish between economic decisions and political decisions. Politics is taking on new and broader dimensions. It must be redefined to take in much more than what has ordinarily been considered political activity. Politics involves making choices and choosing directions, not only for oneself, but for the whole society. In the West, particularly since Machiavelli, a distinction has been drawn between ethics and politics. Now we must ask ourselves, "Is it possible to create new politics without new ethics?" This country is lousy with politics without the slightest trace of ethics. In the recent past people always determined their ethics by politics—if it didn't pay, you changed your ethics. We have to think the opposite way today. If it is bad ethics, it isn't good politics. Revolutionary politics is ethical or it isn't revolutionary.

When the Italian city-states were fighting one another in the fifteenth century, what did they care about ethics? Ethics was completely subservient to politics. Machiavelli said that you can't confuse ethics and politics; politics is a science, value-free. A politician can't be ethical, he said in effect.

Having lived by Machiavelli's rules for five hundred years, we should realize that one of the causes of our troubles is that ethics has for so long been subservient to politics. It is impossible to project a revolution without ethical concepts, or concepts of the appropriate relations between people.

In the new era which we are entering, we must reject any pretense of value-free politics or of politics independent of ethics. No politics can be anything but self-defeating unless they are ethical. The big problem which remains is to decide what *is* ethical.

Politics involves citizenship, the responsibility to a particular polity, the creating of governing structures, of plans, of laws, of leadership—whereas ethics deals with one's social relations with friends, family, and associates, irrespective of citizenship. People have engaged in politics and had no ethics; ethical people have not engaged in politics. That has been the separation up to now, and that is why U.S. politics has been so unprincipled. Most people think of "going into politics." Isn't politics an activity in which everyone should be engaged, an activity not appropriated by an élite? Why shouldn't everyone take positions on issues not just in terms of one's friends, or one's intimate circle, but in terms of the constituency of which one is a member, which includes a lot of people one doesn't even know?

You have to have a conflict before you can have politics. Only when you struggle over an idea, do you reach the level of politics in the sense in which we are discussing it. Politics begins when you project an idea so that people can take sides. *Politics involves taking sides.* It means proposing or supporting particular plans, programs, perspectives which you believe are right. Most people in the United States don't want to be "involved in politics." They say that it's "dirty" or that it means dictatorship or "élitism." But their negative attitude stems principally from the fact that politics means taking sides over issues and conflicting with people over issues—something which they would rather not do. They still have the illusion that things develop automatically—without the need for political decision-making—and that the best government is the one which governs least. Yet many of these same people are the ones who are demanding a strong government to insure "Law and Order."

Up to this time they have thought of government chiefly in terms of the administration of social services. They have thought of the government as a Welfare State, one that takes care of sanitation, prisons, old-age pensions, social security, the lights on the corner. Jacques Ellul in *The Political Illusion* (New York: Knopf, 1967) criticized the readiness of the modern citizen to leave all these decisions to someone else, as if they were purely technical questions which did not involve actual choices or principled decisions. In fact, in all these matters, we are beginning to realize that political decisions *are* involved, and therefore people must take responsibility for making these decisions—not only by paying taxes but by actively deciding what should be done and what shouldn't be done.

Do some people have to get out of Washington for the water in the Potomac ever again to run pure? Should Americans cut down on their standard of living? Who is going to give up what? Are these political or ethical questions? Could we say that the general statement, "People are going to have to give up things in order to have a decent society," is an ethical statement; while the process of deciding who is going to give up what, and the actual making of decisions on a particular policy or for a particular policy, is political? Can we say that ethics deals with principles, while politics deals with the actual decisions, the choices? The governing principles are the ethics, while the decisions as to how to govern, made on the basis of ethics, flowing from ethical judgments, are the politics.

It is necessary to make a distinction between ethics and politics and then to re-unite them, because we are trying to re-establish the concept of polit cs as based upon principles and not only on power. Modern man/woman has been dominated by the concept of means rather than the concept of ends, by the question of *how* to do things rather than *why*, by the concept of politics as a value-free science. Modern societies manipulate people through propaganda so that it is difficult for the average person to proceed from principles. But the fault is not with the propagandists alone; it is with the basic concept of value-free politics which is shared by both propagandist and propagandee. Modern man/woman tends to rely upon external forces (the state or the economy) to resolve problems rather than accept the responsibility of *people* to resolve problems. Many Frenchmen (like Ellul) who have had experience with European Communism now ha e a kind of antipolitical bias, in the sense that they distrust the tendency in modern masses to rely upon the centralized state to resolve all problems. They want to re-establish responsibility within the people—but this cannot be done by turning your back on politics.

What is the relation of personal, human needs to political needs? In the speech previously referred to, Chief Justice Warren talks about the need for political cooperation and accommodation between political systems. But he does not deal with the personal, human need of people for national identity. Without nation-states and nations, people wouldn't exist as people; they would just be persons running around. Cooperation between nation-states is necessary to the salvation of the planet, but that is very different from the utopian idea of establishing a United Nations based upon the abolition of the nation-state.

Nations are created by people with a profound historical concept of where they have come from and where they are going. They are not just the result of schemes for the redistribution of property. In the United States today the great majority of people have no history with which they can identify themselves and in which they can believe. Everything they once believed in about the Declaration of Independence, the Constitution, the Founding Fathers, the Civil

War, has been found wanting. The Vietnam disaster is a culmination to the blows which their concept of themselves as a nation, as a great people, has been experiencing, chiefly under the impact of the black revolt.

The American people need some concept of where they have come from and where they are going as a people. This is a profound human need, one that has to be answered with something more than a concept of the world-state, of internationalism, or the abolition of the nation-state. We certainly need internationalism because weaponry has reached the point where nations can destroy each other and the entire planet, and because we are all dependent on and part of the same ecological system. Internationalism, however, does not deal with the human needs of people.

A new American unity, compounded of diversity, must be created. The United States is one of the youngest of all the nations. It has a brief historical past. (Not that having a sense of continuity from a distant past alone can solve the problems of a nation!)

What does unite Americans or what could unite Americans? We must discover a new basis for American nationhood, one that has nothing to do with who came over on the *Mayflower*. What does a Chinese who came over in 1889 or an Italian who came over in 1910 or a Pole who came over in 1929 care about the Declaration of Independence? They just came over here because it was impossible over there. They were unwilling to accept any longer the tyranny and poverty of Europe and Asia. So they fled from their homelands much as blacks fled from the South. When we ask what is the nature of man/woman, we are asking the question for this time and this country. We are asking "What is an American in the last quarter of the twentieth century?" When we ask "What is an American?" we give the dimension of nationhood to the concept of man/woman, and we therefore add a political dimension to our concept of humankind.

You can't have a great revolution if only one part of a particular nation feels itself involved in the struggle for social change. The entire people must feel that they are fighting against the past and for the future of humanity. As Marx said in *The German Ideology*, "each new class which puts itself in the place of one ruling before it, is compelled, merely in order to carry through its aim, to represent its interest as the common interest of all the members of society, put in an ideal form; it will give its ideas the form of universality and represent them as the only rational, universally valid ones."

If, as we have insisted, a revolution, a great revolution, represents a very dramatic change of direction and therefore an advance in the evolution of humanity, then we should be able to look back upon the French and the American revolutions, and see the drastic departure in the concept of human identity which took place throughout the world. If one is not able to recognize that kind of dramatic transition or profound worldwide advance in human identity, then one can say it was not a great revolution.

Why is politics an art rather than a science? Because science is not marked by that element of creativity which is essential to politics. Politics must involve leadership, and political leadership must be creative. Leadership requires a sense of responsibility, and the capacity to think on a grand scale.

For many years we thought we had the answers to how this country should be run because we were on the side of the workers, and the workers were destined to reorganize society on new foundations. We called that our politics (as opposed to other people's politics). Now we have begun to examine and to explore what principles should govern the relations between people and what human identity is in *this* day and age. Meanwhile, the country's politics has been going to rack and ruin. So we are now challenged to begin relating the principles we have been developing to the sphere of politics in a more concrete way.

Up to now we have thought that politics existed only in a clash between classes. Today we can see that what must be involved in the American revolution is a clash over values. It is not a question of redividing the cake, but of creating a new cake. There is a tremendous clash over what values should be involved in creating this new cake. This is a politics with which few people are familiar, since redistribution of property has been at the root of previous politics.

In the last ten years various liberation movements have come into being. Some of these are still concerned chiefly with the question of redistribution of the cake—how blacks or chicanos or women or young people should share in it. Others claim that their values should be the values of the entire society. But few, if any, of these groups think in terms of their commitment to the whole of society. A kind of absenteeism has developed. Liberation has come to mean separation. All that each group is concerned about is itself. Each one has a concept only of its own rights, although some claim superiority for their values above all others. They have little concern with consistency—hippies, for example, talk about ecology and throw things all over. They act as if they have added to the fundamental "Rights of Man" two other rights, the right to walk away and the right to be internally contradictory. "Do your own thing" is the mood of the liberation movements. All such groups formed on a biological basis—race, sex, age—can only degenerate unless they search for an enlarged sense of their human identity within a historical context. There is nothing intrinsically beautiful about women, blacks, or the young. These are bases on which individuals, cast adrift by a disintegrating society, can come together, and, on the basis of what they have in common, begin to explore and to develop an historical identity.

If you create a collective or a commune with the idea that you will observe ethical standards among your fellows, but to hell with everybody else, you are not being ethical. Yet this is happening all over the place. One group will steal from another because its members are from the most oppressed class in society.

Unless somebody begins to think about the principles on which these disparate groups can discover a new unity, we will not have a revolution or a new society in the United States. In their *anti*-ness today, each sees itself as better than everyone else, as having *the* key. In their separateness they can only degenerate, be they black, female, chicano, or homosexual. They get worse with time, and by their excesses and their lack of concern about the achievements of man/womankind over the ages, provoke middle America into counter-revolutionary positions.

We have to shift what unifies these groups (anti-Vietnam war, anti-racism) away from just *re*jection to *pro*jection, from just *de*nunciation to *an*nunciation. We need to develop projections that have both unity and diversity in them.

Up to now, the tendency has been for each group to view itself in the same way that Marxists have traditionally viewed the working class, as the class with the solution to all the problems of society. Blacks were only interested if you were talking about blacks; they could not see anything in the past as related to them unless it was black. Women's liberation groups have substituted sex for class or race. None of these groups seems to have thought about how all of this is to come together or converge at any point. This has been a period of the disintegration or fragmentation of the social structure. But unless the dividing lines within our society are projected on another basis than those on which each of these groups started, each group is going to become more negative, and the possibility of bringing them together on any basis is going to become harder.

All these groups talk about freedom. What do they mean by freedom?

The civil rights movement was asking for specific rights. These specific rights were what it meant by "freedom." By "Freedom now!" people meant freedom from white domination. But you can be dominated in a thousand ways. When we speak of a specific historical movement like the Uhuru movement in Africa, we are in a sense in less difficulty because Africans clearly meant self-government by "Uhuru." They had in mind an image of national independence. They talked about George Washington, Thomas Jefferson, Patrick Henry. Even in the United States, the early movement for "Freedom now" was very concrete. It was to enable blacks to move about as freely as whites. They were not talking about freedom in the elusive sense in which we are pursuing it now.

Again, using China as a contrast, the idea of freedom does not exist in Asia. Not even in Russia. In these countries the idea of a subjective individual will, separate and apart from the will of the community, from the order of the society, from the external pressures of the environment, has never existed. The historical, philosophical concept of freedom has not existed in Asia. The abstract concept of freedom could not in fact exist separate and apart from the concept of separate individuals, all with wills of their own. Precisely because this concept of separate, individual wills emerged in the West at a time when the individual had a very limited concept of the world and of historical development, it has turned out to be a concept of a very arbitrary type of freedom.

For example, if a child says "I'm free," he/she can then begin to do all kinds of capricious things because his/her freedom has no limits from within. This helps to explain the movement in the late

1960s. When the human nature that you are expressing is limited, while the concept that you are projecting is very vast, there is bound to be contradiction in your actions.

In what sense should we as human beings be free? We certainly don't think that we should be un-free. As human beings, we are free when we are confident of our relation to the world we live in and are not fearful of it. We are also free when we are confident of our relations with other men and women. Freedom comes with recognition of the dialectical inter-relationship between oneself and one's social and physical environment. There are all kinds of extensions of these inter-relationships, but no notion of freedom which frees one from inter-relationships is a valid notion. Freedom is not a *thing* that you get or you gain or you accomplish or you buy. Freedom is essentially a relationship. There is no such *thing* as freedom.

However, what the Western individual usually means by freedom is not a particular political movement—*from* some particular relationship *to* another relationship. Few people talk about freedom in terms of the freedom to move and to act with people in a certain relationship. They usually talk about freedom as being able to do what they please—the freedom of the individual. They are dissociating the individual from any necessity, from any relatedness, because to the Western individual any relatedness is a kind of restriction. That sense of individual freedom, precisely because it was once such an advanced idea and had so much scope for expression in the United States, has haunted us all. The liberation groups are permeated by it because they are all heirs to this tradition. Today we must supplant this concept of abstract freedom with another concept of freedom that is based upon a relation to nature, to other people in society and in the world, to the past and to the future; one based on inter-relationships which are now necessarily a part of our reality, rather than on the illusion of isolated, internal freedom.

In the United States there was more of an objective basis for individual freedom than anywhere else in the world. Hence the concept of individual freedom became more entrenched here. All the liberation groups—blacks first, women and others later—are still prisoners of this concept. They see themselves as part of a sphere of freedom which does not, in fact, exist. Because Americans have lived in a land where it was feasible to think about freedom in this way, they have come to think of themselves as *the defenders of freedom throughout the world—a "chosen people."* What is most objectionable in U.S. foreign policy is derived from the notion that *we* know what freedom is and nobody else does. Therefore *we* are going to give some of it to the world. Actually you can be against U.S. policy in Vietnam and still be just as destructive at home, because you still haven't grappled with and uprooted this illusion of individual freedom.

Politics, freedom, neither of these has ever been seen as a relationship. Each has been seen as a *thing*. There are relationships which permit freedom and relationships which don't permit freedom. Freedom is not a concept which one is free to define for oneself. It is utterly impossible for us to transcend nature because we are a part of nature. If there is no such *thing* as freedom, then we can only talk about freedom *from* what, *for* what, *to* what.

Should people be free at all times to say just what they feel? There are a lot of illusions about that. The idea of the unlimited right to speak—proceeding from the preciousness of this internal sense of freedom—has to be abandoned. All of us are under enormous pressure as revolutionists to defend the freedom of people. When do you *not* defend a person? Where do you draw the line? Do you really believe in public lewdness on the stage? What is appropriate? In the name of an abstraction like freedom, we are destroying other values and relationships of incalculable importance.

All the "free" movements which have developed in the last three or four years are manifestations of this concept of freedom. All of them imply that human beings don't have to make choices. They therefore represent a very narrow, backward view of man/woman.

Our new notion of freedom must be a *social* one. The old notion of freedom has become ridiculous. We see it manifested in the liberation movements, where any restriction is considered a violation of one's freedom. "What right do you have to tell me what not to do?" Am I free to pick up a gun and shoot somebody else? On what basis does one person have a right to kill someone else? What is the difference between rights and freedoms? People say, "I have the right to bear arms, and if you don't allow me to bear arms, you are infringing on my freedom."

Modern man/woman has lost that sense of harmony with nature that the ancients talked about—the sense that nature was here long before human beings and that we are a product of nature and of natural processes. The average man/woman hasn't the faintest notion of that relationship, nor the slightest feeling of humility or wonderment. When he/she asks, "Shall I cut down all the trees because my son needs a new house?" he/she doesn't wonder how long it takes to grow a tree. This is where the notion of harmony with nature enters. You can cut down a tree but you can't make one. You can plant one, but it would take a hundred years before the tree would be worth cutting down.

Just as Americans have an idea of politics and freedom based on the historical past of this country, so we have a unique idea of equality. And just as our ideas about politics and freedom have to be re-examined, so do our ideas about equality.

In many respects the idea of equality should be taken for granted. Men, women, and children are all equal in the sense that they need air to breathe, food to eat, health care. But these are only generalities. Obviously everybody should be equal in many spheres of human life where there are terrible inequalities today. But the idea that everybody is equal is in another respect ridiculous. Every person is a unique individual coming out of a particular background and unique experiences. Some are men, some women; some are musicians, some are craftspersons. Some have lived in the country before coming to the city; others have lived in the city all their lives. Some have had more advantages than others. Many have been exposed to so many things and ideas that they need to live for a period with much less in order to develop their human capacities to create, to reflect, and to select. Some seek responsibility; others evade it. Some think before they act, others just react. There is a wide range of individuals in our society, as in any society, at all levels of development. How do we grasp both ends to pull forth the middle unless we admit, to begin with, that there are actual differences, actual unevenness among people, actual ends and middles, making it possible for some people to create and project the very advanced idea of grasping both ends to pull forth the middle so that the whole society can advance more evenly and thus counter all tendencies to hierarchical and pyramidal structures?

If we insist that everybody is equal already, then we destroy the possibility of development. If everybody is already equal, then all motion stops. That is why those who insist that everybody is equal also believe in a kind of spontaneity as the way that all big changes take place. As with a school of fish, all change direction at one time, presumably because of instinct.

Without the dialectical idea of development accelerated by taking advantage of the contradictions or tensions inherent in actual unevennesses and differences among people, it is impossible to create a concept of leadership based upon a solid philosophical foundation. The idea of human beings all moving simultaneously like a school of fish with no ideas in their heads and without struggling among themselves over these ideas, actually provides the basis for a totalitarian dictator to manipulate people as masses, turning elections into plebiscites which deliver mandates to the leader.

Until now it has been difficult for Americans to recognize how the idea of equality can end up in the reality of mass-man/woman and dictatorship, because the idea of equality was originally won in struggle against rigid feudal inequalities. It was a revolutionary idea at the time. When the Puritans fought for religious equality, they fought for everybody to be able to talk to God without the intervention of priests and bishops. When the idea of political equality was created after the American Revolution, it was conceived as a way in which everyone would have an equal voice in shaping the course of the new nation. First, every white man, then, after many struggles, every white woman, and finally after many more struggles, everyone, regardless of race or sex, could go to the polls. But while we were fighting for the right for everybody to go to the polls equally, the actual unequal development of the society and a new historical reality were being shaped by those who had the most economic power. Eventually these aligned themselves with the military apparatus, as the nation became increasingly entangled in world conflicts, culminating in today's military-industrial complex. So now our political equality at the polls only makes us all equal in political helplessness.

We can only deal with these questions when we understand that ideas themselves are not permanent. Ideas which were once solutions become barriers to advance at another stage of development. There is no such thing as "the truth."

To clarify the question of "the truth," we must first make a distinction between three categories which are usually linked

together as "truth." They are scientific truth, factual truth, and the
ideas called "truths" which are actually convictions held by people
as to what it means to be human.

First, it is clear that science has discovered many valuable facts
about physical realities. Yet someday, someone is going to discover
that something even in this sphere (for example, that the speed of
light by which everything is measured) is, in an Einsteinian sense,
relative, and then all scientific facts will have to be re-evaluated.

Next there is the category which Hannah Arendt has called
"factual truth" in her important essay "Truth and Politics." Factual
truth involves statements about events and circumstances which
have occurred or are occurring to human beings. The opposite of
factual truth is not error or illusion or opinion, but the falsehood or
lie, either of commission or omission, i.e., the deliberate attempt to
deceive. Lying even in trivial matters reveals the arrogant belief that
facts are deniable or can be made "inoperative." Hence the
inevitable degeneration of any individual, nation, or organization
which has a careless attitude to factual truth.

Finally, there is the category of truths which has to do with the
nature of man/woman. Is Man the son of God? This is the sort of
thing people argue over. In this sphere there are no absolutes. Yet for
hundreds of years, most people, and not only religious people, have
believed in "the truth."

The concept that all truths which deal with human identity are
relative and not absolute is indispensable to the revolutionist. In
order to make a revolution, you have to discard the notion that
anything one has previously regarded as truth about human beings is
necessarily true. Revolution is an effort to discover or to create truth,
not to *prove* what is true. It is hard to persuade most radicals of this.
You question their personalities if you question what they live by.
Being a revolutionist for them is living by certain truths, rather than
discovering or creating new truths. The New Left—as distinguished
from the Old Left—started out by trying to discover rather than
prove. But they were empirical and pragmatic in the extreme. The
Old Left had a body of ideas which the masses of people are
supposed to prove for them. So they are happy, gratified, satisfied
whenever the masses do something to prove what they already
believe. All this has nothing to do with being a revolutionist.

Revolutionists do not believe in absolute truth but they do have strong convictions, thoughts which move them. How can you have strong convictions which possess and move you, and yet develop them in relation to struggle, to practice, and to developing reality? The highest level of human creativity is the constant developing and advancing of your vision. But this is a dialectical process, involving a creative relation with reality, which is very different from syllogistic thinking. Syllogistic thinking is a way of proving a statement rather than a way of advancing a vision (e.g., "All men are mortal, Socrates is a man; therefore Socrates is mortal" is a syllogism).

Vision is more than thought. Vision adds to the rational process of thought all the instincts, intuitions, and other untapped qualities in people. That is why vision can't be analyzed in the way that thought can be.

In the attempt to grasp what vision is, we approach the realization that a human being is infinitely more complicated than we have been ready to recognize. The more complicated human beings are, the harder it is to organize, to dominate, to use them. What has distinguished great creative individuals from all others is that they have been willing to accept the challenge of the complicated nature of a human being. Maybe that is why there have been only about two thousand great individuals in five thousand years. Some people are defeated by this complexity; some are illuminated by it; some are challenged by it. This complexity tells us that the evolution of humankind is still going on and will continue to go on. The nature of man/woman, our human identity, is still being discovered, still being created.

So when we are asked "What is truth?" we must make clear that there is no such *thing* as truth. There are different kinds of truth. There are truths which are really scientific facts, used for technical purposes. There is factual truth, or truth-telling as opposed to lying. And then there are truths which are really convictions, having to do with human beings, with change, with development, with values. Convictions are relative, not absolute.

That they are relative means that they are extremely important. It is hard for people to accept this because in the Western intellectual tradition, absolute truth has come down to us as a positive goal to be striven toward, while relative truths have come down as "merely relative," and therefore, by implication, mean, material, negative. This started with Plato, whose anti-mass bias was clear. It was extended by Christianity (to save the souls of the meek and humble). Then science gave it new life. Therefore, it is hard to get people to understand that truths are constantly being created, and that this creativity is in fact the greatest achievement of humanity. We tend to speak of ideas as "only relative" or "merely relative" implying that what is relative doesn't matter too much because it is not fixed, as if only fixed truths were important.

A constant evolution takes place in our concepts, in truths. God was a concept created by human beings. The first gods that men and women created were closer to nature because at the time people lived closer to nature. As we progressively departed from nature, beginning to master nature for the first time within the last few hundred years, we created other, more complicated gods. As we were enhanced in one direction, we were dulled and diminished in another. This is the contradiction, the duality in man/woman. When we crossed "the threshold of reflection," in Chardin's phrase, we began to discover things about our own developing nature. We may think that we have discovered the final truth about the nature of human beings, and therefore we know who and what man/woman is. But we don't. The nature of a human being, present as well as future, is infinitely more complicated than we have permitted ourselves to recognize or to express.

A revolution is to create new truths about human beings and society. There is no proof really that the road you are taking is the "true" one. You have to make it true. Revolution creates new bases of tensions, new unities which will split again into new dualities.

Most people think of the U.S. Constitution as a sacred document, valid for all time. Little do they realize that a constitution is usually arrived at out of a crisis situation.

The U.S. Constitution was no exception to this rule. It was conceived and adopted under a specific set of conditions which had been created by a struggle against another very specific set of conditions (British colonial domination). The writers of the Constitution could not possibly have written a document for all time. That is why, when people today talk about defending the Constitution, in a period of such great social upheaval and rapid technological change, what they are saying is that they are defending the past, when the past itself bears no relation to the new contradictions that have developed, except insofar as it has covered up contradictions and encouraged them to fester. Those who defend the Constitution may be defending the very valid and important principle that citizens of any nation, like members of any organization, must live by some set of standards and procedures in their relations with one another. But insofar as they are defending a constitution which was adopted in a very different time, they are fighting a defensive struggle and cannot possibly win. A constitution adopted so long ago is in conflict with the present reality, and therefore cannot possibly lead us to the new set of relations which is now necessary, and which could not possibly have been within the vision of those who wrote it.

In attempting to use the U.S. Constitution to resolve our contemporary contradictions, Constitutional experts have trapped themselves in the same dogmatism as the Marxists who live by *Capital* and try to make Marx's analysis of nineteenth-century European capitalism fit today's America. Before their very eyes, not only has capitalism developed and created new contradictions for itself, but even socialist nations have developed new contradictions which Marx could not possibly have anticipated.

In both cases, it is not that Marx or the Constitution is wrong. It is that society has changed. At the center of Einstein's theory is the concept of change and relativity, but even Einstein's theory will someday become outmoded. Nothing remains the same forever. All things in our world are relative, because our world has been created by human beings and human beings are constantly creating anew as they become new people. Man/woman breaks from the past; yet it is the same man/woman who makes the break and maintains continuity with those who have come before. Everything around and surrounding us is in motion, the earth, the planets, the sun, the stars, the moon. It is within this universe of movement that we exist. That is why Ansel Adams and Nancy Newhall say, in *The American Earth* (San Francisco: Sierra Club, 1960), "Step ye very lightly on this earth, it is the mother of Man."

We who are concerned about the advancement of humankind must understand that in the dialectical process of development, opposite forces can be brought together in unity. But then a new set of opposites emerges within the new unity, setting into motion a new struggle between opposing forces and thus the basis for further advancement.

It is the contradiction between the deeply entrenched tendencies to rapid economic development regardless of human cost and the now urgent human need for rapid political development which is the root reason for a revolution inside the United States.

Humankind is still in its infancy, and the real potential of humanity for creativity in every sphere—ethical, esthetic, political—has not been tapped. In the past Americans have exercised their ingenuity chiefly in making things to satisfy their material needs. Now we have the opportunity to exercise it in all the other spheres in which human beings obviously have the capacity to create. In the past men and women have only created gods out of their hopes and fears. Now we have the opportunity to create humanity—out of all that we have learned about ourselves and the world in which we live.

In terms of political philosophy and institutions, we should rejoice that the United States is still a nation in its infancy. It took the European peoples nearly ten centuries, from the Middle Ages to the Renaissance, to forge their nations. Not until 221 B.C., a full thousand years after the historical period of the Chinese begins, were all the states of China unified under a single emperor. Our nation is only now approaching its two hundredth birthday. What kind of Constitution should we write for a new America—under the very different conditions of the late twentieth century, knowing the things we know and which nobody could have known two hundred years ago? At some point we all have to grow up and assume responsibility. To blame the Founding Fathers for what they did is as much a cop-out as continuing to bow down before a Constitution written in a completely different world.

10
CORRECTING MISTAKEN IDEAS ABOUT WAR, WORK, WELFARE, WOMEN

Have there ever before been so many people saying, "We are in the struggle," without any common notion of what the struggle is for? Or with so many disjointed and/or sloganized notions of what the struggle is for? The Crusaders knew they were out to make everyone a Christian. Today people in the movement have no unifying idea of what kind of "whole new person" will be created in the process of revolution. And, yet, precisely because in the United States there is such a deep cult of the individual and people have so many different points of reference, we need a unifying view of what kind of more human human being will be created in the course of revolutionary struggles.

In the Russian Revolution it was not so necessary for people to have a concept of the nature of man/woman—i.e., of what humankind has done down through the ages. In the past, acting out of material necessity and in keeping with standards and traditions still remaining from the past, people could respond almost automatically and in so doing advance society. They were pursuing a course of history whose direction was to some degree already set by the pursuit of economic necessities, and which they were in a sense only improving.

In the past we never asked workers whether they were *for* a revolution. The very fact that they rebelled against present conditions, that they thought of themselves as "us" against "them," was enough for us to be sure that they were in favor of the new society. It was not until the United States had experienced an extended period of continuing rebellion, as it has over the last ten years (to the point that rebellious masses now feel that because of the despicable character of present society, they have the right to do anything) that we could arrive at a really serious evaluation of the difference between rebellion and revolution.

Unless we are willing to make this evaluation now, we shall only wind up making excuses, rationalizing why we didn't succeed— which is what radicals generally do. What we need to re-examine is our major premise, which has been that "the masses are ready," and all we had to do was get to them and stir them into motion, whereupon their momentum would bring out the instinctive and elemental drive to reconstruct society which was already within them. Hence the typically radical emphasis on "militancy" as the measure of how revolutionary an individual or the masses are.

Blacks took this assumption even further, particularly after the rebellions of the late 1960s. They assumed that all blacks were really in favor of revolution, or that all blacks were beautiful, which is another way of saying that all blacks are the same. "All blacks are oppressed; therefore all blacks are beautiful." Yet, precisely at the point of greatest apparent unity among blacks, of greatest "black identity," of greatest assumption of the sameness of blacks or of the possibility of uniting all blacks—i.e., in the wake of the rebellions— all the differences that are within blacks began to come out.

It is impossible to overemphasize the significance of differences. For example, if you ask one black, "How would you like to live?" he might say, "I would like to live like Adam Clayton Powell, with a mistress and a house in the Bahamas and a guaranteed salary from Congress." Another guy might answer, "I want a Cadillac and a million dollars in the bank, and I am ready to push dope to get them." Another, "I'd like to live like Martin Luther King." And still another might reply, "I want to live like Cabral, because he was a revolutionist and Martin Luther King was just a Christian liberal."

Each is describing the difference which resides within him; also, of course, the differences inculcated by his father and mother, those instilled in him by the schools, by whom he met or didn't meet, etc. But essentially the differing answers to these questions spring from the essential nature of the individual. Richard Wright was Richard Wright, and the only one of all his brothers and sisters who emerged from oppression; the rest were submerged by it. There was a quality in Richard Wright which said, "I am not going to be oppressed; I am not going to be shaped by my conditions." Revolutionary thinkers, revolutionary theorists, revolutionary leaders or revolutionary individuals who can give leadership are people who are different in this sense. We can't begin to move until it is clear that this is where we are moving from.

What is the despicable character of our society today? In the 1930s you could start out with pure economics. Even as late as 1969, it was possible to believe that you could make a radical change in the social, economic and political fiber of this country within the economic framework. Today you would have to start by talking about the "quality of life." Everything is breaking down. Why? People find it easy to blame the moon program or the war in Vietnam. We are against both; but we also are convinced that not going to the moon or ending the war will *not* stop the breakdown— as long as there has been no serious thought given to alternatives. That is why the question, "Whom would you like to live like?" is such a revealing one. Or "Who do you think is moral?" We have to reveal people to themselves—and also to discover the people who are different, who are not determined by their conditions, who are resolved not to be shaped by them.

We can say that certain things are not worrying the American people as a whole. For example, "inequality" bothers specific groups but not the American people as a whole; and it bothers specific groups chiefly because they "want in." Despite its currency, "quality of life" is too general, too depersonalized a term to describe what is bothering people. It is the kind of word used mostly by professional intellectuals in writing or talking about the prevailing disintegration. On the other hand, the average person experiences this disintegration, this breakdown, this deterioration, in more basic human terms.

People feel that this "falling apart" syndrome is wrong; that it is contrary to the very nature of society; that any given society should be "a coming together" rather than "a falling apart." They feel that the whole situation is beyond human control; that nobody is controlling anything; and that it is wrong for things to be going in all directions with nobody at the helm. If you keep probing people, you find that what bothers them most is the purposelessness, the meaninglessness of their existence. "Why am I doing what I am doing? Why does anybody do anything?" Today the only explanation people can offer you or themselves for what they do is "Why not?" If we begin to realize that this is what is really bothering people, we may be able to arrive at a fundamental conception of what people need and the absolutely crucial role which the search for meaning plays in human life.

What differences matter to us? The first difference is whether a person is or is not making a value judgment of a particular society and of how people are related to one another in that society.

If, in regard to the prevailing disintegration, we were to try to distinguish between what those people (who are different in the way that matters to us) regard as negative and what they are beginning to regard as positive, what they are against as contrasted with what they are for, what they feel is wrong, as contrasted with what they feel would be right, we could say that "determinism" represents the negative. There is a growing feeling that being shaped, being determined, is negative; while shaping, determining, choosing, is positive: that the breaking down of society into classifications and categories represents a negative, while some reintegration, some new holism, represents a positive; that being "faceless masses" or regarding everybody as being the same, represents a negative, while recognizing differences represents a positive.

We have to look at the United States today in fundamental terms such as these—not just in terms of economics, e.g., high prices. In this connection, it is not so much the actual high level of prices which bothers people so much. It is rather that there seems to be no end to the rising of prices. The whole thing seems so senseless. In the United States prices never go down, no matter how much is produced or how much more quickly more is produced. It is the irrationality this represents which is so destructive, since unit costs should go down as more is produced more efficiently. What is so disconcerting is the apparent impenetrability, the meaninglessness, the senselessness of the whole situation. We live in a world in which what is happening seems to be brought about by nameless shadows. We are trying to discover something new about humankind. And until we begin to learn more about this, it is impossible to have programs—because any programs would just be based upon what we have already determined, i.e., on the past. The past paralyzes all of us. A vision is necessary if we are to escape paralysis.

It is impossible to sit down and work out a blueprint of what man/woman wants, or to find the answer by asking people what they want. We have to look at what human aspirations have been in the past and what new contradictions have grown out of the satisfaction of those aspirations. Every aspect of the social world has been created by man/woman. The system didn't make itself. Human beings made it, and while it is true that those with power have the most power to direct the system, it is also true that if most people didn't go along with or participate in the system, it could not continue. Some of the things that human beings have created have wound up around their necks. This has happened many times before. And things will begin to get better only when people begin to realize that what we thought was better is not better, and something has to be done about that.

Seventy-five years of technological revolution have created a completely new situation. The industrial revolution, two hundred to three hundred years ago, did one thing; it completely shattered the world of its time, because prior to that time things had been practically the same for thousands of years. Now all of a sudden, the technological revolution has burst upon us and has done something else. It has given us the means of creating material values without limit. It permits us to pollute our planet. But it also compels us, for the first time in history, to wonder where we want to go. Up to now, people have known where they wanted to go. But where do we want to go now? All of a sudden, we can have Cadillacs *and* food. What the technological revolution does is ask us to ask ourselves some questions which in the past were asked only by very unusual individuals. Now all of a sudden, man/woman in general is being asked, "Where do you want to go now?" Who is going to help man/woman in general to know anything about this? That is why the United States is such an important place. We can have everything we want—then discover that that isn't what we want. What *do* we want?

We are at a turning point in history. We are not just trying to deal with topical issues, topical grievances, such as corruption in the New York City Police Department. The problems of the new epoch are entirely different. They are not just a continuation of the problems of the old epoch: food, survival, a roof over one's head, etc. Obviously we are talking about the United States, not about India, although the solutions we come to here are going to affect the rest of the world.

One of the important things that a revolutionist is going to have to do in the next period is to confront the attitudes that unions represent. Unions, in the most fundamental sense, represent the attitude of "Let's get ours," regardless of what happens to anybody else. Unions also represent the attitude of "Don't work, because by working you increase profits," without considering what the process of work, the nature of work, means to human rationality. What the unions are doing also gives the impression, creates the attitude, that somebody else, the system, can do things for you. The radicals themselves, in criticizing the union bureaucracy, reinforce this attitude. They give the impression that somebody else besides you, the protester, can be held responsible for important decisions.

In all these fundamental ways, affecting the very essence of people's sense of themselves in their daily lives, and hence the possibilities for a new beginning, unions represent all the worst attitudes. It is very difficult to accept, when so many struggles have gone into their organization, that unions today are the culmination of reformism, and that we have reached the point in history (in the United States) where the more you reform, the worse things get. It has never been so before. In the past, it was inconceivable that struggles for higher wages could act to destroy human rationality. Such struggles were progressive in the past in the sense that the changes they engendered advanced everybody in society. But look at the constitutions of most of the unions, particularly the AFL unions. They read like a combination of Karl Marx and the Declaration of Independence. The concepts behind them all antedate the techno-logical revolution.

This is the kind of thing we have to recognize and think about. Unions are not the only examples of this kind of destruction of human rationality, but they are an important example. We are not talking about attacking unions; we are talking about understanding, internalizing, recognizing that we are at the stage in the United

States today where the changes which have to be undertaken are not going to be, cannot be, undertaken by reformists or by people who are thinking about how to "get ours." They can only be undertaken by people who know what they want to change.

The technological revolution is so all-embracing, the powers which are now open to humankind are so great, that we suddenly have to discover what we want to do with these powers. Humankind has never been asked that question before in this way, imperiously. What does humankind want to do with these powers? Are we going to have morality, or are we just going to have greed? The answers which Marx gave to the questions of his epoch are no longer true, no longer adequate to the questions we are being asked in this epoch.

We are not trying to deny Marx, but there is no question that Marxism is limited by the historical determinism which has become identified with Marxist thinking. Most Marxists have believed that if you could only sneak up on the masses and prod them into taking action over their grievances, then, as a result of their objective situation in society and in the productive process, they would keep on acting in such a way as to create a socialist society.

Everything that has happened in the last century has demonstrated that this is not true. We have to abandon the whole concept of the future sneaking up on the masses once they are in motion. We have to repudiate the notion that the ideas or the consciousness of the masses do not matter; that they don't need advanced ideas; that their physical energies and their objective situation in production are all that matter; that the self-interest of workers (or of any social group *per se*) objectively and automatically coincides with the advancement of the human race.

On the contrary, we must not only develop advanced ideas but we must project them, advocate them to the masses, for them to grapple with, grasp, and then turn into a material force to change themselves, society and the world. That is the only way to revolutionary change in the modern world.

Essentially the people who rely upon Marx for theoretical and political guidance are still trying to communicate on the basis of a vision from the past, when in fact the task of the revolutionist is always to communicate on the basis of a vision of the future, a vision which nobody has yet projected. Otherwise we are limited by the past. That is why philosophy becomes so important in periods of great historical transition. One's attitude to specific issues comes out of one's philosophy. For example, welfare is one of the most demoralizing, destructive institutions in this country today. Welfare came out of the struggles for reform, but now it is a permanent fixture which is destroying human beings. We have reached the point where all the reformer can think about is more welfare.

First, we have to recognize that the concept of society's responsibility for taking care of people is an extraordinarily recent phenomenon. Before this era poor people went to the poorhouse or the workhouse. Now suddenly, we are facing the fact that what we have created—because we have come to care more about people—stinks, even though what we have created is a great advance over what existed in the past. How can we expect that in only thirty years people could arrive at the notion that welfare stinks unless we are able to project a notion of what would be better? What would be better than welfare? We must be prepared to deal with this question, recognizing clearly that most folks on welfare are not at this point ready to deal with it themselves, just as most workers are not ready at this point to deal with the question of unions, nor most teachers with the question of education.

This is where the question of differences between people comes in. Because of the differences within people (for all kinds of reasons), there are only a few who are ready to grapple with these questions now. But such differences between people and within people do exist, otherwise society would be made up only of faceless masses. When people put forward their ideas to others, then personal differences are brought out. Controversies begin around positions that matter. Thus, through differences within people, movement is engendered among other people.°

° An example of this kind of position-taking is the pamphlet, *Crime Among Our People*, in which, after describing how stealing and killing have become the way of life in black neighborhoods, and analyzing how this situation emerged out of the failure of the Black Power movement to pose power in terms of responsibility to govern, the people themselves are called upon to change their way of life by valuing people more than things, pledging not to buy "hot goods," holding teach-ins in schools and churches, criticizing any section of the black movement which attempts to commercialize blackness or looks benignly on anyone of any race who steals, mugs, vandalizes, pimps, or rapes, or who pushes drugs or sells stolen goods in any community. Available from Advocators, P.O. Box 07249, Detroit, Mich. 48207, at 10¢ a copy.

We are not talking about objecting to welfare or objecting to unions. We are talking about how one frees oneself from being so wound up with and imprisoned in the past that one can't think about the future, about a new way to live, a new way to care.

What do we tell a person who is on welfare? We can't just say, "Make a revolution, and you won't need welfare." That is just an evasion. We have reforms today that Marx couldn't possibly have envisaged, because they didn't exist in his day any more than television or satellites or trips to the moon existed in his day. We have no doubt whatsoever that Marx would have come to terms with such changes, and made use of them in his analysis of society, if he were alive today. Our job is to try to do what he might have done. The Marxists have failed because they have not been ready to recognize the tremendous changes that have taken place since Marx.

We cannot repeat too often that we have a responsibility to discover and to project new concepts of man/woman that will be appropriate for this period, this specific stage of human development. Seventy-five years of technological revolution have made obsolete some fundamental concepts by which humanity has lived in the past. The technological revolution has completely changed the historical situation, just as the Renaissance destroyed the Middle Ages. The technological revolution is the contemporary equivalent of the Renaissance.

At this historical juncture, as at every great historical juncture, human beings have to bring about a great change in their concept of necessity, i.e., in their assessment of their power as human beings to shape their destiny. At the beginning of the Industrial Revolution, men and women were able to abandon the prevailing concept of religious determinism—that human destiny was determined by God. They were able to recognize that they had created the gods. What we have to get rid of now are the concepts of economic determinism and historical determinism. In other words, we have to stop thinking about human beings as completely shaped, completely determined by their circumstances, by external causes. We must begin to think and to project to others the idea that "we can change the way it is" because, in fact, our circumstances were made by human beings. Just as through technology, man/woman has practically remade the world, so man/woman can remake him/herself. The system is a product of human beings, just as technology is a product of human beings, just as the gods were and the church was. What humankind is going to become, what society is going to become, is going to be determined by us as human beings. We can decide how we are going to be and how society is going to be, but we can't do this until we stop seeing ourselves in the role of creatures and begin to see ourselves in the role of creators, stop seeing ourselves in the role of victims and recognize ourselves as truly self-determining.

It is impossible to build a new revolutionary movement until we have gotten rid of the concepts of economic and historical determinism, as previous revolutions in the West got rid of religious determinism. Man/woman can discover how to make a gun that can shoot thirty miles, but we haven't discovered yet what a human being can become, what we can make of ourselves, because we haven't even asked ourselves the question. So people just think of themselves as victims, and the more oppressed they have been by the system, the more they regard themselves as victims and act like victims.

Once it is clear why we must discover completely new ways to think about ourselves as human beings, then we can become more specific about the fundamental human activities which need re-thinking. Take, for example, the question of work. For the last two hundred years Western man/woman has thought of work chiefly as labor, i.e., as a "job" which you did for somebody else in exchange for wages so that you could live. Work has been thought of in terms of economics, material necessity, material scarcity.

How do we begin re-thinking the nature of work in the wake of the technological revolution, in the era of material abundance? Why does man/woman work? What human value, as distinguished from market- or exchange-value, does work have? Is there a human necessity for work as distinct from a material necessity? Is work necessary, not just to contribute to the totality of goods and services, but to express creativity, to develop human rationality? Is there an ethics of work, as distinguished from the capitalist work ethic?

Marx opened up this contradiction within the work process at the very beginning of *Capital* when he drew a sharp distinction between use-value and exchange-value, between concrete labor and abstract labor. The concept of the human nature of work is even clearer in his *Economic and Philosophical Manuscripts*. As Hannah Arendt points out in *The Human Condition* (New York: Anchor, 1958), "Every European language has two etymologically distinct words for what we have come to think of as the same activity, and retains them in the face of their persistent synonymous usage." Thus, the Germans distinguish between *werken* and *arbeiten:* the French between *ouvrer* and *travailler.* In each case, one word suggests a form of human creativity, while the other suggests pain and travail.

It is only from such a fundamental rediscovery of the human nature of human activities that we can deal with immediate issues like welfare, relations between men and women, war. Until we have made the struggle to re-think our human identity and have arrived at some clarity in regard to it, we cannot bring clarity to others.

At this stage the American revolution consists of discovering what American man/woman wants, now that he/she can have the material things. Only then can we tackle the question of how to achieve it. Our job now is to discover what it is that we want beyond the material. What do we want in our relations with ourselves? How do we conceive our human dignity? What do we want in our relations with each other? It is something beyond the material, but what is it? Now that we can have the material, and know that it isn't enough, what is it that we want? This question is what bothers Americans most; even race relations are an aspect of it. How does American man/woman want to live tomorrow? It doesn't have to have anything to do with how we lived yesterday.

For the first time in history men and women have the privilege of deciding how they want to live. What form should our satisfactions take now? In the past our satisfactions would have taken material form: bigger houses or "a staircase going nowhere just for show," as Tevye says in *Fiddler on the Roof,* more food, more clothes. Now man/woman is wondering, "What are really my satisfactions?" Some people are just trying to get the question into focus; they haven't even begun to search for answers.

The most important thing to do at this point is to project the idea that man/woman can continue creating, that we are still evolving, still in the process of becoming. One of the reasons why the radicals have failed so abysmally is that they think of revolution as a struggle to reach an end, as a closed system rather than as a new beginning. They have not been able to project notions of and for tomorrow.

Tomorrow's notions depend on our recognizing that what we have been trying to achieve is no longer right, that we have to aim for something new, and that the process of becoming will never end.

Determinism is the negation of revolutionism. "My life has been pre-determined. I can't do anything." If somebody says he/she can't do anything, he/she isn't going to do anything. To do anything, you have to believe that man/woman *can* do things.

Obviously we are not asking blacks to believe that they created the white man who brought them into slavery, because they didn't do anything of the kind. But now that they are here, blacks have to be able to shatter the notion that "the man" controls everything that the black man can think or do about revolution. As long as blacks think in that way, they will never be anything but protesters. Our job as revolutionists is to persuade every man/woman: "*You* are the master; nobody else—not the capitalist, not the boss, not the white man. Man is not a victim except as he sees himself as a victim." Only then can people say, "Yes, the problems are enormous; they are formidable, but we can solve them. We can change the way it is." Because if people don't think that they can, they are not going to try. And all we are going to get are sporadic rebellions or bomb-throwing.

We believe that human beings need to live more humanly and that the progressive evolution of humankind has been, in fact, the result of the continuing struggle to put human beings first. But what does it mean to put human beings first? The New Left has been saying this for the last ten years, so that it has become a cliché. By itself, the formulation doesn't sufficiently enlarge our concept of what it means to be human.

What *is* a human being? Is it just any person who didn't drop dead at birth? Some people are more human than other people. Our job is to create within human beings the sense of what it is to be a human being, to help man/woman understand what a human being not only is but has been. A human being is someone who expresses human capacities, creative human powers, and is always striving to express them.

What is a human being? How do we distinguish the human being that we are talking about from the human being the anthropologist or zoologist is talking about, i.e., someone who is just different from an ape? Most people consider evolution to be the biological process by which man/woman over a period of millions of years became a two-legged upright creature from a one-celled animal living deep in the oceans. But we must be able to see the evolutionary process of humankind in a very different sense. Evolution for us today as revolutionists is the continuing struggle of man/woman to transform him/herself into a more human being. (This is one of the difficulties with finding the proper substitute for the words "man" and "mankind." These words have been used traditionally to express a historical creation that goes beyond the zoological, i.e., self-creation, or creation by conscious individuals. This sense of historical creation must be retained in the word we use while at the same time making clear the role that women have played in this process of historical creation.)

There is no point in asking people if they think human beings are more important than things. They are going to say "Yes, of course," but the dialogue will not have enlarged our concept of human identity at all. We must go through a tremendous struggle before we can reach new truths, new convictions about our human identity, and from these truths, these convictions, develop a new vision of what we are striving for as revolutionists. For example, the slogan, "To each according to his needs, from each according to his abilities," may have been a challenge a hundred years ago. Today it is an abstraction because it does not encompass the tremendous creative potential of man/woman which we have to call on today. It projects too limited a view of humankind; therefore it cannot summon up deep conviction.

Which "human being" is abstract, and which is concrete? Most people will say, "I am a human being" or "I am"—meaning "I am living and breathing, eating and sleeping, etc., therefore I am human." But this is really an abstract concept of a human being, a thin, superficial concept, in the sense that it reduces the idea of humanness to its lowest common denominator. People who define a human being in this way haven't given any thought to what it really means to be human. In the course of the last fifty thousand years, we have been going through the process of enlarging our human identity. The concrete result of this historical process is the continuation of that creative struggle to discover what a human being is.

What do Americans really want today? The picture of people

half-satisfied and half-unsatisfied gives a clue. One has the sense of something wrong but can't define it because it is unconscious. It takes the form of depression, a sense of vacuity, of vague purposelessness even when you know what you are planning to do, relations with others that are at once flabby and tense, irritability, self-questioning. "Why am I so tense? Is everybody so irritable?" The answers to these questions, most of them unconscious, have to go into the changing of the society. The unconscious isn't the unknown. It is something which is within man/woman, which is working, and which is tremendously important. Imagination and vision are explosions of the unconscious. Man/woman has the unconscious within him/her. Therefore it becomes our job to persuade men and women that they are fifty times grander than they think they are. They don't really know who they are. They haven't taken the time to envisage, to imagine who they are.

We can't make a Chinese Revolution or a Cuban Revolution in the United States. *We* are going to make a completely new revolution, the revolution of tomorrow, the revolution of an advanced industrial country. The only way we can do it is to shatter yesterday's generalizations about revolution. We have to create completely new aspects of revolution.

The technological revolution of the last seventy-five years poses three areas of problems that have to be surmounted and can only be surmounted by creating something new:

First, there is the technology of production. Automation and cybernation pose totally new problems of work.

Second, there is military technology. This poses the possibility of the end of the nation-state and the end of war. They just don't make sense anymore because they have become so dangerous, as Kathleen Gough pointed out ten years ago in *The Decline of the State and the Coming of World Society* (Detroit: Correspondence Publishing, 1962).

Third, there is the technology of reproduction, of maternity and of child care. This poses a whole new set of challenges that underlie the women's movement. The pill, the fact that we are getting close to over-population and can't go on having so many children, the fact that children live longer because they are no longer carried off by childhood diseases, the fact that abortion is simple and safe—all this means that unless women find a new role for themselves, they will stagnate. This challenges us to change the old relationship between men and women, and poses the possibility of the simultaneous development of men and women. These are *not* "women's" questions, any more than the question of work is a question only of the working class.

Thus, the technological revolution has created critical questions in three spheres: work, the state, the family; economics, politics and social relations. Up to now we have tended to think of these as distinct categories, with economics as foundation and everything else as superstructure. Now we can see how they are inter-related, and we can think about all of them more concretely, in relation to people's daily lives and their search for human identity.

We face all three questions at once. They pose the possibility of a new advance in the evolution of humankind, the possibility of both men and women contributing equally to that evolution as they have not been able to do for the last five thousand years since the rise of the state.

Einstein said that when man split the atom, he changed everything but the human mind. It isn't easy to grasp the essence of that quotation. People usually think that it took an expansion of the human mind to split the atom, and obviously this is true. But how are we going to make the tremendous leap from the kind of expansion of the human mind which it took to split the atom, to the kind of expansion of the human mind which Einstein said did *not* take place?

In a global sense, when the atom was split, the human mind *was* changing. Only it was changing not in the West but in China and Vietnam, the countries sustaining the onslaught of Western technology. In these countries, antidotes or alternatives were being created which were in fact inventions of the human spirit, e.g., great unselfishness, new relations between men and women, a sense of international solidarity, new ways of looking at the relations between people, both inside countries and between countries. So that in China and Vietnam people were not just making Third World revolutions to reach the stage at which the West had arrived. They were advancing humankind to a new plateau.

That is why nobody can become a human being who is not absolutely opposed to the attempt of the United States in Indochina to bomb humankind back to a capitalist way of life.

But we can't go on from there and say, "Therefore the primary task of Americans is to end the war." That is to go from a judgment directly to an action, which is reactive politics. Unless there is a revolution in the United States, the United States isn't safe for the world. But the Indochinese can't make the United States revolution. Americans have to make it. In that sense the revolutionary struggle in the United States takes priority over all other struggles.

Americans have to solve the problems of the world in their own country, precisely because every problem facing humankind is focused in this country. We have a melting pot that didn't melt; we have thoughts that nobody else has; we have a kind of materialism that nobody else has. We are facing all the problems of humankind right here. That is why the American revolution is the most important revolution in the world.

We must remember also that if Nixon withdrew ground troops from Indochina, it was chiefly because the Vietnamese people had defeated the United States by revolutionary struggle and not because the people of the United States changed. An important part of the Vietnamese revolutionary struggle was to undermine the morale of the United States. The Vietnamese carried on a moral struggle, and as a result, that tiny nation was able to defeat the most powerful country in the world. The Vietnamese people are telling the Western world "Don't talk about civilization until you can talk about morality." We have reached the stage in revolutionary struggle, in revolutionary thought, when it is impossible just to talk about facts. We are forced to wonder about morality. That is what the war in Indochina means.

How can we help the American people today to break out of old patterns of thought? We must explore the concept of confronting oneself.

Let us take the example of a garbage collector who doesn't give a damn because he has a nasty job. He spills half the stuff in the gutter and doesn't bother to pick it up. He doesn't think of the rats that will have a chance to feed and breed as a result of his carelessness. A man who has that attitude to his job, no matter what his job is, can't possibly build a socialist society. A man with an attitude like that isn't an asset to any society.

Does it do any good to accuse a man of that kind of "not thinking about society"? Wouldn't it create more movement within him, i.e., more self-movement, if we were to say, "You are doing a lousy job,

and you don't give a damn. That is a hell of a way for a man to live."
Then, when he replies, "Why should I give a damn? I'm being
exploited. All I care about is my eight hours," *we* say, "For your own
sake you should give a damn." What Mao seems to be saying, and we
are still trying to discover how to say in this country, is "You are not
a member of the working class or of any advanced class, if you
behave this way. You are not standing for anything, neither for
yourself nor for society." This is the kind of thing which is involved
in confronting oneself.

There is a legitimate question whether we should continue to use
the words "bourgeois" and "socialist" to distinguish between the
"don't give a damn" attitude, and the attitude which does give a
damn about oneself and society. In favor of its continuing use is the
responsibility of the revolutionary intellectual to recognize the
revolutionary tradition and to define him/herself in relation to that
tradition, to make clear what is being preserved and what is being
changed and why. *We* have to make the definitions. We don't just
throw away words and start afresh because we recognize that the
words came from somewhere. So, through an enormous amount of
effort, we arrive at new definitions of "socialist," what we mean and
what we don't mean by the term, and thereby we also help those
with whom we are working to understand that nothing remains the
same, and how and why changes take place in meanings along with
changes in society. Hence we should clearly establish our definitions
of socialism, boldly accepting our responsibility for redefining it
because of the differences between nineteenth-century Europe and
twentieth-century America, making clear what we mean and what
we don't mean by socialism, bourgeois society, etc.

So we say to a man who is doing a lousy job, "Your attitude to
work is the attitude of this lousy society which you have accepted.
You are thinking only of yourself and not about your job in relation
to your fellowman or to yourself as a creative human being.
Therefore *you* are defining yourself as mean and petty. Just because
this society defines human activity in terms of exchange value doesn't
mean that you have to accept that definition. There is another
attitude to work which each of us has to and can discover for the
sake of our own dignity, our own concept of ourself."

Those radicals who are still talking to workers (including women
workers) of revolutionary struggle in terms of going on strike

completely misunderstand the present stage of society and human development. Going on strike is what workers had to do in the nineteenth century or as late as the thirties in order to get recognition of themselves as human beings. Today, going on strike is what particular groups of workers do to "get theirs," with no concern for anybody else but themselves. Therefore, for revolutionaries today to talk to workers in an advanced country like the United States in terms of going on strike shows absolutely no recognition of the way that the human personality is being torn apart these days because of the lack of a perspective that takes in the whole society and envisages what is involved in the development of a new person.

The Puritan ethic as it applied to work contained a certain rationality. There was not only discipline from without but acceptance of that discipline on the part of working men and women. As we have seen, the Puritan ethic originated with ordinary men and women who for the first time began to hope for happiness on earth. There is no doubt that the Puritan ethic helped make possible the development of capitalism because it disciplined people for work. As capitalism was developing through its exploitation of working men and women, those who were exploited could still see the rationality of their work because they could see the fruits of their labors all around them and feel that they were making a contribution to society.

It is perfectly legitimate to say to everyone that he/she has to contribute to society. What you do contribute may be subject to a great deal of choice or differentiation as the society develops. But, for your own sake, you have to accept that if you want to live, you have to do something, not just *be*, like a vegetable. This is also part of confronting oneself. Those radicals who believe that the Puritan ethic with regard to work has been rendered obsolete by the technological revolution are thinking like the slaves in every society who begin to fantasize about the new society in terms of the leisure and uselessness they envy in their masters. It is dehumanizing to inculcate in people the idea that they can live without working. We have to recognize that, despite the technological revolution and indeed as a result of it, there are a million new things that can be called work. There is no job, no activity, in which you are not relating yourself to somebody, *if only to yourself.*

Today, as a result of the rebellions and the identification of work with slavery and with white oppression, young blacks have developed an antagonism to work which has to be fought, but in a revolutionary way, i.e., by insisting that the socialist attitude to work involves working well. Anyone who says, "I am a victim of bourgeois society, of white oppression, and therefore whatever attitude I have to work is legitimate, whether it be living like a leech or stealing," is accepting the dehumanizing character of bourgeois society or of white oppression. Most people who are just rebelling against the old society think that under the new society they won't have to work. That is why the notion of the relationship of work to human creativity and the very nature of man/woman is so important. Note, we are *not* saying that "If you don't work, you starve." Rather we are saying, "If you don't work, you don't express yourself as a human being."

This is another way of saying that anybody who accepts his/her victimization by society is not going to change the society. All he/she is going to do is remain a victim and perpetuate the society. The socialist ethic of work involves creativity and self-reliance.

We need to examine the nature of work in the past, and what must and can be maintained in the future. Clearly, conditions governing work in the past were very different, and some cannot be preserved. For example, in an agricultural society the nature of work is very much determined by the climate and the seasons. These can't possibly play the same roles in work performed in an urban environment. Yet, obviously, unless we re-establish a human relationship with Nature, whatever work is done is not going to be work that develops society or the individual.

In the past the nature of work involved certain manual skills (handicraft), the coordination and interaction of brain and hand, and a certain amount of creativity and intrinsic joy. Something of this has to be preserved; yet it obviously can't be preserved in the same form in a society that is highly developed technically, where there is no longer the same control by the individual over the tools he/she works with.

In the past we have had work as governed by the whip, either in terms of undisguised force (slavery) or in terms of wages. Obviously we must get rid of this completely. But already, as a result of an economy of abundance, this kind of necessity is no longer with us in the same sense, although a lot of people are still thinking about it in the same terms. We can't move a single step until we recognize that exploitation is actually decreasing, although the human condition of people is getting worse. What are the new necessities for living like a human being under these new conditions? How do we resolve this unprecedented contradiction?

In the past people could see what they were doing as socially beneficial even if what they were doing was for wages or if it was dirty or menial work. The scale of what they were doing was small enough to be comprehensible through the human eye. Cleaning away trash from the railroad tracks meant safety for the trains. Today the huge scale of operations, the destructiveness and wastefulness of so much that is produced, all make it difficult to see one's activity as part of a meaningful whole.

We can say that work is necessary to the development, the expression, the creation of one's humanity. But having said that, we haven't said enough. We have to be more specific about which fundamental ingredients have to be incorporated and which elimi- nated in order that people should be able to develop, to express, and to create their humanity through participation in work. For example, it is clear that one has to have a concept of *purpose*, i.e., that what one is doing, although not necessarily directly utilitarian, is an addition to society, to humankind. There also has to be an element of *self-determination* in relation to the purpose. One must also be able to see the *relevance* of the methods one is employing to the goals or purposes one is seeking to achieve. There has to be some sense of *process*—that doing things takes time and that there is a logical and temporal relationship between various steps of the activity. And there has to be a sense of *workmanship*, i.e., that the quality of the results depends upon the quality of the effort.

It is inconceivable that humankind could exist without work. The new ethic of work starts out in the first place with the idea that work is a necessity for the human personality. But man/woman has struggled for so long against compulsory work that we have lost the notion that if we didn't work, we would not exist as human. We exist at the historical conjunction of the highest point of the mass struggle against labor and the technological revolution which has eliminated the old reasons to work. So we have to reaffirm that people have to work, but they don't have to work in the old way and for the old reasons. We can't look for the new way or for new reasons unless we believe that there *are* human reasons for working. People who want to repudiate the concept of work altogether are not looking for any new way at all. They just want to live on welfare without thinking of how destructive this is to their humanity. Everything creative is work; and ultimately all work is creative. The new ethic of work will include the necessity of working, but the reasons will be new ones. They will have to come from within. So to the kids who say, "I don't have to work, the machine will do it all," we answer, "If you are going to sit around and enjoy the fruits of other people's work, if you can't think of any work you want to do for your community, for other people, for yourself, then you are destroying yourself." At the same time we realize that it is not going to be easy to start the multitude thinking this new way, when they have been used to thinking of work only as a form of slavery.

We need to set up a polarization, an opposition between two attitudes to work. Whether or not one calls these respectively the "bourgeois" and the "socialist" attitude to work is not important as long as we recognize that at this historical juncture, this transition, there are two attitudes: one which is a hatred and repudiation of work, destructive of the human personality, and the other which recognizes work as essential to the development of oneself as a human being.

How did we in the United States get so many people on welfare? Originally the only people on welfare were those in dire need. Then came the Depression and there were lots of people in dire need, so WPA and welfare were created. WPA was conceived as a means of putting the unemployed to work.

After the Depression we cut out WPA; then everybody went directly to welfare, with no socially available means of returning to work. Since that time a welfare culture has developed in this society. People began thinking, "If I can be on welfare and make $350 a month, why should I take a job paying only $550 and have to work at the same time?" People became choosy about whether they would take a job or not. It is going on in millions of cases all over the country. People are using the victimization complex to justify being on welfare.

People on welfare who want to rediscover their humanity are the ones who are in the most urgent need of finding a new, enlarged human identity, a new enlarged concept of themselves as human.

Because when you accept the parasite's role in a society, you are destroying your humanity and destroying society at the same time. We are accustomed to thinking that people only lose their humanity when they kill or rape. But we have to realize that people on welfare are losing their humanity in a very deep sense.

It is all connected. You can't persuade anybody to be a socialist just by yelling about socialism. You have to persuade a person that there is something in the human relations, the human identity, embodied in the concept of socialism that they would want. The new ethic of work involves trying to persuade people, not that they should take dirty jobs and keep their mouths shut, but that unless they have jobs and do the best they can on these jobs, they are demolishing both themselves and society.

If some people just produce garbage and others see their whole lives as picking up the garbage that others throw out the window, it is almost impossible to persuade the latter to do the best possible job in their work. The man who has been working at picking up garbage then begins to lose some of his humanity too. So work has to be related to many other things.

A few years ago we were saying, "All we need is the socialist revolution and everybody will enjoy working for the communal good." Now we know that isn't so. Unless we persuade people to think differently about work in relation to themselves, all we shall end up with will be somebody ordering others to do what has to be done. What we are trying to discover now is how to persuade people that we are going to arrive at that situation unless, by our own choice, we change our minds about what responsibilities we are ready to accept.

We have arrived at this conclusion (we feel it very strongly)—that anybody who doesn't have reverence or respect for work, who rejects work, and who wants to live off other people, is antihuman, antiself, and will never build a new socialist society. We have also arrived at a very deep conviction that work is a way of expressing, developing, creating your humanity, the humanity which is essential to human identity.

We have to find the reason for people today in the United States to want to work in this way, at a time when apparently nobody wants to do anything. Moreover, there are enough concepts from the past in people's minds to justify, legitimize, and validate to their own satisfaction their lack of will and zeal and passion. Whereas people in the past wanted to do such things as build cathedrals under the most difficult conditions, today under much better conditions, people don't want to do anything. We face the awesome challenge of discovering how to give people the will to work creatively under the present circumstances.

Suppose we were to go to some folks on welfare and say to them, "Instead of demanding more welfare, why don't we go and take over all the chores that have to be done in the community, including getting rid of the dilapidated buildings, cleaning up the lots and building playgrounds in them, carrying out campaigns in the community for birth control, administering to the sick and the old, setting up small-scale clinics in the community? *And,* on all those occasions where these activities conflict with those already involved in these activities as jobs, let that conflict be recognized as one which we will have to work out in order to establish new relations."

Can people on welfare do what we have just outlined above? It depends upon whether they feel they want to do it as an expression of their own humanity, themselves. You can't ask anybody to go out and clean up a lot and make a park of it if all he/she is thinking is "Why should I? I am not going to get paid for it. I can sit home and do nothing and get the same amount of money," or who says "My brother is a park worker. If I do that, I will put him out of a job"—even though he knows his brother isn't going to do it because there isn't any money to pay him at the rate he is accustomed to receiving.

Looking back at the old socialists, the Old Left, we can see that they had a historical vision, the vision of a planned economy, although it was very narrow and really not relevant to the United States. Then the New Left came along, without any vision and without any historical perspective. All they had was their activism and their good intentions. What we are talking about now is a historical vision that is relevant to the present age and yet related to the historical past, without which good intentions and activism have no relation to the evolution and advancement of the expanding human identity of the great masses of the people.

Today we have to confront people and challenge them to say what is their conception of a human being and how a human being should live.

By confronting people we help them to deal seriously with questions. We set up positions so that people can begin to grapple with fundamental issues. We state our positions sharply enough so that people can't avoid what is involved for the human race. Not that we expect them to make up their minds immediately. We know that it will take time. But we take positions in order to help people discover what is their attitude to themselves and to other people. We have to confront people very sharply so that they can discover some of their own humanity before they destroy themselves.

We have to chide people, telling them things about themselves that nobody else has been telling them, what they are doing to themselves, making them face themselves as they are. Malcolm X was a master at this kind of chiding. People today don't believe anything is happening to them; they don't believe anything can touch them. We have to combine this chiding with an illumination of where they have come from. Otherwise they can't really have any idea of the self which they are destroying.

When you take positions on fundamental issues, you have moved beyond an abstract discussion of human identity. You reveal to a person what is his/her attitude to humanity and how this attitude must change if he/she wants to be human. You remove from him/her the liberalism which makes him/her a cripple! Positions are a means whereby we get an individual to confront him/herself, to begin to define his/her humanity; whereby we force a person, through ideas, to act rather than just complain. We take a position in order to force a person to take a position, and thereby to take some responsibility for his/her positions. In other words, we establish a framework within which he/she can grapple with him/herself.

Positions enable you to begin discussing with people who have questions on their mind and who are not just blaming others but can make choices. By taking a position on the question of work, we are able to help a person clarify his/her relation to society. At first we may not be able to reach the person who has made his/her whole life and culture one of victimization. But people who are already wondering, who already have a healthy attitude to work, are able to become advocates or proselytizers for something bigger than themselves. They begin to understand that an ethic of work isn't just a personal thing, that it is related to something much larger, the advancement of humankind. The most alienated elements are not going to grasp this early. But the controversy has to start, so that they will not be allowed to go unchecked in their disintegration, and so as to help those who already have some inclination in the new direction to take steps in that direction. The liberals are the worst obstacles to revolutionary struggle because they make it unnecessary for people to confront themselves. Liberalism is the opiate of the people.

A revolutionary must have a profound belief in the capacity of humankind. If we really believe that man/woman has great capacities, our job is to draw upon these capacities as a basis, to accept them, to evoke them. Our job is to enable people to feel their enlarged selves. Man/woman is a remarkable creature. He/she isn't mean, even though he/she is acting mean. He/she is capable of sensitivity, heroism. But ordinary people in the United States have so diminished themselves that they haven't the faintest idea of what people are and what they are capable of being. The only possible way of moving anywhere is by being confident that people are capable of extraordinary dedication, commitment, and creativity. But we can't just exhort them, can't just try to inspire them. We have to bring about a confrontation within them between what they are and what they can be. We do not just open up to them a vision of the positive, but we force them to confront their own negativity. So we have moved now to a stage where we are not just exploring the nature of man/woman but are asking man/woman to confront the negative in him/herself and in his/her present nature with the potential of his/her human nature.

The people of the United States are damaged people. We have to bring about a confrontation between their damaged character and their potential character.

Marx thought he could talk about primitive communism, and that workers, liberated from bourgeois oppression, would behave like primitive communists, with the additional social qualities produced by the organization and discipline of modern industry. Now we are saying that bourgeois society has damaged people, that it has made the most oppressed into the most individualistic, and that the individualism of bourgeois society is now deeply rooted in the character of the most oppressed. The individual who is oppressed has to confront his/her own nature before he/she can even begin to realize the human nature which past creations have shown man/woman to be capable of and create the new society which will enhance this nature.

We have to advance the idea that dividing up the Gross National Product equally has nothing to do with the advancement of humankind. We are projecting beyond the concepts of equality and rights. We are not trying to persuade people to get their equal share. We are trying to persuade them to feel and think and act differently. Since Roosevelt, this country has been trying to give the poor housing. We have succeeded in giving them poor housing, and nothing else. Why? Because there wasn't enough difference in the thought, the attitude, the search. Until we can persuade people to want something more than just more, we are not going to be able to change anything. Anybody who wants to change something has got to be able to change what he/she wants.

Men and women have been fighting one another for hundreds of thousands of years. But they have never really faced the question of man-woman relations before. Today women are saying, "Look, let's stop and face it." Within that facing is involved the key to facing all other human relationships, not only between men and women but in every aspect of our human nature, biological, psychological, economic, political, and social. It is no longer just a question of the particular grievances which women have. What is involved now has to do with the evolution of humankind.

Long before there were classes and races, there was the question of relations between men and women. Obviously only a patriarchal society could have created the myth of woman coming out of the rib of a man. And, equally obviously, the idea that either sex existed before the other is a myth. Both must have existed simultaneously. We could ask, "Why didn't women start raising this question in *this* way at the very beginning? Why did they wait so long, until the last half of the twentieth century?" Because originally, there was a natural, biological division of labor, between men who did the work of hunting, and women who bore children, raised them, and gathered, raised, and prepared the bulk of the food. It wasn't the choice of men that they shouldn't have children or of women that they should. There was no choice—it was a natural division. Women bore and nursed the children and did the menial and creative work that went along with being around the house, while men went out and did the more strenuous work.

Almost all the early inventions, in the passage especially from the hunting to the horticultural stage, were certainly created by women. This includes the products of almost every important craft: pottery, basketry, cooking and storing food, spinning and weaving, sewing, housebuilding, all the equipment for tending babies, medicine. The situation is not so clear in relation to fine arts, for men did paintings depicting the hunting of animals. Almost everything except killing animals, fighting other men, and boatbuilding, seems to have been done by women. There is no question that women invented horticulture and agriculture.

It is only after we get to advanced horticultural and horticultural-pastoral societies (when populations become concentrated on valuable land, around irrigation sites—property that is scarce and fought over) that the military arts become important and men come to the fore. Also we begin to have full-time specialization. In the early period of part-time specialization, spinning, weaving, pottery-making, etc., could be done by women in addition to cooking and caring for babies. But once the art of metallurgy is developed, it is complex and time-consuming enough so that people must work at it full-time; accordingly it becomes a craft which is inherited. Men do it because women do not have the time. At that point the conditions exist for the rise of the state. And from then on, men become the advancers of civilization while women have been more the conservers, the links with the past, the peacemakers sometimes, and the traditionalists.

The natural division of labor was established maybe a million years ago and became a relation of domination with the rise of the state about five thousand years ago. The reason it didn't change sooner was that it has taken all these years to develop the technology which has made the state an anachronism and which has made it possible for men and women to share much more equally in every sphere. So now men and women are searching for what the new relationship should be.

It is obvious that in the earlier stage women must have played a tremendous role in advancing society. Then at a certain stage men took over. It is not a question of whether it was good or bad. It happened. But now we are at a technological stage in which we are free to wonder what is the appropriate relationship between men and women. Who does what? We don't need men for protection in the sense in which we used to. What is the problem we face *now?* It is *not* a question of whether women preceded men or Adam preceded Eve. What do we as people do *now* to advance humankind?

In this search for new relations between men and women, we have a manifestation of the search for new relations between people.

Men and women are different. But that difference does not imply inferiority or superiority. We have to recognize that there has been domination of women by men. But we must also recognize the natural difference between the sexes—which does not mean that we accept domination. We deplore the tendency to believe that the only way to escape domination is to deny difference.

We must be careful not to look for fixed truths about the relations between men and women, when in fact whatever we are going to discover will be created, not found. Precisely because this question is so complex, it is important not to have a concept of absolute truth, let alone one of absolute equality. The only important thing is that we undertake a search for new relations between men and women, having rejected the idea of masculine superiority. Rejecting the concept of superiority, repudiating oppression and domination, is the only absolute truth we need to start with. From then on, we seek relations based on diversity which is complementary and non-antagonistic, rather than equal or dominating.

The women's struggle illustrates the complex relationship between the particular and the universal. Most women have been storing up their particular grievances for years, mulling over them, and now exploding over them. But when they do so, it is not just the sum of the particulars that they are exploding over, but a universal for which they haven't yet found the concept. So that when they are asked what they really *want,* they can't give an answer.

The fact is that during the last hundred years, and particularly the last twenty-five, the division of roles between men and women has lost its objective basis, and women and men have not found the new universal to correspond to the new stage of development.

There are certain roles that can't be changed, e.g., childbearing. We can't say that women and men should bear children equally; nor that since only women can bear babies, women should only be baby-bearers. But it is perfectly conceivable that young women should not bear babies for ten years. In fact, not bearing children for ten years might be just the opportunity that young women need in order to explore and enlarge their humanity.

It is not easy for society to accept a projection like this. A lot of people still respond with the attitudes of a century ago, when every child was needed to help till the land. The previous role of women, that of continual child-bearing, has created prejudices in everyone, women as well as men.

On the other hand, if young women didn't have children for ten years, what an opportunity it would give them to consider what they would like to do, what they would like to become, without bearing the social burden of reproduction! That is what is happening through the postponement of marriage in China. Young Chinese women now have the opportunity during these important years of vitality, curiosity, creativity, to develop and explore themselves. For hundreds of thousands of years, women have spent these vital years bearing children. But what kind of meaningful choices can a girl or a woman make if she has a bunch of kids running around after her, whom she has to feed and diaper? In the old days women didn't have postnatal neuroses, because there was a social reason for the bearing and rearing of children. Today, with the social reasons very much modified, many young women have breakdowns after they give birth, and women in mental institutions outnumber men almost four to one.

Many women claim they are imprisoned by motherhood during these crucial years, but they blame men for knocking them up. Others say they should have sex relations with women instead of men. They see themselves as victims, rather than thinking about and choosing a different path of development. Why don't people practice birth control? Not because the means are unavailable or because the knowledge is unavailable. Until we have persuaded people to think differently, as they have done in China, the woman's question will be seen only as a question of rights which men are depriving women of, instead of as the need for women to develop themselves.

Ten years free of motherhood could be crucial years to develop new relations between males and females of a qualitatively new character, the scope of which we cannot even imagine. Young women would have an opportunity to develop themselves intellectually, technically, politically, artistically, giving them a purpose other than getting back at men. Why can't a young woman or girl say, "I don't want to be a mother until I am thirty years old because I want a chance to think." She can decide that right now. Every woman is free to be free until she is thirty. But first she has to understand that she is the one who decides whether or not she has to be a mother to achieve her human identity. Knowing that society perpetuates and reinforces this concept of woman as brood mare and sexpot, she can still free herself, i.e., become independent of this concept.

Today there is a growing number of teenagers who can't think of anything but having children, and who are, in their early and middle teens, settling for futures as ADC and welfare mothers. How can we get these young women to develop a self-concept which will not allow them to settle for such a future?

"Aren't you married yet? Don't you have any children?" Young women are faced with such questions all the time. They need very different concepts of themselves as human beings in order to stand up against such questions.

When we look at these young girls, we see how far we have to project the concept of self-determining, self-enlarging human identity, as well as how hard the most oppressed masses always have to work in order to grasp and make their own these advanced concepts. But the determination to achieve this advanced state of human identity is what always gives the momentum to the struggles of the most oppressed masses when they begin to reject having their lives shaped by the past. These young girls think of themselves as biological test tubes—it is difficult to go much lower in your concept of self. Many of them don't exist in their own minds as people unless at fifteen they have gone to bed with and perhaps borne a child by a football star or a rock musician.

For a woman today to feel that the only realm in which she is self-determining is as a bedmate or a brood mare is self-denial, not self-determination. Because she is human, she has the capacity to envisage a thousand other ways to be creative. But nobody has projected these to her or permitted her to enlarge her self-concept.

We are not talking about informing these young women how not to get pregnant, although obviously we believe that such information should be made available to them. We are trying to change their thoughts about themselves in order that they will want to live differently.

That is why it is so important to give every child a historical conception of where we came from and how humankind has been developing since our evolution from the ape. Only when one begins to reflect on this can one understand the views he/she has about women.

If you have not begun to think of revolutionizing relations between men and women, it is absurd to talk about changing relations between classes or races. That is why the Women's Liberation Movement is potentially the most revolutionary of all movements, because it asks the most profound of all questions, the question which underlies all other movements: How can we establish new and more fulfilling relations between people? Without dealing with this question, we are not going to solve any others. We can only solve the problems of society by solving the problems of human relations.

As long as we only talk about day-care centers or women getting jobs or men helping women with the housework (all of which are progressive) we are still talking only about reforms. We are not talking about revolution until we begin to talk about women thinking of themselves in different ways; or until women can say, "I want to spend the most productive years of my life, the years between fifteen and thirty, as a human being, doing anything that any man can do. I do not want to be tied down to the biological role which women have played in the past."

In order to break down the many manifestations of male domination, men should not only respect this but they themselves should recognize that they have been part of the pressure to tie women down. Part of the problem is to persuade men that this demand is equally in their interest. To say that men shouldn't look at women as sexual objects isn't very realistic. They are going to look at them as sex objects, but they shouldn't look at them as sex objects only.

A woman has first of all to look at herself as a person. The Women's Liberation movement is ridiculous when it assumes that every time a man looks at a woman he wants to rape her. In the United States almost as many women look at men sexually as vice versa. Our whole society is sex-oriented. "I can make any chick on the block," says the guy. "I can be as tough as any boy on the block," says the girl. Both mean that they haven't arrived at any discrimination in their hearts or minds in relation to themselves.

We are not taking a moralistic position about whether people should have sex or not. We are talking about human behavior of a very dehumanized kind. People behave according to the concept they have of themselves. If theirs is a self-degrading, dehumanizing concept, they will behave in a degraded and dehumanized way.

The concept of love has changed a great deal over the ages. In other times, families played an important role in production and reproduction, and therefore sexuality automatically had a social importance. Today what you do for personal reasons is solely dependent upon your caprice, your whim, your personal feelings at the moment. What people are beginning to wonder is whether one's immediate feelings are an adequate basis for organizing any society.

We are not saying that sex was invented or created by the economic system, but it *did* have economic purposes and a social framework. Infant mortality being what it was (and still is in some parts of the world) only two of many children might survive to take care of their parents in their old age. But that is not the case in the United States.

The Suffragettes were advanced in relation to other women and to the men of their time, but they merely wanted to participate in the man's world, i.e., to vote. Members of Women's Liberation today say, "I don't want to participate in the man's world; I want to discover the proper world." That is why this is such an important movement. When the workers took over the plants in Russia, Lenin said "This is socialism." He thought that changing the relations in production would change humankind. If you change relations in production, you have only begun the process.

We must have confidence in the mind of human beings. What one thinks will shape the changes one wants to make in all relations—in production, with members of the opposite sex, with children, and with other men and women. Many of the objective obstacles which made it impossible or difficult for the human mind to progress in the past are no longer there. We are even more capable than we were yesterday of using our minds creatively.

To use one's mind creatively, one must be ready to take positions and struggle for these with other people. In the realm of man-woman relations, the following positions are a minimum for forward movement:

1. The male-dominated family has lost whatever validity it once may have had. Advancing technology now makes it possible for women to engage in all forms of socially necessary and creative activity. Hence the family structure must be reorganized to become a cooperative decision-making body. Women should be in no way restricted in their right to abortion or birth control. We must fight against and expose as male chauvinist all who use legislation, religion, or politics, in an effort to restrict the right of women to abortion or to practice birth control.

2. The struggle for women's liberation is not a middle-class white question. All women, regardless of race, are victims of male domination. Therefore black women, no less than white women, must participate in the Women's Liberation movement and struggle to help this movement to achieve its potential. Those women who do not fight against male domination are, like blacks who do not fight against racism, "Uncle Toms."

3. Black women are not free from male domination or male chauvinism any more than they are free from racist domination or capitalist domination. Therefore they must struggle against male chauvinism and male domination wherever it appears. The struggle for black liberation does not take priority over the struggle for the liberation of black women from the domination of all men, black and white. Until all blacks are free, no blacks are free. The struggle for the liberation of black women from male domination is the struggle for the liberation of one-half of black people.

4. The black nationalist position on women is completely reactionary. The black movement up to now has failed to attack this position. Too many militants and too many women in particular have ignored or acquiesced in or succumbed to domination by black men, particularly in the extreme nationalist movement that has developed over the past ten years. This acquiescence in reactionary politics has had the most damaging effect on a whole generation of teenage girls who have been persuaded by opportunistic men to have children by them in the name of "Black Power," or the argument that the more children blacks have, the more powerful they will become.

5. A woman does not have to prove herself to be as strong as a man in order to be equal. She does not have to be better than a man, i.e.,

incapable of making mistakes, in order to be equal. Women are one-half of humanity; therefore they should be treated as equals.

6. A revolutionary organization must consciously aim to encourage the equal development and participation of its female members. Any organization which fails on the question of male chauvinism will find itself failing on all other questions.

11

NO PROMISED LAND

The American Dream has become a nightmare. For the vast majority
of Americans, the world in which we move about from day to day
has become one in which the behavior of nothing and no one is really
predictable; where the slightest crack in the system of complexly
integrated operations can cause chaos; where dangers and insecurities lurk on all sides; where carrying out the most mundane and yet
vital tasks—going to the store for a loaf of bread, or coming home
from work in a public conveyance—have become struggles for
survival; where day after day your insides are constantly sweating it
out, even when you appear outwardly calm. Having a good job and
earning the wherewithal to buy practically anything you want has
not brought a sense of security and confidence. If anything, it has
increased your sense of insecurity and helplessness. If you don't have
a job, if you are an older person, you feel helpless and useless.
Nobody cares whether you live or die. On the streets you are an easy
target for muggers, who knock you down and grab your money with
less concern than they would show for an orange crate. Parents work
and make sacrifices to bring their children up with health, skills,
respect for others and themselves, worrying all the time that they

will end up on drugs and/or turn into thugs. Hoping against hope that this will not happen, mothers, especially, read every word of advice they can find on what to do with children, all of which only increases the profits of the publishers and the fears and insecurities of the mothers.

Everybody can see what is happening. Most people only complain and blame it all on someone else. But, more and more, some people are beginning to realize that the road we are traveling can lead only to more isolation from each other, more antagonisms and conflicts, and more alienation from the rest of the world, and are wondering how we can find a new road for ourselves, our children, and our children's children.

The antagonisms and conflicts which have erupted between the races, the sexes, the generations, and between this nation and the rest of the world, are particular manifestations of the main contradiction in the United States. This contradiction lies in the fact that we have not made the rapid political advancement necessary to meet the new problems posed by rapid technological and economic advancement.

The French and American revolutions in the eighteenth century, and the great revolutions of the twentieth century, all show that rapid political development can only take place within the perspective of the evolution of all humankind.

The labor movement in the thirties, and all the movements of the fifties and sixties, the black movement, the youth movement and the women's movement, began by struggling for their own interests, but derived their momentum from the fact that their interests coincided with those of society as a whole. However, when these movements were challenged by the chaos created by their struggles to relate their particular interests to the interests of the entire society and all humankind, they tried to evade this challenge. Instead they tried all kinds of separation, concentrating on the grievances of their own particular group, struggling to get "our share" or "our rights." In the end, each has become an interest group, concerned only with itself. While each may talk about Black Power, Women Power, Workers' Power, in the final analysis each is only talking about separation of powers, or "a piece of the action." None is talking about real power, which involves the reconstruction of the entire society for the benefit of the great majority and for the advancement of humanity. They have each reduced themselves to being a part and lost sight of the whole. By evading their responsibility, they have lost both their sense of ethical judgment and their respect for factual truth. In losing these they have lost some of their own humanity.

That is why so many non-white groups inside the United States expound the nonsense that they are Third World people fighting to liberate themselves from imperialism and neocolonialism, when this is actually the revolutionary duty and potential of the peoples in the Third World itself—Asia, Africa, the Middle East, and Latin America. That is why so many play around with Pan-Africanism and other escapist ideas of geographical separation, while continuing to live in the citadel of capitalism, enjoying the fruits of U.S. imperialist exploitation of the Third World countries. That is why they evade facing the opportunist and reactionary tendencies within their own interest groups, such as black capitalism or the black nationalist position on women or the elevation of rapists and muggers to the status of "political prisoners," despite the obviously corrupting influence of these ideas on young people within their communities. That is why they take no responsibility for the confusion and demoralization which they have done so much to create, not by their concrete struggles but by the myths that they have propagated in the wake of concrete struggles.

This continuing evasion of responsibility on the part of many who were once involved in real struggles in the United States raises the serious question of what kind of human thinking they represent. Since most of them do not view themselves as a part of the capitalist system, and in fact most of them denounce capitalism, one might be led to believe that their thinking is socialist and not bourgeois. But in spreading these political myths of people inside the United States being "Third World," of political prisoners, of Pan-Africanism as a viable solution for Afro-Americans, and of male chauvinism, they are more representative of bourgeois thought than they are of socialist thought. As we have pointed out, bourgeois thought is concerned with what benefits the few or a particular interest group rather than what would benefit the overall society. Socialist thought, on the other hand, is concerned with what will advance the whole society.

This brings us to the question of why we believe a revolution is necessary in the United States today.

U.S. capitalism has developed many tentacles. Through imperialism in its various forms of development—colonialism, neocolonialism, multinational capitalism, and the military industrial complex—it exploits and manipulates the people in Asia, the Middle East, Africa, South America, and even Europe. Since World War II the people of the Third World, i.e., the countries and nations outside Europe and the United States who have been systematically damned to underdevelopment by United States and European imperialism, have been struggling to liberate themselves from colonial and neocolonialist exploitation. In a large part of Asia they are well on the way to achieving this liberation. If, however, the Third World countries do not succeed in completely liberating themselves before the victory of the U.S. revolution, then when the American people make the new American revolution, we will have to destroy every vestige of U.S. domination over the rest of the world before we can regain our own humanity and rejoin the rest of the world in the struggle to advance humankind.

The United States is the citadel of world capitalism, and everybody living in the United States, regardless of ethnic origin, must begin by facing this reality. A revolution in the United States is to take the American people on a new road, in a new direction, to a new and more human form of political, economic, and social relations, among ourselves and with the rest of the world.

When most Americans think about a revolution, all they can think of is a coup d'état, i.e., the overthrow of the government by a lightning blow. If you say you are a revolutionist, they ask if you are for overthrowing the government or the system. But people do not make anything as serious as a revolution to rub out a government or system. The only justification for a revolution is the fact that social, political, and economic contradictions have accumulated to the point that the existing government and the existing institutions obviously cannot resolve them. Therefore it is not so much that the revolution overthrows the government and the system as that the government and the system, by their failure and their misdeeds, drive the people to rescind their mandate to rule. They have lost their legitimacy, their right to continue, because what they do creates more problems and contradictions than solutions.

A revolutionist does not hate the country in which the illegitimate and oppressive system and government continues to rule. Far less does the revolutionist hate the people of the country. On the contrary, a revolutionist loves the country and the people, but hates what some people are doing to the country and to the people. Someone who hates the country and the people becomes a renegade, and runs away. Therefore the important question is not "Is the revolutionist for overthrowing the government?" Rather it is "Do you believe the present government and the existing institutions of this country serve the need of the people to continue advancing their humanity?"

U.S. capitalism today is a cancerous growth on the people of the world. Now the American people need to find another way of life, a superior system which will enable human beings to control technology rather than be controlled by technology. The uses we have made of technology under capitalism have led us to lose our concept of what it is to be human. We have used it to destroy people in other countries, to defile our relations with one another, and to cripple the development of our human capacities.

We, the people of the United States, can only regain our humanity by recognizing how decade after decade we have increasingly separated ethics from politics.

As a people we have had a long history of living on the backs of other peoples in the world, living by the exploitation of Africans, Asians, Arabs, South Americans—all people whom we have considered less human than ourselves. So little have we cared for the humanity of others that the great majority of the American people have been supporting, by our taxes, by our votes, by our silence, the dropping of millions of tons of bombs on people in Asia with as little concern as if we were eradicating roaches in our kitchens. We have bullied or condoned the bullying of the rest of the world in the conviction that we knew more about freedom and democracy than other people. Because it served our immediate interest, we have interpreted freedom as an evasion of political responsibility to ourselves and the rest of the world. We have interpreted democracy as a ritual for evading responsibility or delegating it to others, evading the fact that democracy is a process whereby the great majority of the people engage in the political struggles necessary to arrive at important social decisions.

We have exploited and bombed so many people with our advanced technology for so long that it has become a way of life to us, a monstrous habit like drinking the blood of others in order to fatten oneself. Hundreds of years ago the Pilgrims did not, could not know that what they started out to create with such noble intentions could become so degenerate. But we do know. The whole world knows. Once we had the respect and admiration of the entire world. Now the whole world has witnessed our corruption, our degeneration. It sits in judgment on our actions, while we grow more indecent in our lack of respect for the opinions of the rest of humankind. We have used other people as a dope addict uses dope, always needing a bigger dose, not caring how he/she gets the money to feed his/her habit. We have reacted to other people, other nations, with the mentality of the U.S. Marine Corps. Whenever we were told by our leaders that U.S. interests were at stake, we were ready to go to any lengths to protect those interests.

Now, before our very eyes, in our own living rooms, we can see where all this has led us. In the witness chair of the Senate caucus room, day after day, we see men who are no different from the Goebbels and the Eichmanns in their loyalty to "The Leader," in their use of the big lie, and in the excuse that they were only following orders. The question is not how much the President knew or which criminal acts of conspiracy or cover-up any one of these men committed. The main question is what kind of people had we become, that we were able to close our eyes to what was happening in Washington. Why did we pay so little mind to the emergence of this political machine whose only goal was to perpetuate the godfather? The overwhelming majority of the American people voted for this godfather. They gave a mandate to this godfather who was so sure that he knew what was best for the nation. They knew that this "best" was the indiscriminate saturation bombing of a tiny nation thousands of miles away. They knew that this "best" was setting up and supporting military dictatorships and client states all over the world. They knew that this "best" was glorifying as heroes the kind of men who could drop napalm and millions of tons of bombs on men, women, and children without blinking an eyelash.

Now these much-less-than-human acts, which so many less-than-human Americans were ready to accept in the name of U.S. interests, have come home, in the form of wiretapping, taping, spying, and other kinds of covert activities whose scope is still unknown, by some Americans against other Americans.

For as long as anyone now living can remember, the people of the

United States, because of the special circumstances of this nation's development, have lived by the idea that we are a special people, a chosen people, superior to the rest of humankind and entitled to use other people for our own advantage. Now the time has come to examine ourselves and the universe in which we live. If we don't change the direction in which we have been traveling, if we don't begin to think of living on our own very abundant natural and human resources instead of exploiting those of other nations, we will not only impede the progress of others. We ourselves will be going backwards, in an opposite direction from the historic trend of humankind today.

The whole world is changing. People in China, Vietnam, Korea, Cuba, Guinea-Bissau, Mozambique, Angola, Albania, are already in the process of creating new societies of self-reliant, politically conscious, socially responsible men and women. Inspired by them, other nations are beginning the painful but challenging process of changing their own direction away from the individualistic and opportunist road towards the road of social responsibility. When people and things in the world begin to change and your ideas don't change, don't advance, to keep pace with the changes in the world, then your ideas become reactionary, i.e., obstacles to progress, and you yourself are in danger of becoming extinct.

We have come to the point in history where humanitarian liberalism, which was a great advance in the nineteenth century, has become destructive of human beings. To be liberal means that you are ready to be understanding, sympathetic, and helpful to those who are oppressed, instead of recognizing that what you are doing is encouraging the oppressed to see themselves as victims and to become dependent upon your understanding, sympathy and help. Liberalism is the opiate of the people.

Today we should know that when workers in the United States go on strike for higher wages, they are only a special economic interest group, no different from or more socially conscious than welfare recipients demanding more welfare. In this country everybody, regardless of race, class, or sex, benefits to some degree from the exploitation of the people of other nations. Therefore in the United States when workers or welfare recipients ask for more, what they are doing is providing the capitalists with more reasons to exploit the people of other countries.

Liberals in the United States set up clinics for the drug addict and call them drug abuse centers. But we should know by this time that drugs don't abuse people and people don't abuse drugs. You can't abuse aspirin or cocaine, and cocaine and aspirin can't abuse you. People who use drugs abuse themselves. They try to escape reality and thereby limit their own human capacity to reflect, to struggle, to create. But in the United States we use deceptive phrases like "drug abuse" so that we can evade the fact that people are responsible for who they are and what they are, and people have to change themselves before they can change the society. The more we evade the contradictions that we have created for ourselves, the more we continue to live by ideas which were once advanced but are now obsolete, the more blinders we put on our own eyes, and the more insensitive we become to the mugging, killing, bombing of other peoples. The only Americans who do not share in the shame that Americans have brought on themselves are the native Americans, who are still in the concentration camps called reservations.

The question is how can we confront the people of this country and start them on the painful process of turning away from their selfish materialism and greed.

This critical point, like every critical point in humankind's long history, requires that some people make the kind of projection which will move us out of our present impasse and start us struggling for a new way to live. When a whole nation has lost its sense of direction, its sense of purpose, its sense of history, its knowledge of where it came from and where it should be going, someone has to confront it with the reality of where it is headed and how it can change direction. In this book, we are attempting to project a vision of a new road. We are assuming the revolutionary responsibility for doing so.

The people who accept the ideas and the political direction of this book as a preliminary philosophical basis for the next stage in human development can become the nucleus for the kind of cadre organization which is necessary to project these advanced ideas to the masses and thus set into motion a continuing process whereby the masses, as individuals, can begin to confront the many questions of their relations to one another and the people of the world. These are the questions which they will have to stop evading if they are to become a part of the universal sisterhood and brotherhood of humankind, instead of the vampires and masters that the American people are today.

It is very necessary to distinguish the "we" who become responsible for the creation and development of a revolutionary organization from the masses in general. The "we" are those who accept the responsibility of developing and using the most advanced ideas in order to bring about the most rapid advance in the minds of the masses. "We" are the ones who bind ourselves together with the philosophy and ideology which is a prerequisite to the creation of any body politic, and who then develop programs to project to and from the masses. Without this distinction between the "we" and the masses there can be no movement, because movement depends on diversity, on differentiation.

The people who make up the cadre will come from all strata and classes of society. What will bind them together is that each of them as an individual constantly seeks to develop his/her own socialist outlook and the socialist outlook of the organization, in theory and practice, and as a transmission belt to and from the masses, with the aim of transforming the masses from bourgeois thought to socialist thought, thereby laying the foundation to eradicate from the society every form of exploitation of people by people.

To make the transition to a socialist outlook from the bourgeois outlook, which all of us have because all of us are products of bourgeois society, every member of the organization and eventually every person in the nation will have to begin living on a socialist basis in relation to other individuals, other races, and other nations, regardless of their political system.

The transition can't take place just by stepping off the backs of others with the kind of apology which we are all so adept at making. We have to set an example by our lives. Self-reliance must be the starting point for the organization.

Many people in the United States are unconscious of what they are doing or permitting others to do in their name with the apparatus of the military-industrial complex. Many people want to shift the blame for our shame to the military-industrial complex. But the greed of the American people for material goods far in excess of what they need is what has provided the energy, the fuel, for the military-industrial complex. The apparatus is the external cause. The greed of the

American people is the internal cause. It is this internal cause which each has to examine and replace with another more human identity.

The United States could not have become the citadel of world capitalism if the great majority of the American people had not acquiesced. That is why we have to distinguish the revolutionary potential of the masses and of mass community organizations from the "we" of the revolutionary organization who accept the responsibility for breaking through the illusions by which every American lives and behind which every American hides. As the cadres develop themselves, they go inwards, not upwards, interpenetrating with the masses in their organizations, developing the Fronts within which the masses can learn through practice the purpose, the methods, and the processes of political struggle.

The development of the internal programs necessary to develop the cadres and the external programs necessary to develop the masses can only be undertaken by people who have abandoned the illusion that oppressed masses can develop into self-reliant, self-determining, socially conscious individuals just by spontaneous rebellion.

Only after the organization has made substantial progress in bringing the masses to confront their own contradictions can the steps be taken to confront the external enemy, i.e., those who insist on choosing the reactionary past, in a power struggle. But before we reach this stage, the cadres and a significant section of the masses must have abandoned their concept of themselves as victims and acquired confidence in their own capacity to govern. They must have come to the realization that there is no utopia, no final solution, no Promised Land, and that humankind will always be engaged in struggle, because struggle is in fact the highest expression of human creativity. They must have reached the conclusion that the only belief worth struggling for is the belief, not in gods or messiahs, but in humankind, because human beings have only themselves to rely on in their unending struggle to become more profoundly human.

Modern Reader Paperbacks